South Philadelphia today. Moyamensing and Passyunk Avenues follow Indian trails from the seventeenth century. South Street, once called Cedar, was the southern boundary of the city from 1682 to 1854. Courtesy of The Philadelphia Inquirer / *Map by Roger Hasler*

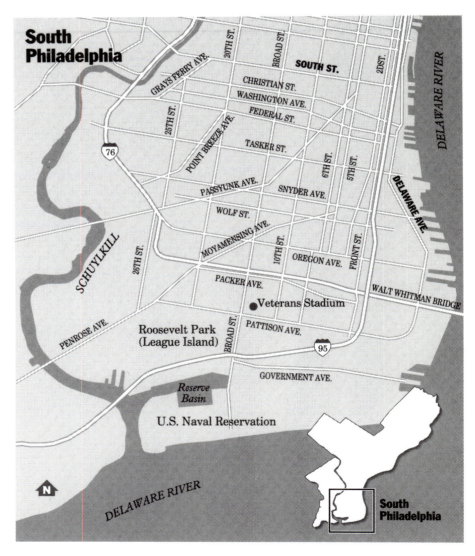

South Philadelphia

MUMMERS, MEMORIES, AND THE MELROSE DINER

Murray Dubin

Temple University Press
Philadelphia

Temple University Press,
Philadelphia 19122
Copyright © 1996 by Murray Dubin
All rights reserved
Published 1996
Printed in the United States of America

⊗ The paper used in this publication meets
the requirements of American National
Standard for Information Sciences—
Permanence of Paper for Printed Library
Materials, ANSI Z39.48-1984

Text design by Arlene Putterman

Library of Congress
Cataloging-in-Publication Data
Dubin, Murray
    South Philadelphia : mummers,
memories, and the Melrose Diner /
  Murray Dubin.
        p.   cm.
    Includes bibliographical references (p.   )
    and index.
    ISBN 1-56639-429-5
    1. South Philadelphia (Philadelphia,
Pa.)—Social life and customs.   2. South
Philadelphia (Philadelphia, Pa.)—Ethnic
relations.   3. South Philadelphia
(Philadelphia, Pa.)—Race relations.
4. Philadelphia (Pa.)—Social life and
customs.   5. Philadelphia (Pa.)—Ethnic
relations.   6. Philadelphia (Pa.)—Race
relations.   I. Title.
F158.68.S58D83   1996
974.8'11—dc20   96-1446

For my parents,
Ben and Mary Dubin,
the greatest
South Philadelphians
of them all

Contents

Acknowledgments

I hesitate to begin thanking people, because I am going to forget someone. A lot of people have been kind to me these past four years. Here are the names of some of them:

George Anastasia, Joe Anderson, Walter Belovitz, Leaden Bernstein, Dan Biddle, Charles Blockson, Lorraine Branham, George Brightbill, Joseph Casino, Dennis Clark, Walt Coughlin, Peter Stebbins Craig, Gittan Davis, Linda Dottor, Frank Dougherty, Bill Esher, Ken Finkel, Jimmy Fox, and Mike Goffredo.

Also, Caroline Golab, Maureen Graham, Mark Haller, Roger Hasler, Margaret Jerrido, Richard Juliani, Tina Kaupe, Hank Klibanoff, Richard Kubach, Jr., Roger Lane, Alice Martell, Pat Mazurek, Randall Miller, Henry Mitchum, Jefferson Moak, Celeste Morello, Kippee Palumbo, Michael Riverso, Joe Russo, Lily Schwartz, Harry Silcox, Carol and Wendell Smith, Joel Spivak, Lil Swanson, Henry Vare, Allen Weinberg, and William Yancey.

The 123 photos in this book would never have appeared without the calm, skill, and hard work of Frank Glackin. And a special thanks and hug to another *Inquirer* colleague, Arlene Morgan, for her insight, suggestions, and friendship. I'd also like to thank Morris Vogel for his comments on the manuscript and for putting me together with the fine folks at Temple University Press. And speaking of fine folks, Temple's Doris Braendel and David Bartlett have been my own personal cheerleaders.

When I tell people that I'm still close to childhood friends from South Philadelphia, they're surprised. We still see each other, play ball together, play cards. Thanks for a lifetime of good times—Bruce and Allen Polsky, Joe Binder, Howard Schwartz, and Eddie Spector.

We spend New Year's Eve with a bunch of friends each year, and none of them are from downtown, but they're special just the same: Molly Layton, Diane and Bill Marimow, Gay and Don Kimelman, Barbara Beck and Larry Eichel, Marianne and Rick Edmonds, Stefanie and Paul Taylor.

I have to thank my children, Alex and Minna. From 1991 to 1995, I said too often, "I can't, I have to work on the book." Through it all, they have been patient and loving and hugged me just the same. Speaking of hugs, no one embraced me more than my wife, Libby Rosof. Not only did she hug and encourage me, she edited me and improved everything she touched. The book has been a temporary focus for me, but Libby is forever.

Preface

I was 12 the first time I went to Red's myself. I was nervous. I had walked from my house on Wolf Street near Fifth to my grandmother's house at Sixth and Mifflin a million times, but Red's was at Ninth and Mifflin, near Bok, and it was way out of my neighborhood.

What Pat's was to steaks, what the Melrose was to diners, Red's was to hoagies. I didn't want to say anything stupid and embarrass myself. But I had to go. Rite of passage, 1959.

So I walked, trying to remember how my father ordered his hoagies. It was a Saturday, so I wouldn't see any of the tough kids who went to Bok, a vocational school. Anyway, I got there okay, walked in, and waited in line. It was jammed, and Reds, an old crusty guy who might have had red hair once, was behind the counter, slicing mortadella like the master maker of hoagies he was. Finally, it was my turn. He looked at me and said, "Wha?"

I understood the language of hoagie loaves. "Mayo, no hot." I had rehearsed the line the whole eight blocks. I did it. I was like the big guys.

He put on the mayo and the meats and more meat and the cheese and the onions and the tomatoes. Then he stopped. I was only a kid, but I was sure there was supposed to be something else on a hoagie. Lettuce. Got to be lettuce. Reds was trying to cheat me, the creep, just because I was from eight blocks away. My mouth went dry. I didn't know what to do. He was wrapping my hoagie. Finally, I croaked in a small voice, "Isn't there supposed to be lettuce?"

Reds stopped and looked at me like I had just asked for the escargots. His eyes got small and dark as hot peppers. "Look, you want meat or you want lettuce?" I gulped and said nothing. He gave me my hoagie and I got out of there.

Reds' response was typical and emblematic of South Philadelphia. Lots of food, not pretty food. Pasta, not parsley; substance, not appearance. Never were a lot of ways to make South Philadelphia's skinny two- and three-story rowhouses look fancy on the outside, but inside people could fix things up.

The reasons may be historical. Besides being Philadelphia's first neighborhood, South Philadelphia is the oldest ethnically and racially mixed big-city neighborhood in the nation. The downtown Spring Street area of Newport, Rhode Island, is a few years older than South Philadelphia, but not many would call Newport a big city. The North End of Boston is a seventeenth-century neighborhood, older than even Newport, and Boston is certainly a sizable city. But the North End never had a substantial black population. Baltimore? No, not as old. New York City? No existing residential neighborhood as old as South Philadelphia. Nothing in the South, nothing comparable anywhere.

Small homes are the rule, so people have lived outside as well, extending their living space beyond the confines of a narrow rowhouse. They sat on chairs and porch steps, bragged about their kids, griped about the city, and, over the years, the community grew closer. The low-rise repetition of rowhouse after rowhouse gave the neighborhood a "settled quality," a sense of stability. It didn't matter whether it was Grays Ferry or Second Street or the Italian Market area; the ethnic neighborhoods of South Philadelphia were a successful adaptation by immigrants to a new land, as immigration experts and local historians Caroline Golab and the late Dennis Clark have observed. And the ethnic familiarity in the neighborhood allowed the labeling of strangers. So strangers stayed away.

There was never a strong reliance on the city. South Philadelphia has water on three sides, making it almost a peninsula. The fourth side was another boundary, the city itself, and that was more a historical barrier than an opportunity. When William Penn founded Philadelphia in 1682, Swedes had been living in South Philadelphia—then called Wicaco, "pleasant place" in the Lenni-Lenape language—for about 35 years. But Wicaco was south of the city's boundaries, so none of its residents were part of the new city. In the 1700s, Wicaco would become known as Southwark, named after a working-class community near London. As the century progressed, the only communities south of the city between the Schuylkill and Delaware rivers were Southwark, Moyamensing, and Passyunk. In 1854, all the communities within the county were consolidated into one municipal entity—the City of Philadelphia. That transformed the three distinct communities south of South Street into one neighborhood stretching from river to river. Using 1995 as a baseline, South Philadelphia has been outside the city far longer than inside—172 years to 141. In the year 2026, the numbers will even out.

I didn't know from barriers and history when I grew up there. I didn't know about the Swedes, the first Europeans to live as a community in South Philadelphia. I knew Passyunk and Moyamensing not as township names, but as avenues, slanty streets with names that were hard to spell. I didn't know that South Street used to be Philadelphia's southern boundary and that my house on Wolf Street would have been in the suburbs before 1854. But I did know about appearance and substance.

I remember the first day I voted. The polling place was Bennoff's barber shop. I had been there many times because my mom worked at the polls. Now, I would finally vote myself. Brownie, the Democratic committeeman, gave me a big handshake and showed me into the polling booth. Then he showed himself in. I had known Brownie all my life. He was a nice man. He showed me what levers to pull, and then he pulled them. It happened so fast, I didn't say a word. Brownie handled it as if it happened every day. Appearance again was not important. Who delivered the votes was.

Urban America started here. This was the first 'hood, and more than 300 years later, it remains, more than anything else, a collection of two- and three-block sections within a much larger neighborhood, a much larger state of mind. Ask a South Philadelphian where he comes from, and he'll say his corner or his parish or simply, "South Philly." He will not say Philadelphia, because the connection is to the smaller entity, the community. The community is bread, meat, and cheese. The city is just so much lettuce.

I've been to reunions of former South Philadelphians, men in their sixties and seventies whose faces light up like pinball machines when they see old friends. These people are tied to one another, tied tight because they survived together. Only now do they understand that they grew up sharing an environment that taught them how to live, that their friends from South Philly would be the best friends they would ever have. At the reunions, they laugh and cry together, unafraid to show emotion. Their names are suddenly Yoogie and Fishy again. They remember each other's mothers. Nobody asks about today. Yesterday was better. They were all the same then.

One last story, courtesy of Frank L. Rizzo, the former mayor who grew up in South Philadelphia.

In 1991, he was running for mayor again. It was a spring day and he was marching in a neighborhood parade in Manayunk, in the northwest end of the city. Fastidiously dressed and groomed as always, he waved to well wishers on both sidewalks as he walked up Main Street. Occasionally, he would walk over to a knot of fans and more than once was kissed by an exuberant woman shouting, "We love you, Frank."

After one of those forays, a reporter who had been following Rizzo for weeks noticed that he had lipstick on his cheek. The reporter knew how careful he was with his appearance and quietly told him about the lipstick. Rizzo put his arm on the reporter's shoulder and whispered: "As long as it's not on my shorts."

Substance over appearance, one more time.

South Philadelphia

MUMMERS, MEMORIES, AND THE MELROSE DINER

The Broadway, just off the
corner at Broad and Snyder,
was the neighborhood's
fanciest movie house, located
across from South Philadelphia
High School and at a stop for
the Broad Street Subway. On
this November day in 1949,
South Philly's own Mario
Lanza was on the marquee.
Courtesy of the Philadelphia
City Archives

Introduction

Before there was a Philadelphia, there was a South Philadelphia. Before the gray asphalt and brick rowhomes and the candy stores on the corner, there were creeks and fruit trees. High reeds, grasses, swamps, and oak forests covered the land. Sturgeon, perch, and catfish were in the waters, and deer, turkeys, and beavers were on the land and, in the beavers' case, in the water as well. Islands pocked the rivers like brown and green turtle shells. To the south, the confluence of the Schuylkill and Delaware constricted the land like a neck.

But I never knew *that* South Philadelphia until I read about the seventeenth-century landscape in a history book. And I would never have read that book if I had not been writing this one.

The history of an urban neighborhood, especially one that stretches as far back in time as South Philadelphia's, is not a story often told. When neighborhoods are discussed, people generally just care about what they can remember and what they have seen, and not what happened a century or two before. Forget about the past being prologue to the present. History does not often stretch beyond personal memory. Just off the northwest corner of Broad and Snyder is a fast-food place, but I remember when it was the Broadway movies because I went there as a child. The relationship between landscape and memory is clear to me there. The relationship is less clear when it comes to the Oregon Diner. As far as I remember, it was always at Third and Oregon. But I know my father told me that there was no Oregon Diner once, that there used to be dumps and shacks.

We do not often think about memory—and what happened before memory—in terms of urban areas, and we rarely *see* history there. Not in the neighborhoods. There, the old store is the old store and nothing more.

Historical connections never had much currency on the street corner because history was not apparent. What history? That old store is history—it was the first Italian-owned business on the 700 block of Fitzwater Street and signaled a change in the neighborhood from Irish to Italian. So much of what is the sinew of South Philadelphia is rooted in what happened before, sometimes way before. From Pennsport west to Point Breeze, history—the people and events within memory and beyond it—touches people's lives today.

Take politics, for example. The stereotype of the South Philadelphia

3

politician is that of a money-grubbing, deal-making, ethically challenged opportunist. Clearly, that broad-brush description is unfair to honest elected officials. But it would be easy to name downtown pols who could slip into that stereotype like an old suit.

One reason political figures in South Philadelphia continue to have that reputation in the 1990s stretches back to the 1850s. Back then, one of the city's premier politicians was a violent, conniving bully of a South Philadelphia Democrat who held on to power for half a century, even though Philadelphia was under Republican control for much of this time. William McMullen protected immigrants from the city uptown, getting them jobs at the Navy Yard and keeping them out of Moyamensing Prison. He ignored the law and became more powerful. He set the tone for the politicians to come.

And people wonder why so many entertainers come from downtown. Well, the first theater in the state was in South Philadelphia, back in the 1700s. George Washington may not have slept there, but he did sit and watch the show. Edwin Forrest, the first great American actor, grew up in South Philadelphia. Performing has been part of the culture in South Philadelphia for 200 years. In fact, if Philadelphia has a performing tradition, it was born south of South Street.

Some of what happened before memory clearly has had an effect on people's lives, but not everything. It would be foolish to draw connecting links to every historical event. For instance, Thomas Jefferson, while Secretary of State, lived in a rented home on the east banks of the Schuylkill in the Grays Ferry section of South Philadelphia for five months in 1793. Jefferson met with Pres-

The availability of work drew immigrants to South Philadelphia. Cutting cloth, wrapping cigars, hauling cargo, selling fruit, cleaning houses—residents did it all. Joseph D. Evancich worked along the waterfront during World War II. Courtesy of Joseph D. Evancich

ident George Washington there once. A fascinating historical morsel, especially for Grays Ferry residents, but not an event that influences people's lives in that community today.

Another aspect of the neighborhood that South Philadelphia residents don't often consider is its reputation, and that is not a veiled reference to 13-year-old girls with big hair or tough guys in tee-shirts named Tony. No, this is more basic. People *know* about South Philadelphia across the country. They've heard of it. An image comes to mind. Think about the big-city neighborhoods in this country that have been well known for years and years—not just known in a specific geographical region, but known all over—and the list is a short one. Harlem and the East Side of New York would head the list, and the South Side of Chicago would be included. Then, a pause. Not Beverly Hills. It's a city, not a neighborhood. And not the Watts section of Los Angeles, because few knew about it before the riots of the 1960s. Haight-Ashbury in San Francisco similarly had no national notoriety before the flower children of the 1960s. The only other neighborhood that would be included on that list is South Philadelphia.

One reason for the recognition is that South Philadelphia is old. How old? Well, people from three counties came to pray in a South Philadelphia house of worship in 1677—a blockhouse that would later become Gloria Dei "Old Swedes'" Church. That's five years before Philadelphia was founded. South Philadelphia has had a long time to develop its singular identity, an identity separate from the city's. Philadelphia was a walking city until well into the 1800s, but South Philadelphia was outside the city, too far to walk to. So city residents did not often stop by to visit. But people did come. By 1696, Grays Ferry Road was used by travelers crossing the Schuylkill.

South Philadelphia has often been defined by its ethnic and racial mix, and in the early 1700s, an ethnic mix was already present. Irish immigrants had begun to settle near the waterfront in Southwark, working as rope makers, riggers, and mariners. Germans joined them, as did the Dutch and English, some Swedes, and a smattering of others. Little development in or out of the city went west of Fifth Street. The laborers and the poor lived in the narrow streets, back alleys, and rear courts of the city, but the poorest lived on the city's fringe—where Southwark was. For the next 290 years, immigrants would stream into Southwark and the surrounding lands of Moyamensing and Passyunk in an urban migration that was duplicated nowhere else in the nation. No other big-city neighborhood would receive this particular mix of immigrants, Irish and African American, Jew and Italian, and more.

By the Revolutionary War, Southwark had more than 750 houses, a handful of small businesses, and more than 1,200 people. Those numbers do not include the small population that lived further south and west in Moyamensing and Passyunk. Included among them was George Gray, who ran a ferry across the Schuylkill. At the time, Broad Street ended at South Street, the eastern end of Washington Avenue was called Love Lane, and civilization was still having trouble crossing Fifth Street. About half of the black population of Philadelphia County lived south of the city. With people finally moving west of Fifth, Passyunk grew to nearly 900 people and Moyamensing to about 1,600. In the last 20 years of the 1700s, the eighteenth-century version of the Mummers— among South Philadelphia's earliest performers—were celebrating New Year's with unorganized parades and gun shots in the air.

It was not called red-lining back then, but the first half of the 1800s saw continued residential segregation in the city by class and race. That meant more and more poor people—Irish and blacks among them—were living outside the city in Southwark and Moyamensing. The Irish Catholic influx into Philadelphia in the 1840s and 1850s sparked a residential movement south and west, past the swamps and the forests, across Broad Street, to Grays Ferry, where a new cluster of Irish worked along the Schuylkill docks. City residents were moving too, but their path was to northern and western suburbs, and they did not often stray south of South Street. And while the Industrial Revolution was beginning, factories and mills were generally small in Southwark, Moyamensing, and Passyunk, so city residents had no reason to come south for employment. South Philadelphia stayed isolated; South Philadelphia stayed poor.

But it did not stay the same, because the look of the streets and neighborhoods began to change. The city was slowly changing from a pre-manufacturing to a manufacturing center, and the effects could be seen south of the city as well. Shot Tower, a high-rise structure designed to manufacture ammunition for sportsmen, was completed in 1808 at Front and Carpenter Streets and used in the War of 1812. Railroads ran along Washington Avenue from river to river, connecting the two ports, and coal yards lined the street. Empty land was slowly filling up. Outdoor food markets opened on Moyamensing Avenue near Washington, on Bainbridge near Fourth, and on Fitzwater near Eighth. The nation's first naval ships had been built in South Philadelphia, so it was fitting that the Navy's first training academy was built on Grays Ferry Avenue near the Schuylkill in the 1830s. Despite the coming of industry and mechanization, south of South Street in the early 1800s was still more country than anything else, colors more green than gray, with gardens, meadows, and ponds outnumbering the mills, factories, and foundries. Large sycamore trees on 11th Street shaded Washington Avenue. The trees served as a "hedge and fence all the way to Passyunk [Avenue]. Parker's Garden ran across 10th Street, fronted by a double row of Linden trees."

Southwark's and Moyamensing's first Catholic institutions opened to serve a growing church-going Irish population. St. Philip de Neri, on Queen Street near Second in Southwark, and St. Paul's, on Christian Street near Ninth in Moyamensing, began filling their pews in the 1840s. And the growth in commerce led to an improvement in creature comforts, especially for travelers on the Baltimore Pike coming north into Philadelphia. Now they could spend the night at the Point Breeze Inn or the Passyunk Inn, both along the Schuylkill.

Crime and violence were growing in South Philadelphia as well. In the 1830s, the neighborhood's first penal institution, Moyamensing Prison, was ready for business at 11th and Passyunk. Religious, ethnic, and labor strife marred the 1830s and 1840s. Anti-immigrant political groups, often with Irish Protestants among them, picked on the incoming Irish Catholics. Actually they did more than pick—they discriminated, attacked, rioted, and murdered. And just about everyone, Irish Catholic and Protestant included, treated the growing black population even worse. A list of South Philadelphia firsts would have to include the city's first race riot.

Race and ethnicity were not the cause of all the disruptions. Coal heavers on the Grays Ferry waterfront, tired of working more than 10 hours a day, walked off the job. Moyamensing textile workers wrecked the handlooms of anyone who refused to honor their strike for higher wages. More and more southern blacks were coming north to escape slavery and to find jobs, and more and more Catholics were fleeing the poverty of Ireland and landing at Delaware Avenue. Housing became less habitable. Slums formed. Soup kitchens and relief agencies opened. Moyamensing Prison was booming. South Philadelphia's image was secure—it was a dangerous place.

Robberies, muggings, and assaults happened daily. The area was plagued by two kinds of gangs, unorganized street-corner gangs and those organized enough to run bribery and extortion rings on the waterfronts. Volunteer fire companies fought each other to get to fires first, and they strong-armed residents to pay for fire protection. Philadelphians were wary of crossing South Street, and so were the police, who had no jurisdiction there. Red-light districts shone so brightly in Southwark and Moyamensing that a published guide to bawdy houses declared that South Philadelphia had some of the best and the worst, naming names and addresses. Tourists came, as did out-of-town writers. Southwark and Moyamensing were notorious.

By 1850, nearly 39,000 residents were squeezed into Southwark's one square mile. Moyamensing, more than twice as big, had about 27,000 residents. And Passyunk, on the outer banks of South Philadelphia, had just 1,600 people in its nine rural square miles. The 67,000-plus residents in the three communities were a sizable chunk of the county's population, but considerably fewer than the 121,000 living in the city.

The inclusion of South Philadelphia into the city in 1854 did not change life a great deal. No beneficent municipal hand welcomed the poor neighbor from the south. Fourth to Ninth, Lombard to Fitzwater, was known as the infected area before the consolidation, and that did not change. The housing

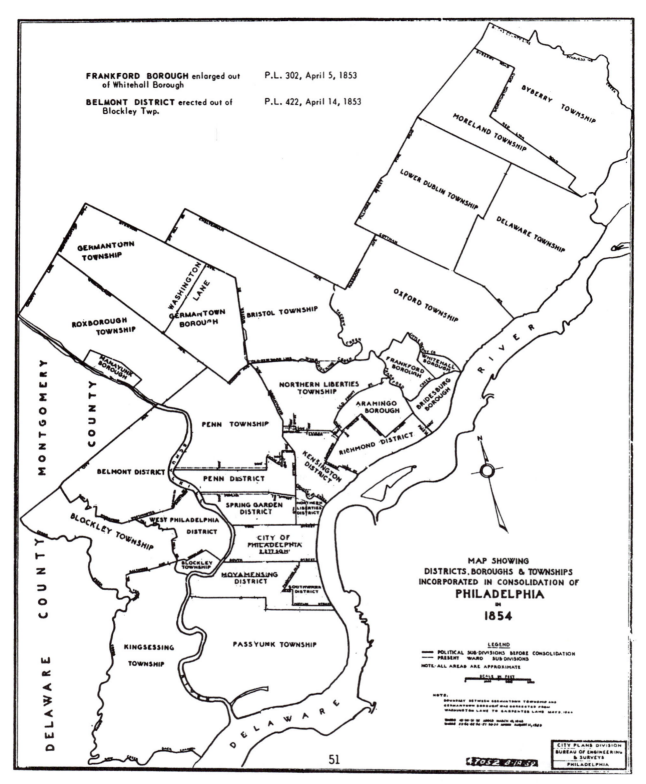

MAP SHOWING
DISTRICTS, BOROUGHS & TOWNSHIPS
INCORPORATED IN CONSOLIDATION OF
PHILADELPHIA
IN
1854

The city and surrounding townships in 1854, before consolidation created the modern boundaries of Philadelphia. Southwark and Moyamensing townships were smaller than Passyunk but had far more people. From "Genealogy of Philadelphia County Subdivisions." Courtesy of the Philadelphia City Archives

Everyone downtown has a picture somewhere of their grandparents, the ones who were born in the old country. This is one of those photographs—Maria and Augustus Maranca, parents of Sue Bruno, whose husband's name was Angelo. Here they are in 1939 with Michael, their grandson and Angelo and Sue's oldest child. Courtesy of Jean Bruno

remained overcrowded, the sanitary conditions awful, and disease a constant worry. A new city police force patrolled, but the streets continued to be dangerous.

By 1857, 500 children were attending St. Paul's parochial school, but no children attended public schools because there were none south of South Street. Transportation became easier when the first street railway began operation on Fifth and Sixth Streets in 1858, taking riders from Morris Street in South Philadelphia north 36 blocks to Berks Street, and back again. The cost was five cents, and 46,000 riders used it every day. Black riders were not welcome.

Philadelphia in the 1800s was a city full of people connected to their communities in powerful ways. Unlike New York, Chicago, and Boston, the city never offered incoming immigrant workers a rooming-house district. Blacks from the South and Irish immigrants did not live in large, high-rise tenements, as they did in other cities. No, newcomers plopped down in the neighborhoods, renting terrible housing in rowhouse communities. Polish, Italian, and Jewish immigrants would later do the same thing. Much of that housing was in South Philadelphia, because that is where the ships that had carried them from Europe landed or where their fellow immigrants came after landing in New York or elsewhere.

And they wanted to be there because they were not simply "huddled masses yearning to breathe free." That famous description suggests that nineteenth-century immigrants settled anywhere they could. That was true for some, but most immigrants knew exactly where they were going when they landed at Ellis Island or at the foot of Washington Avenue. A neighbor or relative from the same village or town or shtetl had come before. Work was available. Pulling on them was a migratory chain, not an abstract dream.

People began to buy the inexpensive homes. The neighborhood grew, and its identity strengthened. Like lived among like, and a threat to the neighborhood became a threat to the individual. And while South Philadelphia was often defined as an Irish neighborhood or an Italian neighborhood, it was never overwhelmingly anything but working class and poor. No ethnic group ever numerically dominated in the 1800s. Yes, there were Irish and African American pockets during that time, but neither group ever came anywhere close to 51 percent of the population. The Irish were already residents when the famine in Ireland brought a flood of newcomers in the late 1840s and 1850s. Jews and Italians did not come in large numbers until after the 1880s, but South Philadelphia already had a church full of Italians and a synagogue full of Jews in the early 1850s.

Before the century would end, Italians, Irish, blacks, and Jews would all be living together, each with its own community and each with its own social and cultural institutions. Ethnicity changed from block to block, but the neighborhood was shared, sometimes peacefully, sometimes not. In 1861, the focus of inward South Philadelphia was forced outward. War does that. The Civil War also focused national attention on little South Philadelphia.

Southern slaves already knew about the neighborhood. Philadelphia was the center of free black life in the nation, and the southern end of Philadelphia was the epicenter. So they escaped north via the Underground Railroad and found themselves in a neighborhood full of Union soldiers.

The train station at Broad and Washington was bustling with soldiers heading south to Washington and coming home to the Northeast. The volunteer hospital across the street treated the wounded. Many of the Union soldiers arriving in Philadelphia had come from New Jersey, New York, and the New England states. South-bound trains arrived at switching points like Tacony or Camden, New Jersey, where the soldiers boarded Delaware River steamboats that brought them to Washington Avenue for the short march to the station on Broad Street. Once they left the ferry, thousands and thousands of soldiers were introduced to South Philadelphia and to "Brown's."

Historian Frank Taylor writes: "From the beginning of this movement of hurrying soldiery, the patriotic families living in the vicinity of the Navy Yard offered refreshments to the extent of their limited abilities." The need grew, and a grocer and fruit dealer named Barzilai S. Brown began getting the foodstuffs necessary. Local residents found an old boat shop on Swanson Street south of Washington Avenue and opened a hall for soldiers to eat and rest.

Known first as Brown's, it later was called the Union Volunteer Refreshment Saloon and grew into a facility large enough to feed a regiment, with the cooking and serving done by volunteers from Southwark. "Seven barrels of coffee and 15,000 cooked rations were often made in one day. . . . The Second Maine Infantry arrived at one o'clock upon the morning of May 31 and found the hot coffee, beef and bread all ready for them, much to their surprise and delight."

The Quaker City String Band in their Minstrel Days costumes outside City Hall on New Year's Day in 1965. Courtesy of John Walsh / Quaker City String Band

Brown's was ready for the Second Maine because the neighborhood knew when troops were arriving. The military would telegraph ahead when a troop train left Jersey City coming south. When the message was received, a small cannon under a flagpole on Washington Avenue near the waterfront was fired. The troops were coming.

In addition to food and drink, the volunteers at Brown's provided writing paper and envelopes. The soldiers' gratitude was expressed in thousands of letters home, "many of which were printed in distant newspapers." The reputation of South Philadelphia spread.

After the Civil War, residents began to stretch out in South Philadelphia. Streets as far south as Packer and Curtin now appeared on maps. In 1868, the St. Charles Borromeo Church opened on 20th Street, between Montrose and Christian, in an area described by a church publication as "wilderness." That same year the city sold League Island to the federal government for one dollar,

11

The Melrose Diner in 1941 and waitresses Dot Seaman (left) and Dee Wayana Lawrence (right). The way the story goes, Seaman persuaded a friend, Helen Tierney, to come work at the diner and Tierney later married the owner. Courtesy of Richard Kubach, Jr.

hoping that the Navy Yard would relocate to the southern end of Broad Street. The flag was not raised on the new facility until 1876 because it took that long to fill in League Island and construct a yard big enough for the Navy—about 800 acres and five miles of waterfront.

The foreign-born population of Philadelphia peaked in the 1870s as the Irish influx slowed to a trickle. Over the next 30 years, many foreign-born Italians, Jews, and Poles would move into the slum housing in South Philadelphia that had belonged to the immigrant Irish in the 1840s. The Mummers became more and more popular, and life appeared to be opening up below South Street. Among the openings were the Penrose Ferry Bridge and a more modern Grays Ferry Bridge, a church for Polish Catholics at Second and Fitzwater and another for German Catholics at 26th and Tasker. In 1899, the Graphic Sketch Club opened in South Philadelphia, the first free art school in the country. Not a bad way to conclude a century.

The new century began with a population boom as South Philadelphia grew to more than 282,000 in 1900—60,000 more than in 1890, and more than four times the population 50 years before. Nearly 10,000 of the newcomers were black, increasing their percentage to more than 6 percent.

More black residents was not the only change. Just 43 South Philadelphians were born in Russia at the time of the 1880 census, but by 1900 the figure was 17,429. Italians saw a 12-fold increase over the same 20 years, from 1,193 to 14,540. While there were still more Irish than any other ethnic group, their

The 600 block of Mifflin in 1943, with the Alterman family outside taking pictures. The three boys are cousins and playmates. That's Sam's boy, Arthur, in the front. Behind him is Stanley Dubin, son of Mary Dubin, Sam's little sister. Donnie, Lou's son, is in the back of the line in front of his father. Courtesy of Mary Dubin

number diminished in that period to 24,718 from 27,036. It would never be close to 27,000 again.

Into the 1900s, and we find ourselves within the grasp of memory again. In addition to an archival history of the neighborhood, this book contains the memories, in words and in photographs, of 52 current and former South Philadelphians. Each chapter has their voices. People who loved the neighborhood and people who hated it. People who can trace their lineage to the 1800s and people who settled in the 1950s. People who would never leave and people who would never go back.

I go back. I still enjoy the Mummers Parade. I eat at the South Philly Bar and Grille on 12th Street, and at the Triangle Tavern, across from where the prison used to be. I take my kids for water ice at John's at Seventh and Christian. They eat with a spoon. My daughter likes the Melrose Diner. My son likes Geno's Steaks better than Pat's. We visit my mother on Wolf Street. I show visitors the Italian Market.

When I grew up there in the 1950s and 1960s, it was a neighborhood of Jews, Italians, Irish, and blacks. Today, there are just a few hundred Jews left, but there are still plenty of Italians, Irish, and blacks. A new immigrant group began trickling into South Philadelphia in the 1970s. By the 1990s, the influx of Southeast Asians had transformed Eighth Street near the Italian Market, first an Irish street and then an Italian one, into a Vietnamese thoroughfare. And Seventh Street north of Porter, once a Jewish shopping strip, had become the home of Cambodians and Vietnamese. Though visible in the community, Southeast Asians add up to just 7,000 residents, barely 4 percent of the population.

In the long view of history, no one should be surprised at their arrival. They are but another immigrant group come to Southwark, Moyamensing, and Passyunk searching for work and a new home. And like so many others before them, they have established places of worship. The city's first Cambodian and Vietnamese Buddhist temples are downtown. The Vietnamese temple is not far from the Italian Market, and the Cambodian temple is just about a mile south of the first ethnic church in South Philadelphia, the blockhouse where Swedes began praying in 1677.

1
Irish

South Philadelphia was the city's first ethnic ghetto, and the Irish were its first residents. The image of the neighborhood was partially shaped by the image of the Irish: poor, tough, white, uneducated.

But those are not the only Irish and neighborhood images that have reflected off one another over the years. There is the Catholic church, begun by the Irish but so large in the lives of so many Christians in South Philadelphia. The Catholic church is one of the neighborhood's three institutions—the mob and the Mummers are the other two—and the Irish have been instrumental in the creation of all three. Each linked people and community, neighbor to neighbor. Each gave the neighborhood a different feel.

Irish Quakers arrived in Philadelphia with Penn's first settlers in 1682. Some indentured servants who arrived that year were Irish, and probably Catholic as well. Irish settlers trickled in during the late 1600s and early 1700s, and about 30,000 Scotch-Irish from the north of Ireland—most of them Presbyterian—steadily arrived from the 1730s to the 1770s.

It is difficult to pinpoint when the Irish began to move south of South Street, but late in the 1700s is likely. For it was about that time that a "pattern of residential segregation by economic strata began to emerge," according to historian Billy Gordon Smith. And it was about that time as well that poor workers began to settle in the "fringe areas" of the city. The poorest white workers were the Irish, and fringe certainly defined Southwark, the district south and east of the city limits.

In fact in 1797, the same year that John Adams was sworn in as the second president of the United States in Philadelphia, the county of Philadelphia had one of its early political-ethnic controversies. The supporters of an unsuccessful state Senate candidate blamed the "deluded masses" of a particular Southwark neighborhood for voting the wrong way and causing his defeat. That neighborhood was known as "Irishtown."

By 1800 there were more than five thousand Irish-born in the city, and by 1850 a concentration of Irish workers lived in Southwark and the larger South Philadelphia district of Moyamensing. From 1790 to 1840, 70 percent of the immigrants arriving at the port of Philadelphia were Irish. Most of the Irish in the city and county before the 1820s were Protestant, but after 1820 an overwhelming majority of the arriving Irish were Roman Catholic. South Philadelphia was, at different times, a population center for both Irish Protestants and Catholics, but the Irish of both denominations lived elsewhere as well, in communities such as Kensington, Northern Liberties, and Spring Garden.

Some Irish were wealthy, but they were not the Catholics, and they were not the residents of Southwark, Moyamensing, Passyunk, or Grays Ferry. By 1840 Irish men were providing the unskilled work—known as donkey labor—needed on the Schuylkill and Delaware waterfronts. They were now working and living at the western and eastern ends of South Philadelphia.

As the first third of the 1800s melded into the mid-century, change came to the Irish community in South Philadelphia. Some of the change was positive, the first signs of prosperity and of institution building—increased home ownership and a growing, prosperous Roman Catholic church. But it was also a time of increasing enmity and violence toward the Irish, a time of continued labor, ethnic, and religious unrest, growing poverty, and more and more arriving immigrants, rural people who had never before lived in an urban environment. They would become known as the famine generation. No white immigrant to Philadelphia would be treated as badly.

The poverty of the 1800s did not end there. John Pooler, born in 1926, doesn't remember much about how his grandparents were treated, but he knows they didn't have a lot of money. Their home was a squatters' community east of Front Street.

"My grandparents were very poor. They raised poultry, pigs, and they had a livery stable. They put up the animals for these guys with the drayage business—haulers, the teamsters at that time. . . . They had about 10, 12 families in Martin's Village. It was predominantly Irish, but I remember Tony Torelli, the lamplighter, he lived there, too."

People romanticize their childhoods, but Pooler says being poor was overrated.

"My dad worked as a stevedore during the Depression, but there wasn't much work along the waterfront. We had to learn to like potato soup. Everything was hand-me-down. I had to put cardboard in the soles of the shoes. . . . We couldn't go to different movies, couldn't get the clothes that kids had from other areas. Wasn't too many well-to-do people in our area."

By the early 1800s, the Irish were caricatured as drunken illiterates. They had the worst jobs and lived in the poorest housing of any white residents. The women were maids. They were overrepresented in the almshouses and in the jails. And the good citizens of Philadelphia were afraid to go south of South Street where the Irish lived because of the street crime.

Blacks and Irish both lived in despicable housing in the same alleys and courtyards of South Philadelphia, but they never shared a community. In 1832, 1834, and 1842, there were riots between them in Southwark, Moyamensing, and Schuylkill. The violence would persist for much of the century as each group competed for the most menial of jobs and as the Irish tried to maintain a tenuous hold on political power. The relationship was not improved when blacks were later used as strike breakers by the railroads and shipping companies. South Philadelphia's ethnic intermingling was a continuing cause of violence as residents fought for jobs, status, and their piece of the asphalt.

On the labor front, about three hundred Moyamensing Irish handloom weavers walked off the job on January 11, 1843, marching through the community and breaking into the homes of scab weavers to destroy their equipment. Irish immigrants often worked 16 hours a day at the loom to earn three dollars a week, but factories and manufacturers demanded lower wages. Similar violence occurred in Kensington and continued sporadically until the Civil War, when the handloom weavers disappeared into the factories.

There was more violence involving the Irish in 1844, and religious and ethnic bigotry were the primary causes. The year before, while Moyamensing weavers were striking, Native-American organizations formed in the city to restrict the power of immigrants, especially the growing number of Irish Catholics. (These groups had no connection to American Indians; "Native" referred to people born in the United States.) They advocated longer waiting periods for naturalization, restricting public office to the American-born, and teaching the Protestant version of the Bible in the public schools. Dublin-born Bishop Francis Kenrick had aroused their ire in 1842 when he demanded that Catholic children no longer be forced to read the King James version in public school. Which Bible to use became a public issue that would not die.

At an outdoor Native-American meeting in Kensington on May 6, 1844, a riot occurred. How it began is unclear, but bricks and stones were thrown, fires were set, shots were fired, and people died. More fighting occurred the next day in Northern Liberties. When the two days of rioting were over, two Catholic churches had been burned. True to their image as brawling, Irish tough guys, many of the dead and wounded had come from Southwark to be part of the fighting.

Employment discrimination against the Irish was everywhere. Many job postings said, "No Irish." The poverty was apparent, too. In 1849, a cholera epidemic struck the city and surrounding areas, killing 386, with many of the dead in Irish neighborhoods like Southwark and Moyamensing. That year, the Board of Health in Moyamensing found "badly located houses, crowded by occupants, filthy and poor, without ventilation or drainage, or receptacles for refuse, or supply of water, or the common comforts of life."

Also that year, the Society for the Employment and Instruction of the Poor opened the House of Industry at Seventh and Catharine Streets to assist poor residents. In 1855, more than half of the people it helped were Irish. While the caricature of the drunken Irishman was an exaggeration, insobriety was a problem. Contractors routinely gave Irish workers part of their wages in whiskey. In the 1840s, the Catholic church in Philadelphia began to rail against drinking. "The saloon keeper is America's danger and disgrace," said one Catholic prelate. But within the neighborhood, the saloon keeper was a man to be respected, and the saloon was an important institution, a social center where you could hear gossip from Ireland and learn about jobs, "an oasis of camaraderie for the worker, the unemployed, the troubled and the calculating. . . . the arena for political discussion and confederation," as Dennis Clark described it.

In Irish enclaves throughout the city, the corner tappie, or saloon, performed a vital social function, acting as a clearinghouse for news of jobs and politics as well as a center for neighborhood gossip and the latest tales from Ireland. The McGrail Saloon was on the northeast corner of Front and McKean in 1901. Courtesy of the Philadelphia City Archives

The national Total Abstinence Union had its headquarters in the city. The 1870 city street directory listed temperance meetings on Monday and Thursday at Second and South, Wednesday at 19th and Bainbridge, and Friday on Washington Avenue near Third. Tuesday must have been a day off. The 1875 St. Patrick's Day parade featured 39 temperance society marching units.

Not all the news was bad news. By 1851, about half of the property owners in Moyamensing were Irish, and some may have even been slumlords. Since it is unlikely that the famine generation were already home owners, an Irish tradition of home ownership must have begun quite early.

Philadelphia, in the midst of a significant industrial expansion, in no way resembled the Irish countryside, but the farmers and herdsmen fleeing the famine kept coming on ships sailing from Derry and Liverpool. They opened stores, laid railroad tracks, sweated in leather factories, unloaded ships, tended bar, built houses, and hauled cargo on the wharves. Most of the Irish in 1851 were unskilled laborers. An examination of the other occupations held by Irish immigrants in Moyamensing in 1850 lists 32. By 1870, that number had jumped to 72, including occupations like machinist and carpenter, plumber and policeman.

As the Irish of South Philadelphia—and all of the city—began to own their homes and earn more than a dollar a day, they began contributing energy and money to the Catholic church.

In 1850, before the consolidation of city and suburbs, there were five Catholic parish churches in the surrounding county and 12 in the city. That more than doubled to 36 churches in 1870—a rate of growth much faster than in Boston, which had just 20 churches and five mission chapels in 1870.

A 1921 photograph of the clergy at St. Gabriel's Church, 29th and Dickinson, in Grays Ferry. Father John Rooney, seated in the center, was the third pastor at St. Gabe's and was assigned to the church in 1920 after six years at St. Philip's in Southwark. He died not long after this picture was taken. Courtesy of the Reverend Francis Cortese, St. Gabriel's Church

South Philadelphia's first Catholic church was St. Philip's. The first Mass was celebrated in 1841, and the church opened a school in the basement that same year with Mr. McGowan teaching the boys, Mrs. Conway the girls. The church was attacked three years later in the Native-American riots. St. Paul's, the first church in the Moyamensing district, was completed in 1847. Known today as the Italian Market Church, it was built on Christian Street just west of Ninth at a time when there was no Italian Market and there were not many Italians. It was an Irish church.

The movement of the Irish south and west through South Philadelphia can be followed by looking at when and where new churches opened. After St. Paul's, it was St. Teresa's in 1853 at Broad and Catharine, where "there was nothing but grazing land" to the south and west. The church served as a temporary hospital after the first Battle of Bull Run. The Annunciation parish opened in 1863 at 11th and Dickinson. The neighborhood, known as "Cowtown," was described "as little better than wilderness." In 1868, St. Charles Borromeo opened on the west side of 20th, between Christian and Montrose. The neighborhood was also described as wilderness, "more brick clay ponds than houses, more frogs than people." The Irish kept moving farther and farther south. St. Monica's, on Ritner Street just west of 17th, opened in 1895, and the last Catholic church built in South Philadelphia in the 1800s was in the southeast corner of the community. Construction began in 1896 at Our Lady of Mount Carmel at Third and Wolf Streets. Which is not too far from where the grandparents of John Pooler settled when they arrived from Belfast in the late 1800s.

The Neck was the rural squatters' community at the southeastern edge of South Philadelphia, below Oregon Avenue about where Third Street is today. The main drag was Stone House Lane. This June 1924 photograph shows the unpaved street and the wooden houses. As far as anyone can remember, there never was a stone house on Stone House Lane. Used with permission of the Temple University Urban Archives

Pooler grew up on the 2300 and 2400 blocks of South Lee Street, below Front near Ritner. His grandparents, Martha and Thomas Pooler, and their nine children lived nearby in Martin's Village, a tiny squatters' community just east of Front.

"My grandparents didn't live in a shack. It was real nice. It was wood and brick. Had about four rooms downstairs. Had a big parlor. The upstairs had about four bedrooms, but they had an outhouse. Plumbing wasn't in existence back in them days. . . . It was mostly an industrial area that surrounded them. They had a place across the street that used to creosote railroad ties.

"My grandfather was a big, strapping Irishman, and always with a suit and a hat when he come up into the city. Well, that's what he called the city, coming up out of Martin's Village past the railroads."

When John Pooler was 14, his parents moved to the 100 block of Gladstone. It was 1940 and the Poolers hadn't moved very far, but now they owned their first house.

"We used to walk all over, to Market Street, up to Broad Street, down by the coal pier on Delaware Avenue and go swimming, Pier 124, way below Packer Avenue. South of Oregon Avenue was the Neck, Stone House Lane. That was another squatters' community. They never paid any rent or anything. We'd walk down Stone House Lane, where Third and Oregon is today, toward the Navy Yard, climb a big embankment where there was more railroad tracks, and we'd sit and watch the Navy planes come in over our head and land at Mustin Field.

"They had a couple of swamps there. Do a little fishing, and we used to do a lot of swimming. They had an artesian well, and it was bitter cold in the hottest day of the summer. The guys from our neighborhood were one of the few allowed down there. The Neckers didn't like too many intruders."

Front and Gladstone was an Irish neighborhood, and Pooler's three brothers went to parochial school at Mount Carmel, but he went to public school at Sharswood because his mother liked the kindergarten. Italians and Jews lived nearby, and he remembers little conflict. Blacks lived a block or two away, north of Oregon on Howard and Hancock. "They were the nicest people. We all got along."

He graduated from Furness Junior High and went to work at the Delaware River Jute Mill, Front and Shunk, for a dollar an hour. "I was what they call the bobbin boy. When the women filled up the bobbins with the jute, I'd go along with this big carton and throw the filled ones in there and bring back the fresh ones and put them on while they were working on another machine."

Childhood wasn't all deprivation and hard work. There were the feathered and sequined marching Mummers, New Year's celebrants who date back to the Philadelphia of the 1700s. The origin may not be Irish, but in the South Philadelphia of the 1900s, going up the street on New Year's Day was very much an Irish rite. Even today, with Mummers clubs spread into the suburbs and New Jersey, the spiritual home of the Mummers is still the Irish end of South Philly.

Pooler was only six or seven, but he remembers. "My aunt and mother, they knew a lady on Broad Street across from St. Ags [St. Agnes Hospital], and we used to stay in the warm house and watch. All the bands would perform right there and then we went down to Second Street. It was wonderful, just to see everybody being so happy, everybody, what would you say, admitting their sorrows and downfalls from the past year.

"I used to be a page boy for the Gallagher Club, holding one of them big captain's capes, freezing to death for a dollar all day. I was eight years old. Must have been 1934."

A year later, he switched to the League Island Comic Club. "I changed because I used to see them do some wenches out there. It's a good time. I just danced around with the brass band." Men who dress as women routinely appear on afternoon talk shows in the 1990s, but men and boys dressing up as women has been routine in the Mummers Parade for more than a hundred years. Pooler's parents had no qualms because boys throughout the neighborhood were dressed and parading as wenches on January 1. His mother did draw the line, however.

"I asked my mother about gilding my shoes gold. No way, she said. I had to get down to the dump and find an old pair of shoes, bring them home, clean them up real good, and put the gold gilt and sparkle stuff on it."

In 1942 he joined the Quaker City String Band, and he's still there. President five terms, and a lot of years marching up the street with his banjo, third from the right in the front, the number-one line. He's strutted as far away as Cuba. "Then we come home from there and the revolution started. I guess they didn't like string bands."

21

He married a Grays Ferry girl in 1946, got a job at a printing plant, and stayed in South Philadelphia, moving near 24th and Snyder. A little far from the Quaker City headquarters on Third Street, but he still gets down there most days. Retired from the printing plant and the Navy Yard, he's done better than he expected.

"I never thought I'd be able to buy a home, raise three kids, and retire from two different jobs. I don't have to worry about anything now as far as money coming in. I got good Social Security. I get a check from the Navy Yard. I get one from the Warehouse Union and one from the Disabled Vets. And the wife's on Social Security, so we do all right. We're able to take the kids out, treat them good. They're down here for dinner almost every Sunday, and that's what we look forward to."

And he has his Mummers tapes. He's recorded every string band performance since the 1974 parade. "These people around here think I'm crazy. I play string band tapes all day. I like them and so does the wife, so that makes it easier. Down at Wildwood, we sit around the pool with my tape recorder and I play string band music."

John Pooler may have played in the Neck as a boy, but Jimmy Fox lived there. Born in 1924 near Second and Jackson, he was the second-oldest of five children born to Helen and James Fox. His father's parents were born in Ireland, his mother's in Poland. Years later, when he was strutting for Quaker City, and even later, when his son was its musical director, he suspected his mother was rooting for the Polish American String Band.

His dad was a rigger who put large safes in big buildings. His nickname was Harp, and everyone in the neighborhood knew him because he was also a part-time bartender. When Jimmy Fox was seven or eight, his parents separated. His mother was broke, and she and her children moved six blocks south and a world away into a house that her mother had on Stone House Lane in the Neck. He was still in grammar school at Mount Carmel.

"Our address was 3200. There was no individual numbers. The whole Stone House Lane was no longer than five or six blocks of mostly wooden houses, a good 20 feet apart. I don't remember a stone house. If there was ever a big fire, it would have wiped Stone House Lane out."

He liked not being next door to anyone. "You had your own home. Whatever you did in the yard to keep it nice, it showed. That's what I liked about it. And everybody had a dog. If you was a stranger walking down, that dog knew you didn't belong, and you'd hear dogs barking all the way down the road.

"We had a real nice house. . . . We had plastered rooms and all, wallpapered. One story, wooden clapboard, that's them boards that's over one another. When you would go to paint it, it would just suck the paint up like nobody's business. You could go through five gallons of paint on one side of the house, if you didn't keep it painted every once in a while.

"The bedrooms were wallpapered. The kitchen, we had linoleum on the walls, then painted on the top like you see a lot today. We had a great big stove that you cooked on, wood and coal with a big oven on the side. No running water. As you came in the house, we had a porch that went along the front and

The Quaker City String Band had high hopes in 1969 for the Wizards of Love costume, but the club finished seventh. That's Jimmy Fox to the right with the sax, his son, Jimmy Jr., in the center, and Fox's little brother, George, with the bass on the left. Jimmy Jr. was 13 when this photo was taken on Broad Street. He went on to be Quaker City's musical director. Courtesy of Jimmy Fox

down the side. . . . It was one bedroom, two bedrooms, three bedrooms, a living room, a kitchen. . . . When the weather was right, we had a summer kitchen. It had screening so you had plenty of air. We lived for the most part out there. Once we got up and ate our breakfast, we didn't have to come back into that house until it was time to get ready to go to bed.

"Just one outhouse. That was my job, being the oldest boy. Not bragging or anything, my mom took care of the whole five kids. She was on top of you every minute. That outhouse was clean like our bathroom is today. Always scrubbing the seat, always smelled real clean. You put lime down underneath."

To the west of Stone House Lane was the sand and silt dredged from the bottom of the Delaware River. "Every Sunday, we would play football either on the Donnelly Field or on the sand dike. We made fields on top of the sand. The Donnelly Field? A little bit south of us going toward Pattison Avenue, right in back of people called Donnelly."

Neckers were poor, and it was sometimes embarrassing for a child to say that's where he was from. But only sometimes. "It was considered the country, and my classmates wanted to come to Stone House Lane. We had pigs, goats, rabbits, chickens. You don't have that in what we called the city. Anything above Oregon Avenue was the city."

And in the city, it was not always clear where the Neck was. When he told

Bill Partridge and his big brother, Fred, in front of their house at 22nd and Curtin in 1926. Courtesy of Bill Partridge

classmates at Southeast Catholic High School at Seventh and Christian that he lived on Stone House Lane, many did not know where it was. "I would say I live down The Neck. Some of them called me a Two Streeter. I'd tell them I'm a Necker. They would say, Where is that? I'd say, 'It's between Second and Third, south of Oregon Avenue.'"

Many of his neighbors were Slovak, but there were Irish families as well, including the Sullivans, the grandparents of former U.S. Representative Michael "Ozzie" Meyers. "His mom lived right across the road from us. She's a Sullivan. They knew we were a fatherless family and they always helped us out. Everybody was that way."

The Neck was the last frontier in South Philadelphia, the stop sign for those moving south to find a cheap place to live. Only the poorest went that far.

The Fox family moved out of the Neck and into the city in 1942, when Jimmy was 18. Not too far into the city—about seven blocks from their house in the Neck. The Walt Whitman Bridge was being built. "Everybody had to get out. They were starting to put in the footings of the bridge. We moved to 2621 South Third Street. That whole 2600 block, nearly all Neckers settled there. We moved in January . The very next month, I went into the service."

When he was a boy, the Mummers intrigued him. "How come everybody put their foot down at the same time? The heavy drum beats and the left foot goes down. They were in cohesion. I was fascinated."

After the war, he learned to play the saxophone and was recruited to join the Broomall String Band. He went up Broad Street for the first time on New Year's Day. "It was the Snowflakes, a beautiful suit. They had Frosty the Snowman in front of us, and that was one of the songs we played. . . . I loved going up the street. I felt like I was King Tut. . . . One year, we got as high as eighth prize. Hey, that was great for them. I'll never forget, it was the Banjos suit."

He was president of Broomall, but switched to Quaker City in 1954, about the same time that he married and moved to Southwest Philadelphia to be closer to his job driving a truck. He's brought three sons into the band. The 1974 parade was the last time he went up the street, but he's still a part of it.

"I'm the welfare officer. We do a lot of playing for crippled kids. We go to the Variety Club Camp and our young guys play ball against their counselors. The kids are lined up on the first-base and third-base side in wheelchairs and all like that. Close your eyes for a minute, you wouldn't know that they were handicapped. Don't get me wrong. I'm not a holy roller. I walk off to the side and I look to the guy upstairs. I say, 'You allow me to be part of this.' And then we play music for them. . . . I get a kick out of it."

Bill "Wimpy" Partridge remembers selling kerosene as a boy to Jimmy Fox's family. He grew up on Penrose Avenue when it was still farmland. Outsiders may have thought the land south of Oregon Avenue and west of Broad was the Neck too, but it wasn't at all like Stone House Lane.

"People called it the Neck, called it Magazine Lane, called it Nanny Goat Hill, Sunburn Hill, Gooseshit Hill, but we called it the Village. . . . This wasn't really part of the Neck where the squatters were. The people up here owned the land or worked on the land. This was the farm belt."

Born in 1921, he was the youngest of 12 children. The family home was a rented farm house at 24th and Hartranft, where the Passyunk Homes public housing project is today. His father, Tom, hauled paper in a six-horse team from the waterfront to Curtis Publishing.

"This here was down 20 feet here. This is all filled-in ground. This was all farmland. You could see from here to the river." He looked out the window from his home near 21st and Penrose, the only single house for blocks, an old brick reminder of another time. A hotel is on one side, Passyunk Homes on the other.

"I took my shoes off when I come home from school at summer vacation and never put them back on again until September. I went to Bregy, Vare, Southern. The kids at Southern didn't mess with us. We were a little too hard for them guys. You got a country boy, he's pretty tough. . . .

"We needed something, we went to the city. Seventh Street had everything. Them fellas down there, they was personal friends. Robbins, he made all of our soft hats. Point Breeze Avenue, we'd walk there. That was a promenade on a Saturday night."

Partridge is half-Irish, half-Welsh. His mother died when he was an infant, and the family fell apart. He had to live in a stable for a while and was ping-ponged between relatives. His wife remembers those days.

"I used to go in the store with my mother and buy him a loaf of bread and bologna. I stole blankets out of my house to give it to him so he'd be warm.

League Island was the park and the beach combined. Bill Partridge and his girlfriend, Elsie, are on the left in this 1939 shot. Courtesy of Bill Partridge

He really had a very hard life," says Elsie, his wife. They've known each other since they were children, and married in 1942, just seven days before he went into the service. He came home to a changed community.

"We had a cow barn right off where 22nd Street is now—22nd Street was nothing but a cinder road. When I come out of the Army, home from overseas, I got off at the North Philadelphia Station, took a cab, and I come down here. I see this highway, Penrose Avenue, I didn't know where the hell I was at. It was 1945 and the Village was gone."

He and his new bride moved a few blocks away to 18th and Moyamensing. They stayed 23 years. "I hated it. I hate what we call a city. You hear the people next door arguing all the time. So when we found this place was up for sale, we bought it."

Bill Partridge was a foreman for Gulf Oil for 40 years. He's retired. "I've done okay, I made something of myself." The band keeps him busy, but not too busy to talk about South Philadelphia and the way it was.

When Veterans Stadium was a dairy farm; when a trolley took you from South Philadelphia to Chester; when truck farms were more plentiful than trucks; when he caught carp in Shad Brook at League Island Park and sold it for a nickle to the Jewish merchants on Seventh Street; when he ran so fast that people called him a "whipper," and how "whipper" became "Wimpy." The

This 1943 picture of the married couple Bill and Elsie was taken "in the city," at a photography shop at Broad and Porter. Courtesy of Bill Partridge

memories made him laugh and the memories made him cry. He and Elsie celebrated their fiftieth wedding anniversary in November 1992. He died a month later.

Partridge, Fox, and Pooler, three working-class sons of three working-class fathers. John J. Cox is still another Irish son of an Irishman who sweated for his livelihood downtown, but his life has been decidedly different. First he is a priest, formally the Reverend John J. Cox. Second, he comes not from the eastern end of the neighborhood, but from Grays Ferry. And, third, probably no Irish name is better known or brings back more memories to as many former teenagers in the 1950s, '60s, and '70s as that of Father Cox.

For Father Cox was the overseer of one of the most important and long-lasting social events the community has ever seen. From 1957 to 1974, he controlled chaos and preserved Christian values at the Saturday night dances at Bishop Neumann High School.

"We would have a thousand teenagers, and as high as eighteen hundred when we would have a disc jockey. . . . Danny & The Juniors and Frankie

27

Avalon and Fabian were making records. The record distributors wanted the kids to buy them. For several years, we had almost an entertainer a week. Didn't cost us anything."

Born in 1928, he grew up in Grays Ferry, the only child of parents who also grew up in Grays Ferry. He went to the Saturday night dances at Southeast Catholic when he was a student there. On Fridays or Sundays, he'd dance at St. Aloysius, 26th and Tasker, not far from his home on 29th, between Reed and Wharton.

"We got dressed up. Ties and jackets—plaid jackets were popular. At South Catholic . . . there were more girls than boys, but it wasn't like a grade school dance where the girls stayed here and the boys stayed there. I danced—I still do.

"Those three dances a week, that was your entertainment, because the rest of the nights you were doing schoolwork. . . . Dances, that's where boys met the girls and girls met the boys. You saw them Friday and Sunday at St. Al's, or you saw them Saturday, and you didn't see them during the week because you weren't allowed out for the most part. None of us, even in senior year, had cars. So if the girl you met was from Mount Carmel, Third and Wolf, and you're on 29th Street, you got a problem."

The 1300 block of South 29th Street was overwhelmingly Catholic, and more Irish than not. Most of his friends went to parochial school.

"There were some Lithuanians. In that day, out of those 50 houses, maybe two were Italian. King of Peace Parish, which is at 26th and Wharton, the Italians went there. The Irish went to St. Gabriel. We did have some Germans on the block because of St. Aloysius. The German parish is mixed now, but at that time one parent had to be of German descent to go there.

"Polack Town was down near Snyder Avenue, 29th, 28th Street. There was a black block right behind us. Called Gunther then—now it's the 1300 block of Dover. That's been black as long as I can remember, but not the whole block. There was interplaying, as far as kids were concerned. It wasn't a matter if you're black, get out of here, or you're white, or any of that. They grew up there. They referred to themselves as the Northern black. Then some of what they referred to as the Southern blacks began moving in, and some of the kids I grew up with, their parents moved out. . . .

"Before high school, I don't think most of us knew where north of Market Street was. . . . Where Tasker Homes is now was totally empty. A haunted house was way back there, but I don't know of anyone who ever went back there. We were forbidden."

His father, John, was an auto mechanic who didn't own a car. He earned eight dollars a week. His mother, Martha, worked at Molly Dolly, a doll clothes factory at 25th and Grays Ferry, and then at the Quartermaster's. Her parents came from Donegal.

"People thought it was a special neighborhood back then partly because a lot of people who lived there were family. You could have 10 people in the same family in 10 different houses on the same street. They didn't move in those days. Mary Jane got married, she might move two blocks away."

A lot of his old neighborhood is falling apart, he says, but his mother's street looks the same.

"My mother is 90, and down the street there are little kids, eight, nine years old, and if they see my mother by herself, they will come and make sure she gets into the house safe. When she used to carry groceries, they would run, take the groceries from her, carry them. She would go to give them a quarter. 'Oh, no, Mommy says we're to help people.'

"Mom had a simple lock problem. A young fella down the street was a locksmith. The guy next door called him. He took the whole thing apart, fixed it, put another lock on, a security lock. Mom said, 'How much?' He said, 'For what? You're a neighbor.' That's it. You're a neighbor."

Combined with the reputation for neighborliness, Grays Ferry also possesses a reputation for racism. Right or wrong, some outsiders see it that way.

"When it was a white neighborhood, sometimes it would be a revenge-type thing. Someone would say that Jimmy got beat up by a black kid, and they didn't care if the next black kid through was the right one or not. That would happen. But as the years went on, I think the opposite was more true, black kids beating up whites, picking up trash cans and throwing them through windows."

Father Cox, who would become the principal at Neumann, later moved to Southwest Philadelphia and a post as pastor at St. Clement's Church. He condemns racism on anyone's part. "The Irish have enough fights among themselves. They don't need anyone else to fight with."

He was ordained a priest in 1953 and began teaching at South Catholic a year later. The school moved and was renamed Neumann in 1956. Two years later, he was running the dance. He had 15 students helping. "We had someone at the door with a screwdriver checking for taps on the shoes 'cause we had a brand new gym. They had a choice, either take them off or go home. We don't need your quarter. Later on, it went up to 50 and eventually a dollar."

Girls couldn't wear pointed high heels; boys had to wear shirts, ties, and dress pants. The girls usually were from Southern or St. Maria Goretti. The boys all came from Neumann. The dance was 8 p.m. to 11.

Father Cox's booming voice could be heard in the gym with or without a microphone. He'd stand on the top of the bleachers. "If you really wanted a thousand kids' attention, first of all you stopped the music and then you would say, 'Jimmy Jones in the back, shut up.' There may not have been any Jimmy Jones, but everybody turns to see who was talking. So as they turned, you said, 'Now the rest of you shut up, too.'

"I would be up in the stands with the spotlights on. If halfway across the court there was a couple getting a little too friendly, I would meander down and all of a sudden be between them. What would I say? Well, it depended how close they were. If they were very close, the stock line was, 'I am very, very much in favor of Christian conception, but not on the dance floor.'

"If it was a sophomore girl, she would go blank, 'cause she'd never heard a priest talk like that. Secondly, depending how close they were, I would take my hand and go right down between them and tell them that there had to be that much between. When the Twist came in . . . we forbade it because it began to get a little too racy. Some of them decided to do the Twist on some other number. In the darkness, I would say on the microphone, 'I think over in the

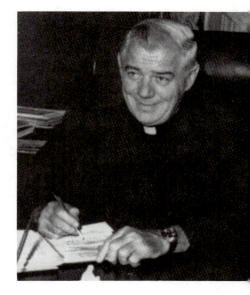

The Reverend John J. Cox in 1978. This yearbook picture shows him as principal at Bishop Neumann, after his days as the dance master of the Neumann Saturday night dances. From The Crystal / *Courtesy of Bishop Neumann High School*

29

corner you better cut it out, 'cause I'm on my way.' They weren't there when I got there."

Girls' drinking was the biggest problem. Drugs were not yet a concern in the '50s and early '60s.

"The same two women that sold soda when I was in high school were still chaperoning when I was running the dances, Amelia McGlocklin and Catherine Russ. For the girls' bathroom, we used the two women and two parents. If there was a girl sitting on the sink, they'd say, 'Would you please get off?' If the girl gave a flip answer, she would just come out and say, 'Father, green dress, blonde hair, on sink, fresh.' I would kick the door open and say, 'Girls, you have 30 seconds to get decent 'cause I'm on my way in.' Of course, the woman would always be ahead of me. I would get the young lady, get her outside, tell her to call her parents and have them pick her up, and station someone with her till they picked her up. Then I would tell the parents. In those days, you wouldn't see that girl for another month, six weeks. The parents would discipline her at home, so you didn't have to do anything."

Sometimes, the boys, yes, those young men from Neumann, were a problem as well. "If someone did have a few beers and was going to get a little rambunctious, then I pulled them out and had one of the faculty members call his parents if it was serious enough. If it wasn't . . . most of the time the old shoulder was what I used. The nerve right across, you grab that, they really jump. They'll go down on you, especially up from behind. They're not expecting you and you hit that nerve, then real quick squeeze and they're down. Whenever it happened at the dance, they didn't even ask who was there. They knew 'cause that's the way I handle things."

Grays Ferry's Joseph Slavin has never kept an eye on a thousand dancing teens, but he has operated a corner deli, taught school, sold real estate, directed a senior citizen center, performed on the guitar, counseled deaf children, and been a plumber. Now he teaches in a parochial school.

Like Father Cox, he is an Irishman from Grays Ferry. But the similarity stops there except for one more thing: like so many others who grew up poor in South Philadelphia—Irish or not—the church was central to their lives. So much of the history, so many of the memories, were shaped by ties to the church.

Joe Slavin was born in 1947, oldest child of Joseph Patrick Slavin and Regina Scanlon. His father's grandfather, Michael, arrived from Kilkenny in 1880 and settled in Grays Ferry.

He grew up at 1426 Napa Street, between Reed and Wharton, 30th and 31st. "There were kids all over. Summer nights just seemed to go on forever. . . . Not only did you have your own family, but you had the people on your street who were your extended family. Feeling of safeness. I had the back room, which overlooked the driveway, and I remember waking up mornings to the rag man's call. It was wonderful, in memory anyway, this sound. Horse and wagon coming up the driveway, calling, 'Rags.' I used to beg my mother to give him some. I don't know whether I thought he would sing better or louder or what. I remember a man with a saxophone. He would play and you used to be able to throw pennies down. He would catch them in the mouth of the saxophone.

"When I was a little older, six or seven, there was a wood shop on the corner of 31st and Wharton, and they would leave out the old scraps of wood they didn't want. Saturday ritual, we would go to the movies, pay a dime at the Earle Theater on 28th and Reed. Whoever was playing that day, when we came home that's who we were, Prince Valiant or John Wayne, or Errol Flynn in *Robin Hood*. Those pieces of wood became our swords, our guns."

A bartender's son, he lived in a porched, two-story brick and wood house with a driveway, but no car. "The hardwood floors I remember. My mother had this very old fur coat, and I used to pretend the coat was the boat and the floor was the water."

His father died when he was seven. "The church was part of life. One of my memories of my dad was being taken to St. Gabriel's Mass on Sunday morning. It was the night he got sick. I just remember holding his hand and going to church, and he had to leave to go to the men's room after he started throwing up. That was the beginning of a heart attack."

Uncles and aunts helped the Slavin family survive. After his father's death, the family moved to 26th Street, between Tasker and Morris, formerly his mother's parents' house. "The church on the corner would ring bells at 6 o'-clock in the morning, 12 o'clock in the afternoon, 6 o'clock at night. The ringing of those bells was my timepiece till I was in high school. If I can get in the house before the bells ended at 6 p.m., then I was okay."

The church was St. Aloysius, and by then it was no longer for Germans only. Irish boys like Joe Slavin prayed and went to school at St. Al's. If you had asked him where he was from in those days, he would have said St. Aloysius Parish.

"You know, I didn't know anyone who went to public school. It seemed to me that everyone was Catholic and everyone went to St. Aloysius or St. Gabriel's or King of Peace, and everyone went to Neumann. . . . I remember when I was in seventh or eighth grade, going to a Protestant church on 22nd Street to go bowling. I was very skeptical. . . . I didn't know what the people would look like. It turned out to be an extremely pleasant experience."

Point Breeze Avenue was where his mother shopped. "We called it the Lane. Ostroff's Candies was there and had fantastic milkshakes. I would get my school shoes at Edmonds, and it had this little machine you would walk into that would take an X-ray of your foot, which is probably a bunch of baloney. There was a real 5 & 10, where for a nickel or dime you get a goldfish in a bag. I remember the wooden floors."

His mother's two sisters lived near his house, and he had the keys to their homes. "When I was nine or ten, it was like having three homes. Everybody would just come and go. I knew who my mother was, but there was also these other important adults who had just as much authority over me, Aunt Ann and Veronica."

During high school, he worked at a butcher shop, a fuel oil company, a printer. After Neumann, his uncle got him a coveted apprentice spot inside a plumbers' union local. He said okay, even though he didn't know a screwdriver from a crescent wrench. Most of the apprentices had worked summers or had dads who were plumbers, but he was plumbing with the best of them by the fourth year. Despite his skill he did not like it, because plumbing had nothing to do with who he really was. He was going to enter the seminary.

It was the late 1960s, Bobby Kennedy had been shot, and the idealism of the Kennedys and Martin Luther King sparked a generation. He wanted to give something back. "I don't think I realized it at the time, but how does one be of service? Coming from the background that I came from, you become a priest, and so I entered the Norbertines. They're the fellows that run Neumann and had an abbey in Paoli. It was not an intellectual decision by any stretch. It felt right, I did it."

Two years later, he knew he had made a mistake. That was not the best way for him to be of service. After a number of jobs, including some folk singing, he met and fell in love with Barbara Batyko, a former nun who was a school counselor. Before their wedding in 1976, he was offered a job as complaint and referral coordinator for the Grays Ferry Community Council.

He still lived on 26th, but he didn't know much about the racial problems in the western end of the neighborhood or the community council, both of which seemed to be in the newspapers every day. "This is important about our neighborhood—it's a boxed-in area. You have 25th Street, where the railroad is, it's almost a dividing point. You have the Expressway, you have the river, and that's it. It's a box. Living on 26th, to get out of that box, I would go up 25th Street to get on the Expressway. To go into town, I would go up 26th and onto Washington Avenue. I never had to go out toward 29th or 30th."

He took the job on a temporary basis, thinking he'd be there six months. He stayed five years. "The job was wonderful. I was given a free hand to resolve problems. We did thirty-five hundred to four thousand complaints and referrals a year, anything from 'My street light is out' to 'My son is on drugs.' " Slavin also helped start, and was the director of, the area's first senior citizens' center, the William A. Barrett–Nabuurs Center, named after a politician and a priest.

He knows what outsiders think of the residents of South Philadelphia neighborhoods like Grays Ferry and Whitman Park, areas where there has been trouble between blacks and whites. When he meets someone from elsewhere, Joe Slavin says he lives in South Philadelphia, not Grays Ferry, until he gets to know them better. The perceived racism is an issue he has wrestled with.

"I could take you there, and people would know you're a stranger, that you are not part of the community. Grays Ferry, it's very much a village. Everyone knows everyone. . . . You have this community of Irish, and it's very easy for the society at large to see their own faults in this group, and take it out on them. If we're talking about prejudice, that exists not only in South Philadelphia, but in our city, our state, and in our country. It's part and parcel of America."

He disagrees that his neighborhood has more racial problems than other parts of the city. "Perhaps what you have is people who are uneducated and express themselves honestly, without couching their terms behind lawyers as the people in Society Hill did [when redevelopment forced black residents to move]. . . . The people in Grays Ferry—I don't want to say that they are poor.

They're not, but there's a lot of elderly without pensions that survive on Social Security benefits. They can't move. This is their home and that's it.

"On my block, on Corlies Street, we have three black families. When the families first moved in, I think there was some . . . fear. What are they going to be like? Who are they? There was that fear of the unknown. They are our neighbors now."

Long-time black and white residents generally have gotten along, he says. "The white people don't think of them as black, or different. They're part of Grays Ferry, been there forever. When you can put a name on someone, when you see a young fellow on the corner and you know his parents, you don't have fear."

His home is down the street from a housing project, Tasker Homes. "On Friday and Saturday nights, you can hear the automatic weapons going off in the project. My kids have verbally expressed and have written about the fear that they have when they go to bed.

"Who lives in the project? Blacks. I can intellectually say I realize that this is not all the black people in that project, but if you want to get down to a nitty-gritty common denominator, well then, it's in the project, *ergo* the blacks, so you are afraid. My car has been broken into twice. [People saw that] it was done by black kids. What did that mean? It means there are some black kids in our neighborhood that are going to rip you off. Other people are going to make it more simple, which is—watch out for all of them."

He adds that the worst problems with neighbors on Corlies Street have been with renters not taking care of their homes. The worst renters were "always white and always obnoxious."

His memories are not tainted with adults talking about race. His parents never did. His memories are better than that. "My uncle was off Tuesdays, and he used to take us out to the Melrose Diner for dinner sometimes. I remember the painting as you first come in. Here was a place far away from home that had this [city landscape] picture that I knew. Their baked beans were great. And Horn & Hardart. Each Christmas, we would go into Wanamaker's and see Santa. . . . Then we go out to dinner, and it was usually Horn & Hardart at 12th and Market. . . .

"After my dad died, all of my aunts, uncles, and relatives would wind up at our house Christmas Day. That would go on from about 12 o'clock in the afternoon till sometimes . . . we'd be singing till 1 or 2 o'clock in the morning. Music was a big part of our life, songs from the '20s, the '30s, even the '10s. . . ."

He went to church Christmas Day, and every Sunday, and sometimes more often than that. Joe Slavin was an altar boy. "They had something called an all-night benediction. . . . It would go in shifts, but at least one person had to be in church at all times, and it would run for 24 hours. Often, I would be in there at 1 o'clock in the morning and sit through the night, because the person supposed to take my place never came. You weren't angry with them. The quietness, smell of the wax, smell of the wood from the church, it was almost a gift that you were given to have that time by yourself there. That's the way

Jean DiElsi (in the center, with the dark hair), hugging Melrose Diner maintenance man Jack Hyland at a Christmas party inside the old diner near 16th and Passyunk in 1948. Courtesy of Jean DiElsi

it was looked upon, as a gift from God that the other people didn't make it. They don't do that anymore because it's not safe."

Jean DiElsi, from an Irish family, has always felt safe and comfortable in South Philadelphia.

"My husband always said he wanted to go to Jersey and I said, Go, because I'm going to stay here. I have a sister in Jersey, but it's not for me. . . . I like being in the city. I like jumping on the bus to get in Center City. If I feel like walking with a shopping bag or going up Passyunk Avenue, I do it. I couldn't do that if I lived in Jersey or wherever.

"And the people are nice. You go out, you bump into people. Hello. How are you? How do you feel? Where have you been? Other places, they don't even know you're alive. We had people that lived next to us when we were little, their name was Enderman. They were German. He wanted to go to California, and they went. Believe me, she used to write and call my mother and say, 'I have neighbors, I don't even know what they look like.' So I know people are never that friendly in other places."

Jean DiElsi, youngest of five girls of Regina Ward and Edward McLaughlin, was born in 1925 on the 2600 block of Chadwick Street, between 16th and 17th near Oregon Avenue. Her father drove a truck and delivered cookies for a while.

"I didn't know I was poor during the Depression, because my father worked at the cookie place then, and he would bring five-pound boxes of cookies home. I didn't know that they were the cookies that dropped, and the company sold them to the workers for 25 cents. I thought we were rich."

(*above left*)
Edward McLaughlin and his wife, Regina, leave their house to attend the 1946 wedding of their daughter, Jean. Courtesy of Jean DiElsi

(*above right*)
The newly married Sam and Jean DiElsi pose at Oregon and Chadwick in 1946. Courtesy of Jean DiElsi

She knew that the people who lived in Girard Estates, just to the north and west of them, were more "well-to-do," but it was no big deal. She could go swimming in the lake at League Island or at the pool at 24th and Wolf. The Plaza Theater was at Broad and Porter. The corner store had ice cream. And the neighbors were nice. "I don't think there were two people who wasn't Irish. Let's put it this way: It was Gilligan, it was Farley, it was Harkin." Not everyone was Catholic, just nearly everyone.

She left school at St. Monica's in the 10th grade and found a job selling shoes at the Blum Store, a department store at 13th and Chestnut. For two years, her boss was Mr. Weinberg. When he decided to leave for another job, she decided to leave first. "He was really a nice person. Some of the other people I worked with were really snobs, and I couldn't tolerate that. Why were they snobs? I guess because I was from South Philly and they weren't."

It was 1943, and she was 18 and looking for work. She found it quickly, working as a cashier at the Melrose Diner. Jean DiElsi is not one to make drastic changes in her life. She still lives on the block she grew up on, and she's still working—now as a waitress—at the diner, located at the intersection of Passyunk, Snyder, and 15th.

Back then, the diner was on Passyunk Avenue, near 16th. "It was the only diner around, and it was open 24 hours. If you went to dances, everybody would go to the Melrose Diner afterwards. That was the big thing. No, there was no Mel or Rose. It was named after a can of tomatoes.

"The owner, Mr. Kubach, didn't like to hire people who were very young. He liked somebody who was married and had a lot of responsibility. I told him that the ad in the paper didn't say a certain age, and I told him I couldn't come work right then because I wanted to give Mr. Weinberg a chance to get somebody else. And he said, when I left, he wanted me to come work there."

She started out as a cashier on the night shift, but began working as a waitress in less than six months. Today, she works just two days a week. More than 50 years at the same job, and she is not Melrose's oldest employee.

"It's like family. It isn't a job. When I first walked in there, I found so many people that were so pleasant and went out of their way to make me feel at home. I'm talking about the man that owns it. I'm talking about the people that work there. . . . The bosses, they don't make you feel like they think, 'I gotta put up with her today.' If you're out sick, they call, ask you how you feel. 'What can we do for you?' "

She's waited on former Vice President Walter Mondale, Liberace, Eddie Fisher, Eddie Fisher's brother-in-law ("a very nice fella"), and Frank Rizzo, when he was a police detective and when he was the mayor.

"We had a lot of people from TV shows, like that show *Alice,* you know, the waitress in the diner. Yeah, Linda Lavin. Skinny, skinny, skinny. In fact, she amazed me when they asked her about eating something that was a starch and she said, oh, no, she was under contract that she couldn't gain no weight. The whole staff was in at that time, hanging their mink coats up. I tell you, I've seen number writers, and I think their wives dress beautiful and they are more down-to-earth people. People that are in shows and all, they have that little air about them. They'll never give that up. I mean, I waited on [mob bosses Angelo] Bruno and Chick Testa and all of them. These were all down-to-earth people, and I'm sure they had a lot of money. . . ."

She met her husband, Sam, when she was 14. He was a kid from the neighborhood, an Italian kid. They married seven years later at St. Monica's. It was 1946.

"My neighbors gave me more flack than anybody. They said, Why aren't you marrying your own kind? And I said, 'Well, it just so happened, I fell in love with him. I didn't fall in love with my own kind.' And I said, 'My mother is accepting it. My father, and Sam's mother and father, too.' My mother was very much the kind that said, Look, if you like somebody and they're nice, you play with them. Don't worry if they're Polish or Jewish, or whatever. We were not allowed to say, 'Oh, that dirty dago,' or something."

Sam and Jean were following a long South Philadelphia tradition of Irish–Italian intermarriage that dates back to 1877 and the wedding of John Raggio and Mary Leary Brown at St. Mary Magdalen de Pazzi Church. They lived with her parents for 22 years, and no one complained. She and Sam vacationed in Florida, Virginia Beach, the Poconos. He died in 1979; they had been married 32 years and had no children. Today, her Chadwick Street block is still full of nice neighbors, and the Melrose is still home.

"When I was a little girl and people would ask me where I was from, do you know what I would say? I'd say, 'I live in the best part of Philadelphia.' Where's that? they'd say. 'South Philadelphia.' "

2
The Arts

The clergyman had not crossed the ocean to listen to voices like these. He insisted that the congregation pay attention and follow his direction. When some members ignored him, he fined those foolish souls for "untimely singing." He probably was not aware of it, but the Reverend Andreas Sandel, pastor of Old Swedes' Church, was setting a standard—music was not to be trifled with in South Philadelphia. It was 1702.

Now, more than 290 years later, some things have not changed. Music is still taken seriously in South Philadelphia, all sorts of music. And anyone is likely to sing.

Walk about a mile south of Old Swedes' with baritone and music teacher Elliott Tessler and his dog on a Friday night. "A bunch of guys were hanging out. . . . They yelled to me, 'Hey, opera, our buddy sings.'

"And this big guy comes out of the crowd and he says, 'Are you the guy that sings?'

"I said, 'Yeah.'

"He said, 'Do you teach?'

"I said, 'Yeah.'

"He said, 'I'm looking for a teacher.'

"He was singing for some competition. And at 12 o'clock, around all his beered-up buddies, this fella sang an excerpt of an oratorio on Second and Mifflin."

An oratorio on Two Street in 1992. It's not just polkas and banjos and rock and roll downtown. South Philadelphia is contraltos and clarinetists, painters and playwrights, film directors and Broadway stars, musicians and singers, so many singers. It is also authors and songwriters, bandleaders and dancers, and a Pulitzer Prize winner. People perform in South Philadelphia. Choose your simplistic explanation—It was a way out of poverty. It was an escape from anonymity. It was their only form of expression.

Well, this explanation is even simpler. People downtown were not afraid to enjoy themselves, and one way to do that was to sing and dance and play an instrument. Remember, there were no strangers, so who was going to laugh at you? Not your neighbors. They were rooting for you. They really were. As a little boy, I used to imitate Johnny Ray singing "The Little Cloud That

Cried." I was awful. The only key I knew was off, but I sang anyway on the street corner.

Performing is a tradition dating back to the 1700s and theater on the corner. In the 1800s the Mummers began strutting. The 1900s have seen everything from tap dance to do-wop to comedy routines on the corners. That performing tradition crossed ethnic, religious, and gender lines. Sometimes the tradition survived despite those lines. It had to do with being from South Philadelphia. It had to do with making your own fun, because you couldn't afford to buy enjoyment. You had to create it.

South Philadelphia comedian and musician Cozy Morley: "Kids on the corner, that was a terrific thing for young guys to do. Because it threw everybody out. I was different around that corner than I was at home. I became a silly, funny kid. Everybody had their own little role to play, and one thing led to another. Some of the guys went on to really big things. Jack Klugman and Joey Bishop did really well."

Not only is there a history of performance and the arts in South Philadelphia, there is a story of historic performance. It was on another corner, South and Leithgow Streets, that the first play written by an American author and performed by professional actors was staged in 1767 (officially, of course, there was no America yet). *The Prince of Parthia* was the play, and Thomas Godfrey, Jr. was its author.

The location of the Southwark Theater—the nation's first permanent theater—was no accident. While open-minded about religion, the local Quakers were not fans of the theater and permitted none in their city. But the south side of South Street was beyond the city limit. So was the north side of Vine Street, but the eighteenth-century theatrical district, such as it was, was in South Philadelphia.

The British, of course, had had a theatrical tradition of their own. During their occupation of the city, Howe's Thespians, named after a man better known for his military leanings than for his theatrical ones, often performed inside the Southwark Theater, with the aforementioned general watching from a special box draped in British red.

Another general, George Washington, also enjoyed the theater, though it is unlikely that he was there on the same nights as his British counterpart. When Washington attended, the theater company often performed a comedy, *The Poor Soldier,* and made certain that his seat was not obstructed by the building's wooden pillars.

In 1779, the state legislature, unhappy with the goings-on on South Street, banned theatrical performances. But it was not that easy to stop the show. Rather than advertising the comedy and dramas of the day, the Southwark Theater instead publicized the forthcoming "comic lecture in five parts on the Pernicious Vice of Scandal." In other words, *The School for Scandal*. The show went on, and the legislature repealed the law in 1789.

The neighborhood's cultural heritage is often overlooked when the past is examined or memories are dredged up, but the history of arts and entertainment is as eclectic as the people who settled in its neighborhoods. The Graphic Sketch Club, now the Fleisher Art Memorial on Catharine Street, opened in

1898 as the first free art school in the nation. At St. Martha's House, a provider of services to the community's poorest residents, adults met weekly in the Eighth and Snyder building to study Shakespeare. The year was 1904. Ferruccio Gianninni opened Verdi Hall, the "Met of South Philadelphia," on the 700 block of Christian Street in 1905. The Dunbar Theater, the city's first black theater, opened just a hoagie or two north of South Philadelphia at Broad and Lombard in December 1919. The all-black cast's first performance was *Within the Law*.

Youngsters downtown do not grow up knowing that the city's first theater orchestra or free art school was in South Philadelphia. But they often do grow up with an appreciation and acceptance of music, and a willingness to perform.

Donald Montanaro, born in 1933, is the associate principal clarinetist with the Philadelphia Orchestra, and an orchestra member since 1957. He grew up at 20th and McKean.

"Music was such a part of everything. My sisters were always singing, or we would be listening to music, and we knew every song that was popular. The Earle Theater on Market Street had these big bands that would come through, and my sisters would take me up there. I saw Glenn Miller, Jimmy Dorsey, Tommy Dorsey.

"I just liked music. We had a player piano. My brother studied the violin, and then he had a trombone. Two of my sisters studied the piano. They would do the dishes together, harmonizing and singing. My father loved to sing. South Philadelphia, a lot of people play instruments. I just wanted to play an instrument. How I even decided on the clarinet is beyond me."

Montanaro had music lessons at Settlement Music School, a South Philadelphia institution that gets too little credit historically for the role it played in nurturing talent downtown. But when his teacher left, he somehow managed to get Jules Serpentini, then a Philadelphia Orchestra member, to tutor him. It was 1946, and Montanaro was 13.

"There was a very musical family across the yard. They lived on Emily Street. The father was a barber, but he played a good clarinet and he had played at theaters. One of the sons, John, played the clarinet, and the other one played the oboe. The clarinetist was four or five years older than I. His father had a heart attack, and left the mother with eight sons and pregnant with a daughter. And Serpentini took this boy, John, he was very talented, and taught him for no charge. So I approached John."

And John Genovese, who would later join the San Francisco Symphony, approached Serpentini. Montanaro had his lessons. Then, like so many talented young musicians, Montanaro joined the orchestra at South Philadelphia High School led by Jay Speck.

"Jay Speck was not only a tremendous musician, he was a brilliant man and a fine person. . . . I would go in and try and catch him. If I heard a piece of music on the radio, I'd sing the melody and say, 'What's this?'

"He'd say, 'Oh, you stupid boy. You think you got me there.' And he would always tell you what it was and what key it was in. He really had a way with us that really gave us the desire. . . . He put on wonderful concerts. And he would become very annoyed if somebody would not behave right. 'All right, no rehearsal. I won't conduct today.' He would walk off. And we'd say, 'Oh, come on, Mr. Speck, let's have our rehearsal.' We looked forward to it.

"At one time, the Philadelphia Orchestra played in Miami Beach. Jay Speck had retired down there. We arranged to have a luncheon with everyone who had gone to Southern with Jay Speck. There was quite a big bunch of us. David Madison was there, Frank Costanzo, Harry Gorodetzer, Sam Gorodetzer. Joe Lanza and Louie Lanza, how can I forget them? Oh, Lou Rosenblatt, Armando DiCamillo, Leonard Bogdanoff, Adelchi Angelucci. I'm sure there were more than that."

Though the clarinet is certainly not the instrument of choice for youngsters, Montanaro's neighborhood was full of clarinet players.

"It's like an infection, if you put it in a negative way. It spreads. Look, it was John Genovese on Emily Street, and then I came along. On Mifflin Street, there was another fellow, Guido Mecoli, who also went to the Curtis Institute. Then there was Vito Capaccio, who went to the San Antonio Symphony. These are all clarinet players within a four-block square. And Genovese's brother is the oboist with the Boston Symphony Orchestra.

"Most of us, we went to South Philadelphia High School. Jay Speck, he was very inspiring. For example, today if you grow up in a poor neighborhood, maybe the way out is basketball or boxing. It's some type of talent. Well, not too many of us wanted to become boxers. Music was our way. People like Frank Sinatra, girls would scream over them. Artie Shaw, Benny Goodman, these are people that we really looked up to."

Dance was the way for Henry Meadows and LaVaughn Robinson.

Robinson, born in 1927, grew up on 19th Street, between Bainbridge and Kater, and later lived around the corner on 18th Street. He was the youngest boy of 14 children.

"My mother did her cooking on a woodstove in a shed kitchen with a hardwood floor. . . . I was always the one that followed her around in the kitchen. She taught me how to time-step. It was more or less to give me something to do. I was like seven years old.

"We come up during the Depression, and everybody was tap dancing. You had a lot of women who would tap dance. Bill Robinson used to come through now and then. He was a good friend of my mother's. He would stop at the poolroom on 15th and South. And at the Attucks, 15th and Catharine. It was a small hotel."

Henry Meadows does not remember being taught. He just always could dance. Born in 1923, he grew up on the 1900 and 2000 blocks of Montrose, and remembers dancing on the street as a 10-year-old to make money to buy clothes. He was not the only child dancing.

"The Nicholas Brothers, Fayard and Harold, went to school with me. They went on to be big. I met LaVaughn dancing. He had good feet. We had one fellow named Bill Graves. He's dead now. Ed Sullivan used to have him on his program. Then we had another fellow named Miller that played one of them big tubs. It had catgut, and he would play that like a bass. We used to go out every Friday and Saturday, but not Sunday. We'd start off at 15th and South and draw big crowds. First we'd all start out together, and then each of us

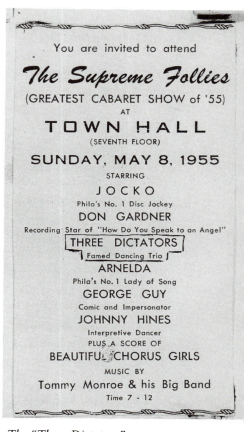

You are invited to attend

The Supreme Follies

(GREATEST CABARET SHOW of '55)

AT

TOWN HALL

(SEVENTH FLOOR)

SUNDAY, MAY 8, 1955

STARRING

JOCKO

Phila's No. 1 Disc Jockey

DON GARDNER

Recording Star of "How Do You Speak to an Angel"

THREE DICTATORS

Famed Dancing Trio

ARNELDA

Phila's No. 1 Lady of Song

GEORGE GUY

Comic and Impersonator

JOHNNY HINES

Interpretive Dancer

PLUS A SCORE OF

BEAUTIFUL CHORUS GIRLS

MUSIC BY

Tommy Monroe & his Big Band

Time 7 - 12

The "Three Dictators" were LaVaughn Robinson, Henry Meadows, and their childhood friend, Howard Blow, another South Street hoofer who danced with Robinson for 20 years. Courtesy of Henry Meadows

41

"The Dancing Jets." It's 1957, and the original threesome has changed because of dancer Howard Blow's illness. From left to right, Henry Meadows, Eddie Sledge, and LaVaughn Robinson. Eddie Sledge's daughters went into show business as singers—ever heard of Sister Sledge? Courtesy of Henry Meadows

would challenge. We had guys we'd pay to take the hat around and collect money. We were kids. We loved dancing."

And they did not just dance on South Street.

Robinson remembers his friends saying, "Let's go to work. And we called that buskin'. Buskin' was going to work, tap dancing. At that time, they had a lot of bars that was up around the Tenderloin. We would go in them bars and dance.

"The musicians would tell us when to come, when it be a lot of people, because we always gave them a piece of the action. We used to go in all the bars that was down Eighth and Race, and they let us pass the hat around. We used to make good money."

Robinson and Meadows went all over the city dancing. But they always came back to South Street. They had fans there. Neighbors supported them. Friends cheered them on. "You remember how you used to see break dancing on the street? It was like that with tap dancing. You could walk from 23rd and South to Fifth and South, and you would see on just about every other corner a different style of tap," remembers Robinson.

"And when you went around in the little streets like Kater, Naudain, say like 8 o'clock. You know how they had them street lights shine down, be like a spotlight? The dancers at night would be around them street lights, and it'd be about maybe 15 or 20 dancers dancing, taking chances. This is what you did."

Robinson and Meadows have danced off and on with one another for more than 50 years. Between them, they have performed with everyone from Cab Calloway and Tommy Dorsey to Frankie Avalon and Frank Sinatra. On stages from Paris to Atlantic City.

When they haven't danced, they have cleaned ice rinks and worked in restaurant kitchens. They both still dance, and Robinson teaches as well. They are part of a South Philadelphia era, the era of the Clark Brothers from Grays Ferry and the Nicholas Brothers and the Condos Brothers, all part of a time when people danced outside the Pep Bar to the music inside, when dancers performed at the Standard Theater on South just east of 12th, when the Two Bit Club, 16th and Fitzwater, was the spot visiting performers flocked to after hours.

The era is gone; the memories are not.

Robinson: "During the time that we came up, we could look at another dancer and tell what part of the country he was from 'cause every part of the country had their own style. Like if we go to one of the clubs and they had a tap dancer, right away after that first 16 bars, you knew where he was from, Detroit or Pittsburgh or Chicago.

"There was a Philadelphia style, but most of the dancers was from South Philly. You had good dancers come out of North Philadelphia like Honey Coles, Bill Bailey, but mostly your dancers hung around Broad and South. Like you had the Condos Brothers, Steve and Nick. Nick Condos was the one that married Martha Raye. They were a white team, but they hung mostly with black guys 'cause they came from 11th and South. There was a theater down there called the Standard that had black shows. Their father was a Greek, and he had a restaurant across the street. Steve and Nick was affiliated with all the dancers and they learned how to dance. And they got real big in the late '30s, early '40s.

"Steve and I became good friends. And we was all together last year [1991] in Lyon, France, and he had a massive heart attack and dropped dead in the dressing room underneath the stage. He was 72."

Local dancers used to be celebrities. Henry Meadows remembers: "They looked up to us. During those days, people respected you for what you did. When we come in town, they made you feel like somebody. Anytime they showed a movie with the Nicholas Brothers at the Royal Theater, 16th and South, oh boy, their names was over top of Betty Grable."

It's been many years since he's danced downtown, but people still remember Henry Meadows. He was waiting for a bus not too long ago when he saw a woman and a little girl staring at him. "When I got ready to get off the bus, the lady says, 'Sir, didn't you use to dance down the Two Bit Club?' She told me that she was telling her granddaughter that I was famous."

Many South Philadelphia entertainers are famous today or were famous at one time. Many were popular singers, such as Buddy Greco, Frankie Avalon, James Darren, Fabian, Al Martino, and Eddie Fisher.

Only two still live in the Philadelphia area. Chubby Checker is in the suburbs, about an hour from downtown. Bobby Rydell has a home maybe 35 minutes from the house he grew up in. He left South Philadelphia at the age of 21.

Singer Frankie Avalon drew crowds wherever he went in the 1960s, and South Philadelphia was no different. This crowd came to see and hear the hometown favorite at Bishop Neumann's Christmas Dance in 1960. From The Crystal / *Courtesy of Jim Kilrain*

"I had no place to put my clothes, the clothes I would wear when I started to become successful, tuxedos and this and that and shoes and shirts and ties. No room to hang anything."

Rydell, born Robert Ridarelli in 1942, told his friend, Dr. James C. Giuffre, that he was outgrowing his home, the house he lived in with his parents and grandparents.

"So he says, 'I'll show you where I live. You may like it.' So we came out and there was a house—this house—just being built on speculation. And we walked through it, and I saw a little sunken living room, a little raised dining area, and the bedroom had a sunken tub."

The transition from city to suburb was not easy.

"My clothes had to be taken to Bambi's, 'cause there was nobody up here who could clean clothes. Buy meat up here? No, no. Got to go downtown, go to Maglio's, buy the sausage.

"Now, the people that I thought were really going to get lost up here were my mom's mom and dad. But my grandmother would say, Look how nice, you got the trees, the creek in the front, the birds are singing nice. My grandmother and grandfather loved it. My mother, it took her a good three years to get adjusted. Me, I missed the bar across the street, the trolley car."

Though South Philadelphia is thought of as one neighborhood, it is really dozens of tiny communities. A Cantrell Street resident might never set foot on Catharine Street, just a couple of miles away. Rydell never strayed too far from his neighborhood. "I was 2400 South 11th, Fabian was 2500 South 11th, but I never knew him as a kid 'cause that was another corner. He went to Southern, I went to Neumann. Half a block away, I never knew him. . . .

It's 1948, and it's a wonder that Bobby Rydell has stayed so thin. This is his mother's mother, Lena Sapienza, filling him with the filled cookies that she made in the basement of their house on 11th Street. Rydell is having hot chocolate with his cookies. Courtesy of Bobby Rydell

"Eleventh and Moyamensing, George's Candy Store, that was our hangout. Go in there for sodas, the Wurlitzer, play the records, all old 78s, smoke cigarettes. . . .

"My fondest memories are the Colonial movies, 11th and Moyamensing. It was the last neighborhood theater. They built condos there. Every Saturday, go from 10 in the morning till six in the evening and see 25 to 30 cartoons, one feature-length movie, a couple of serials like Flash Gordon, Captain Marvel, Red Rider, and Little Beaver, the Three Stooges, Abbott and Costello. It would cost 10 cents. I'd go with my buddies—Louie Cioci, Joe Priore, Anthony Animal, his real name is D'Ambra. And we'd pack our lunch, peppers and eggs, meatball sandwiches, and get Coca Cola, maybe some Jujubes. That was big back then, Jujubes.

"I went to the Broadway, Broad and Snyder, maybe two times. This was a big movie already. And on Sundays, the guys and the girls, we really went heavy. We went in town to the Mastbaum, the Stanley. We're talking about foyers and chairs, lounge seats."

Rydell remembers his house. Good memories. Four bedrooms, marble steps in the front. Not a stoop. Steps. People in South Philadelphia say "steps." "I can remember my mother and my grandmother with the scrub brush, cleaning the steps. It was a two-story house, with a cellar and a coal bin where the coal truck would come. It wasn't a basement, it wasn't a music room, it was a cellar, and it was extremely clean. It had two parts. The front had the coal bin. Then my grandmother had a real big table where she would make all of the homemades, the ravioli. All of the dough stuff was rolled with the rolling pin. And my drums were down there. . . .

"In the back, we had a swinging door to the second part. My grandfather had two wine barrels where he made wine. . . . We didn't have a TV. The first TV that I got I won on the Paul Whiteman *TV Teen Club.*

Popular Dance Orchestras

A Gala Private Party

"Where Every Party is a Banquet"

FRANK PALUMBO'S CABARET-RESTAURANT

Famous for Food Since 1884

PHILADELPHIA, PA.

824-830 Catherine Street

Floor Shows Nightly

Private Room for Banquets in an Atmosphere of Friendly Hospitality

MAIN DINING ROOM — SEATS 800 PERSONS

Palumbo's was where everyone went in South Philadelphia— part nightclub, part institution, always with the good gravy. This 1933 advertisement appeared on an oversized postcard. The second woman from the left is Kippee Bozzacco, who would later marry the owner's son, Frank. Courtesy of Kippee Palumbo

" . . . I think the first time we ate in the dining room was with Sammy Davis Jr. We went to see him at the Latin Casino, and he said, 'When are you going to invite me to the house for some dinner?' I said, 'Sammy, any time you want to come.' So Sammy Davis comes, and my grandmother cooks him chicken, Italian style. And then, I swear to God, she gave him watermelon for dessert. She figured black people like to eat watermelon."

Rydell's parents live with him. He has two grown children. All of the other South Philadelphia singers who became successful left for California years ago.

"When I grew up, it was my mom, my dad, and my mom's parents. So it was a lot of love and warmth and respect in our house. The Lord was good to me and my career, and still has been good to me. And I wanted my children to grow up the same way I did, with grandparents. To have that feeling, that love, that warmth, that respect. It's all South Philly here."

Another place that was "all South Philly" was Palumbo's, the venerable Catharine Street restaurant and nightclub that opened as a hotel for Italian immigrants in 1884 and offered entertainment for more than 70 years, making it the oldest nightclub in town until a fire destroyed it on June 20, 1994.

Palumbo's former bandleader Carmen DiPipi, better known as Carmen Dee, joined the band as a 16-year-old saxophone player from South Philadelphia in 1945, and became its leader in 1961.

"When I left high school, my music teacher said they needed a saxophone player at Palumbo's. I'd heard of it, but it was at Ninth Street and I lived at 13th Street."

He took the 12-block walk from 13th and Dickinson to Palumbo's. It was like nothing the teenager had ever seen. "We had production shows. Every other week, the show would change. We had rehearsals during the day, we had a line of girls. We had comedians, singers. One of the acts was Nelson Eddy."

Carmen Dee left twice, once to go on the road, once to play at another club. He was at Palumbo's when the band featured 29 musicians, and he was there at the end, when there were six.

"I worked here in '45, '46, came back in '49, and stayed till 1953. They used to book an act a whole season because we had different people every night. Two shows a night. Fantastic. I came back in '59, been here ever since. . . . Up until the '70s, we were always busy. We had Durante come here, we had Sergio Franchi, Vic Damone, Tony Bennett. Vic Damone and Tony Bennett weren't that big then. They would work for thirty-five hundred or four thousand dollars a week, whatever, because it was still a paycheck for them, and because not everybody could work Vegas, only the select few. What hurt is the casinos, and Atlantic City and Vegas paying the big bucks. Today, an entertainer could go work just two nights a week and make $10,000. How could Palumbo's afford to give an entertainer $10,000?" Instead, Palumbo's offered banquets, with a comedian and a singer as the show.

The band used to work seven nights a week, but one or two was more like it in the 1980s and 1990s. It was okay. Carmen Dee has a nice house in South Philadelphia. He's been married 40 years. He's been on stage with the best: Jimmy Durante, Fat Jack Leonard, Mel Torme, Perry Como.

And once, just once, with Frank Sinatra. Frank Palumbo, who died in 1983, was a friend of Sinatra's.

"Frank Sinatra used to come here all the time and have dinner. He came here once, the girls from the Red Cross were having a luncheon. Frank Palumbo asked him if he'd make an appearance. He was working with Tommy Dorsey at the Earle Theater. He came in and went upstairs and sang two songs with the piano player. I was in the band. They had to carry him down the steps, the women were screaming so loud. That's the only time."

Audiences scream and applaud for entertainers, but the public's reaction to the visual arts is always more restrained. In South Philadelphia, that reaction is barely audible. Despite an institution like Fleisher, the free art school, there is little popular tradition of painting or sculpting, and the other visual arts have grown downtown despite a feeling that they were almost effete. Everyone hears about Marian Anderson and Mario Lanza growing up, but not Salvatore Pinto, or his brothers, Angelo and Biagio, perhaps the only well-known South Philadelphia artists. It is unlikely that the Pintos received the same neighborhood support as a singer or dancer. Nevertheless, Salvatore Pinto exhibited successfully across the United States and Europe in the 1930s.

Artist and jewelry maker Tony DiRienzi never heard of the Pinto brothers when he was growing up in Tasker Homes. His family did not have much money, but public housing did not have a stigma then.

"Tasker Homes? It was like a family. I had two aunts within a few doors. My father's sister. My father's brother. I had one of my mother's sisters close by. And one of my mother's brothers lived across the street. Everybody in the neighborhood seemed related somehow. I remember 31st Street from Wharton

Carmen Dee at 16 in 1943, wearing his first long-pants suit, two years before he came to Palumbo's. Note the peg pants and the Roadmaster bicycle. The picture was taken on the 1400 block of South Clarion. Courtesy of Carmen Dee

47

(above)
Bandleader Carmen Dee's favorite performer at Palumbo's was Jimmy Durante. Everything was fun when he was on stage. Here Durante clowns with a bad toupee in 1972. Carmen Dee is on the left with the baton. Courtesy of Carmen Dee

(right)
The two Franks, Palumbo and Sinatra, eating pasta, circa 1942. Though Sinatra performed only once at Palumbo's—informally and unannounced—he often stopped by to eat and see his friend, Frank Palumbo, who was best man at Sinatra's wedding to Ava Gardner. Courtesy of Kippee Palumbo

It's the summer of 1950, and everything is okay on Patton Terrace for five-year-old Tony DiRienzi and his mother, Sarah. Inside Tasker Homes, sidewalks are clean, grass is green, and the sun is shining. Later that year, Tony would get polio. Courtesy of Tony DiRienzi

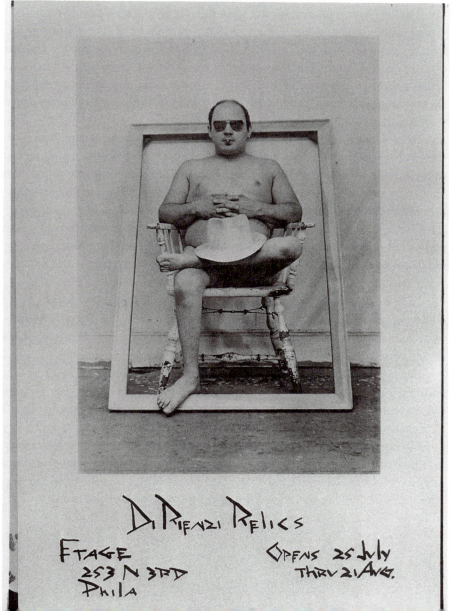

This framed photograph of Tony DiRienzi, his wry comment on Italian machismo, was used to advertise a show in 1976. The painter, sculptor, and jewelry maker easily slips between the world of art and the world of South Philadelphia. He once put on a casino night to raise money for the Pennsylvania Academy of Fine Arts. None of the Academy artists or art historians could deal blackjack or run a craps table, so he brought along some guys from downtown. They did it all, and everyone got along. Courtesy of Tony DiRienzi

to Grays Ferry Avenue was predominantly Italian. The street from Wharton to Reed and to Dickinson was Irish."

He left Tasker Homes against his will in 1950. He was six. He had polio.

He was in a hospital and convalescent home for a couple of years. When he was able to return home, his family had rented a house on the 700 block of Reed. Later they moved to the 1900 block of McClellan, between Moore and Mifflin. Unlike most young men downtown, he never had an intersection to call his own.

"I never found my corner. . . . I could plug into 20th and Moore. And then my cousins lived at 26th and Tasker, and I hung there for a while. I hung around 31st and Wharton, and then I had friends who would hang at 16th and Jackson. . . ."

He learned as a child how to make jewelry and to work with metals as part of his occupational therapy. He liked it and he was good at it. As a young man, he apprenticed with artist and jewelry maker Wesley Emmons. None of DiRienzi's friends or neighbors were artists.

"When I showed them my stuff, they couldn't relate. . . . The only one who really encouraged me was my grandmother, my mother's mother. She gave me support, but she gave everybody support. . . . My whole family's perspective about art was, it's a luxury, it's not something you take seriously. I was always talking about going to law school, and my parents were focused on my becoming a lawyer. . . . They weren't happy when I went with Wesley because that was a real bohemian atmosphere. I came in contact with a lot of other artists and I felt very comfortable. I was uptown then, and I would imagine it was threatening for my parents. It's a very blue-collar kind of sensibility down there."

He went to Temple, majored in pre-law, kept making jewelry, and married Dorothy Haitz in 1966. His mother had died the year before. "The last thing she said to me," said Dottie Haitz, "was, 'Don't let him be an artist.' The University of Pennsylvania Hospital. She died of pancreatic cancer. 'Don't let him be an artist, promise me.'"

Dottie didn't listen, Tony didn't listen. The new couple moved to an apartment on Seventh Street, between Moore and Mifflin. He insisted on staying downtown. The neighborhood may not have been nurturing toward his art, but it was nurturing in other ways.

"I'm always hungry, I could walk off and eat somewhere. If I was tired, I could go someplace. If I was broke, I could go and get some money. My family wasn't involved in my art after a while. They don't know that part of my personality."

But his family did not cut him off. They did not embrace his art, but they continued to embrace him. "My earring is 25 years old. The shit that I had to put up with about that. But my aunts and some of my uncles, they said, That's all right, he's an artist."

He taught jewelry making. He had shows of his art work. He got a master's degree. He taught sculpture. He kept making jewelry. They traveled. They had two children. They moved to the 700 block of St. Albans Street. She was making more money, so he stayed home and took care of the house and the children. He was a 1970s house husband in a place where there was no such thing. The neighbors?

"I was comfortable. . . . We didn't talk about art. We had a rapport. And if I made some new crepes or manicotti, I'd send some over to the neighbors. One woman sent over some of her cake. It was that kind of exchange."

Dottie: "I was a principal income woman. I was not home with the children; that's what was considered strange. They didn't know how to talk to me. I don't cook. I don't talk about drapes, cleaning the house, and I wasn't from South Philly. I was the person from Mars. *He* could talk about gravies."

They do not live on St. Albans anymore—the house was too small—but remain downtown on 11th near Ellsworth. DiRienzi says he "feels very comfortable down here. There's kind of a dichotomy. When we were in St. Albans Street, there was a very provincial perspective—our neighborhood, our kind. There was a kind of cushion inside of there. But at the same time, there was a recognition of a broader perspective, though not an acceptance.

"I remember some friends coming to our place, artists from Center City, and we weren't there. My neighbor came out and says, 'Oh, Tony and Dot aren't there. They won't be back till 5:30. Come in and have a cup of coffee, sit down, let me tell you . . . ' They were delighted by that. I like that kind of attitude even though they would be horrified about some of the blasphemous content, the irreverence in my work. They still accept me. They still relate to me, and I can relate to them in some way."

Sometimes in the summer, young people relate to baritone Elliott Tessler by sitting on the steps of his home on the 300 block of McKean and listening to the born-again South Philadelphian practicing inside. He started downtown, moved away, and then came back.

"I'm not a celebrity, I'm a minor curiosity. If Pavarotti lived here, he would just be a minor curiosity, and probably because he was fat more than because he sang."

No, people know Pavarotti because he sings. Elliott Tessler sings too, sings very well, but he has never been able to make a living at it. For the past 25 years, he has made his living as a deli clerk at Pathmark.

He began to sing as a boy when he heard the voice of another South Philadelphian. "I was enthralled with Mario Lanza. I was about 10 when I heard him in *The Great Caruso,* either at the Jerry or the Jackson movies. The songs I could take or leave, but that voice, utilized in opera, did it to me. So I tried to imitate him. . . ."

What he learned from Lanza records, he used when chanting his bar mitzvah haftorah. He was praised. He began studying at the Settlement Music School.

His family had moved to Oxford Circle in 1951 when he was three. His father died when he was eight. He spent weekends and summers with his grandparents on McKean and Galloway Streets. He thought of himself as a Northeast guy.

"But my street smarts came from South Philadelphia. You got more of a slice of life. . . . The Northeast was antiseptic. South Philadelphia was always fun. When I was a kid, the milk was delivered by horse-drawn carts. The same milk company delivered in the Northeast, and they delivered in trucks. There was a fish man who pushed a cart with iced-down fish. And the ladies would come. He would put down the cart and would clean the fish right there. He would scoop and put the fish's guts in a hole in his cutting board. But where did the guts go? Into the street. I don't know why he bothered with the hole.

"There was a guy, an organ grinder with a monkey. These were regular guys in South Philadelphia. These things you read about in books or see in movies. I would tell my friends in the Northeast, I see these things. They were really happening in South Philadelphia."

While attending college, he decided to change his major and study music full time. His mother was not happy.

"She had a hard life. She was looking forward to me singing part time, and completing some four-year liberal arts program and . . . doing something where the rest of my life would be guaranteed. She was afraid that I might be 43 years old and have to work part time as a delicatessen clerk.

"I transferred to the Musical Academy, it was on 16th and Spruce, where the Garden Restaurant now is. The students? Either talented kids from South Philly or no-talent dilettantes from the Main Line. We're talking 1966, '67.

"My education was interrupted when my presence was requested in the Army. It seemed as if they were having this problem in Vietnam, and they

Elliott Tessler's grandparents operated a candy store at the corner of McKean and Galloway, just a few doors from his home. It seemed like there were stores on every corner in 1953, when this picture was taken. That's Elliott with the holster in front. His grandmother, Dora Chodoroff, is behind him. The rest of the family is his uncle and aunt, Jack and Eleanor Chodoroff, and their daughter, Ann. Courtesy of Elliott Tessler

needed one more kid. I was going to turn the balance of the war. It was 1969. How could I deny my country?"

He came back in 1971, finished his education, and began to sing professionally. "I sang all over the country in opera. I always maintained a cantorial position here. It was always my luck to get into something just as it was going down for the third time. As everybody was bailing out, I discovered the Catskills. I sang under a nom de plume, Michael Templar. That was for all the popular music. I was like a poor man's Jewish, slightly chunky Sergio Franchi. My agency would send me, filling in for ailing baritones. And I was a pretty decent musician, a decent grasp for the repertoire, so it wasn't too hard on me. I'd sing in small regional theaters."

He continued performing until 1984, "till I blew out my cords. I was doing opera, cantorial, and popular music at the same time. I was in rehearsal here for an *Aida*. A pretty decent part, Aida's father. And I was in the Catskills. It was Passover, the big week, and we wanted to make a nice impression because you might sign for anywhere between 30 and 70 concerts for the summer. And I had the seders to sing in Philadelphia. Between a cold and singing three different kinds of music, I had a cord hemorrhage."

So he rested. He taught, did some voice-over commercials, and continued donating his services as a cantor to a small South Philadelphia congregation. Over the years, his voice has healed and he is singing again. He moved back to South Philadelphia. He is serious about his teaching, about his music. He has not given up. Pathmark is part time, to survive. It is a concession. "When it comes to music, I don't make those concessions."

There are South Philadelphia entertainers, like Elliott Tessler, who are not very well known. And there are those, like Lanza, who are known worldwide. But there is one entertainer, just one, who is well known only in the Philadelphia area. He is a local phenomenon, a comedian and musician by the name of Thomas Francis Morley, born in 1926 at 1240 East Moyamensing Avenue, and known to three generations as Cozy.

The house on Moyamensing Avenue had no gas or electric or water. When he was seven, his father, a stevedore, moved his wife and three sons to 440 McClellan Street. His parents were poor, but they bought him a banjo.

"I was very frail, shy, introverted, very pixie-looking. All my uncles were into strength, manhood. They worked along the waterfront, picked barrels up, threw cargo around. When I got the banjo, I'd go into a little room. I was frightened to play in front of anybody. My uncles, they'd say, 'Hey, what's wrong with the kid?' I used to sit upstairs and practice.

"I was with Fralinger String Band. They were raucous guys, drinking guys. I love the string band guys. They're not strong musicians. It's like a choir. One guy individually, he can't sing, but in a choir he sounds terrific. And those guys, they did it for nothing. Never got a dime. They would leave their instruments and let me take them home. It was like a boyhood dream playing all these things. . . ."

When World War II began, all the young musicians went into the service. Cozy Morley was 15 and suddenly in demand.

"I played music on weekends. . . . We once worked in the Community

House in Stone House Lane. That was known as the Neck, and they had squatters. They got no services from the city, nothing at all. They built a community center. Three of us played from eight to midnight on Saturday, and got three dollars. If you went down to Oregon Avenue today, and made a left on Fourth, Fifth, Sixth, or Seventh, that's where it was, all little winding roads. I'll never forget the bathrooms. Outside, there was a big hole in the dirt. That was the men's room. The ladies' room was a hole in the dirt, but they had it covered somehow."

He played drums and banjo and guitar and sax downtown at private clubs. His nickname came from a friendship with an older man from the neighborhood. "People always saw us together and assumed it was Cozy Dolan and his son. They called me Cozy. I'd say, 'That's not my name.' And they say, You don't have to be ashamed of your father. 'But I'm not ashamed, because he's not my father.' The more I would say, the more they'd call me Cozy."

Graduated from high school in 1944, he began playing with bands in clubs uptown on Walnut and Chestnut Streets. "And then the bands would break up. They always broke up. Then you get with another band. I thought I'd get my own band, and we were doing real good. We were called the Cozy Morley Quintuplet. Quartets like the Mills Brothers were popular. Bands would learn songs where they sang together, harmonizing.

"I didn't want to sing. I used to get petrified. My throat would get dry. I forced myself. I had a high voice, and people would laugh. I'm trying to sing real nice, and they're laughing. So, I figured, geez, at least I got them laughing. Then I used to wiggle my ears and play the instruments and stick pratfalls and fall off the stage. But every group that I worked with resented that, 'cause they were serious musicians. Then these guys quit. They couldn't stand me. Said I'm a show off, a hot dog. . . ."

And so he went out on his own in 1948, with a combination of music and comedy.

"I used to pull out a little notebook and read the jokes. I'd say, 'Here's a good one.' Just read the jokes and people would laugh. Then, sometimes, I'd put it back in my pocket, and I would tell some jokes. 'Bring that notebook,' they would holler.

"My jokes were very corny, silly little jokes. 'If your nose is on strike, would you pick it?' And then I did funny dances. I'd imitate the silent movies, move real quick. And then I sang and played instruments. That was my act. In the beginning, I got $10 a show. It was a lot of money. I always thought that people kind of felt sorry for me. Something's wrong with this guy or something. My stomach was always in turmoil, but I kept pushing and pushing and pushing."

He hasn't traveled much—to Boston a couple of times in the '50s, to Albany, to Canada. He didn't want to travel. It was lonely. No one knew him. Downtown, everyone knew him.

"Of the years as a comedian, if you lump them together, I don't think it would be six months on the road. Today, I work as far south as Wilmington, as far the other way as Trenton. If I go more than 35 miles in any direction, no one has ever heard of me.

"Music is my first love. I think I'm a better musician than I am a come-

Cozy Morley counting the evening's receipts at the Club Avalon in 1973. He bought the North Wildwood club in 1956. "I made so much money, it was mind-boggling. The club sat 1,200, and it had no amenities, absolutely nothing. The chairs were busted. In the ceiling, a 25-watt flood light would go on—25 watt in the ceiling. And when people would go to the bathroom, I'd say, 'I didn't bring no paper in there. I put a roll in two weeks ago, and it went like that.' Everybody would laugh." Used with permission of the Temple University Urban Archives

dian. I don't know why they laugh, but they laugh. My act is so disjointed. I tell a Polish joke, and then I tell a joke about an old lady, but they don't go together. But I just tell the joke, and people laugh, and then I go to another joke.

"They like me. All the older ladies, I'm like their son. And the older men, and now I even got that rapport with the kids, too. It's unbelievable. I work the same places, and they call me back. No, the jokes have hardly changed at all. And the same people come to hear them, and then they tell me the one I left out. Then they tell me a joke, and I go up and I tell it."

Ask Cozy Morley or Bobby Rydell or another entertainer why so many big names came from South Philadelphia, and you'll get a different answer every time. It's the Italians. It's the Italians and the Jews. It's the corner. It's the poverty. It's the water.

It's the history. The tradition of performing goes back more than two hundred years. Mummers didn't just walk up the street, they performed, and they performed first in South Philadelphia. The Southwark Theater was on South Street, not Vine. The Settlement Music School was on Queen Street, not Queen Lane. Verdi Hall was on Christian Street. These were institutions that supported, encouraged, taught, showed the way. Downtown, the reaction to people performing is often a shrug and a simple "Why not?"

So *How Many Performers Really Are There from South Philadelphia?*

What follows is a long list of singers, writers, dancers, actors, comedians, conductors, and musicians. Look for a pattern connecting talent and ethnicity and you won't find it. Sure, there are lots of Italian singers, but there are Jewish and black singers as well. Jewish comedians? Absolutely, but there are Irish and Italian comedians, too. Black dancers are named, but so are Greek dancers. The only pattern here is geography; everyone lived downtown. The only class of performers intentionally omitted are Philadelphia Orchestra members. Their numbers are simply too large—as many as 100 current and past orchestra members come from South Philadelphia.

The list is limited to people who were well known at one time, or were involved in some entertainment or artistic effort that was well known. Clearly, well known to you may not be well known to me. Anyone with wisdom to offer to improve the list, please drop me a note in care of Temple University Press. My thanks to the many people who helped compile these names, and a special thanks to Bill Esher and Mike Goffredo.

- **Al Alberts,** *lead singer of The Four Aces, three of whom were from Chester*
- **George Anastasia,** *author of two books about the mob in South Philadelphia*
- **Marian Anderson,** *famous contralto, who died in 1993*
- **Frankie Avalon,** *singer, formerly a member of Rocco and the Saints*
- **Freddie Bell,** *singer, leader of Freddie Bell and the Bellboys*
- **Joey Bishop,** *comedian. His dad's bicycle store was on Moyamensing Avenue.*
- **Jerry Blavat,** *radio personality and disc jockey, the Geator with the Heater*
- **Ben Bova,** *prolific, award-winning science fiction author*
- **David Brenner,** *comedian, moved to West Philly when he was about seven*
- **A. Seymour Brown,** *real estate agent. He wrote the lyrics to "Oh, You Beautiful Doll."*
- **Joe Brown,** *sculptor, Southern grad, creator of athletic sculptures outside Veterans Stadium. His brother was a boxer.*
- **Michael Buffer,** *boxing announcer who has become a celebrity with his trademark "Let's Get Ready to Rumble!"*
- **Bill Carlucci,** *of Danny and the Juniors. He sang "At the Hop."*
- **Alphonso Cavaliere,** *orchestra conductor for Broadway's* Hello, Dolly *and* Zorba the Greek
- **Chubby Checker,** *born Ernest Evans, the singer who popularized "The Twist"*
- **Clark Brothers,** *dancers from Grays Ferry*
- **Condos Brothers,** *dancers from 11th and South*
- **Ted Curson,** *jazz trumpet player*
- **James Darren,** *singer, actor, director. His grandmother lived next door to Bobby Rydell's family.*
- **Peter DeAngelis,** *songwriter and arranger*

56

- **Joey DeFrancesco,** *organist, toured with Miles Davis as a teenager. Father, John, an organist, too.*
- **Buddy DeFranco,** *clarinetist from 17th and Tasker*
- **James DePreist,** *orchestra conductor, nephew of Marian Anderson*
- **Albert DiBartolomeo** *wrote two novels set in South Philadelphia.*
- **Enrico Di Giusseppe** *sang at the Met in New York.*
- **Fred Diodati,** *Four Aces lead singer after Al Alberts left*
- **Danny du Val,** *acrobat, performed on* Ed Sullivan Show *and at Palumbo's.*
- **Charles Earland,** *jazz organist*
- **Fabian,** *the singer with the hair*
- **Wilhelmenia Fernandez,** *soprano, actress (*Diva)
- **Larry Fine,** *of the Three Stooges, from 3rd and South*
- **Linda Fiorentino,** *film actress. One of eight children*
- **Al Fisher,** *of the comedy team Fisher and Marks, from 11th and Fitzwater*
- **Eddie Fisher,** *singer, had his hair cut at 5th and Vollmer*
- **Joey Foreman,** *actor, comedian*
- **Edwin Forrest,** *actor, America's first stage star*
- **Arnold Fox,** *physician, author of* The Beverly Hills Medical Diet
- **Sunny Gale,** *singer, one hit—"Wheel of Fortune"*
- **Kenny Gamble,** *record producer, co-founder of the "Philly Sound"*
- **Dusolina Giannini,** *sang at the Met in 1923*
- **Vittorio Giannini,** *violinist, composer, Dusolina's brother*
- **Charlie Gracie,** *singer, 8th and Pierce, recorded "Butterfly"*
- **Buddy Greco,** *jazz, pop singer, former classical pianist*
- **Frank Guarrera,** *baritone who performed at the Met, from Ninth and Reed*
- **Heath Brothers:** *Percy, jazz bassist; drummer Albert; and Jimmy, flutist and saxophone player*
- **Dom Ierra,** *comedian, appeared on HBO*
- **Albert Innaurato,** *playwright*
- **Jaye Brothers, Phil and Jerry,** *comedians, singers. Jerry had one hit, "Ragmop."*
- **Kitty Kallen,** *big band singer*
- **Irvin Kershner,** *director of* The Empire Strikes Back
- **Jack Klugman,** *actor on stage, screen and television*
- **Joseph Kramm** *won the 1952 Pulitzer Prize for drama for his play* The Shrike.
- **Eddie Lang,** *born Salvatore Massaro, jazz guitarist*
- **Lanin Brothers,** *bandleaders Howard, Lester, and Sam*
- **Mario Lanza,** *singer and movie star, used to drive a bus in Wildwood.*
- **Frankie Lester,** *vocalist, bandleader (real name: DeVito)*
- **Hy Lit,** *radio show host, lived downtown until he was 12.*
- **George Litto,** *film producer (*Blow Out, Dressed to Kill)
- **Bernie Lowe,** *co-founder of Cameo-Parkway Records, which recorded "The Twist", "Bristol Stomp" and "Wah-Watusi"*
- **Man Ray,** *big-time artist and photographer, lived in Paris, grew up near Fourth and Carpenter, died in 1976*
- **Gloria Mann,** *18th and South, singer in the '40s, '50s*

- **Bob Marcucci,** *songwriter, discovered Fabian.*
- **Grace Markay,** *singer, from 13th and Reed*
- **Guy Marks,** *comedian, born Mario Scarpa*
- **Micki Marlo,** *singer*
- **Al Martino,** *singer, actor* (The Godfather*)*
- **Pat Martino,** *jazz guitarist, dropped out of Southern in 10th grade.*
- **Mary Mason,** *"Queen of Talk Radio," is Beatrice Turner from South Philadelphia.*
- **Henry Meadows,** *tap dancer, still lives downtown.*
- **Cozy Morley,** *comedian, musician, owner of Club Avalon in North Wildwood for 32 years*
- **N. Richard Nash,** *wrote screenplay for* Porgy and Bess.
- **Joe Niagara,** *radio disc jockey, dance host*
- **Nicholas Brothers,** *tap dancers*
- **Bob Pantano,** *disc jockey, from Sixth and Wharton*
- **Lisa Peluso,** *soap opera actress* (Loving*)*
- **Vincent Persichetti,** *classical composer and department chair at Julliard*
- **Florence Quivar,** *mezzo-soprano from 22nd and Wharton, sang at the Met.*
- **Tony Reese,** *half of the comedy team Pepper and Reese*
- **Peter Mark Richman,** *actor. He was fullback for the 1944–45 Southern football champions.*
- **LaVaughn Robinson,** *tap dancer and teacher*
- **Joe Roman,** *actor*
- **Bobby Rydell,** *singer, musician, good half ball player*
- **Jodie Sands,** *singer ("I Love You With All My Heart"), formerly Eleanor DiSipio*
- **Jimmy Saunders,** *band singer, sang at Steel Pier.*
- **Vincent Scarza,** *director of the 1985 Live Aid show*
- **Vivienne Segal,** *Broadway actress* (No, No, Nanette, Pal Joey*), died at the age of 95 in 1992.*
- **Dee Dee Sharp** *sang "Mashed Potato Time" for Cameo-Parkway.*
- **Georgie Shaw,** *singer*
- **Dick Sheeran,** *longtime KYW-TV reporter from 1828 South Hicks, was in the 1957 Southern graduating class.*
- **Joseph Stefano,** *film writer* (The Black Orchid, Psycho*), from Broad and Reed*
- **Lou Stein,** *piano player, played with Patty Paige.*
- **George "Bon Bon" Tunnell,** *1930s, 1940s band singer*
- **Charlie Ventura,** *saxophone player, from Ninth and Kimball*
- **Joe Venuti,** *violinist and bandleader, played with Paul Whiteman.*
- **Stanley Weintraub,** *author and expert on George Bernard Shaw*

Not mentioned is one film star who did not live in South Philadelphia long enough to be included—Sylvester Stallone, who passed through as a child.

3
Blacks

Robert Neverbegood is a name few Philadelphians know, but the black history of the city begins in South Philadelphia with him. He was a servant of Patrick Robinson, a Swedish settler who owned 100 acres of land. Robinson listed Robert Neverbegood as his Negro servant in a 1683 census of the Passyunk district in what is South Philadelphia today. A Swedish landowner named Lasse Cock also listed a Negro servant, but never included his name.

Up until then, there had been no record of the full name of a black man or woman residing in the Philadelphia area, either before or after William Penn's arrival. So Neverbegood—one wonders what he did to deserve that name—is the first black resident whose name we know. He may have come from the West Indies on a Dutch ship. But there were other blacks in the area before him. In 1639, authorities in Manhattan sentenced a convict to be sent on the first ship to the South River to live "along with the blacks." The South River was the Delaware. Later, a black man named Anthony was in the service of Swedish governor in Tinicum. Though no Penn colonists brought black slaves with them in 1682, at least one, James Claypoole of England, asked before he arrived if he "might have two Negroes . . . for cutting down trees, building, plowing or any sort of labor that is required in the first planting of a county."

Large numbers of farm workers were not needed for those first plantings because the farms were far smaller than Southern plantations. A few were usually enough. But as many as 13 Negroes worked on Henry James's farm in Moyamensing in 1688. Indeed, for more than 250 years farm work brought black men and women to South Philadelphia. Listen to Lillian Fauntleroy, born in 1911, a longtime resident of Dover Street in Grays Ferry:

"I was born at 1702 Washington Avenue. There are no homes there now. . . . I was raised on the 1000 block of South Chadwick. . . . My parents came here from the South when they were school age. My grandparents came up here because things were so hard down there, in South Carolina. They came here so they could go to New Jersey, where you could go picking. There was work there."

The Quaker influence kept Philadelphia from becoming completely at ease with slavery, but it took more than a century after the city was founded for slavery to be ended in the state. The state passed law after law in the 1700s to curtail the freedoms of black men and women. Liquor, firearms, intermarriage, and activities as simple as meeting together in small groups were all regulated or banned. A preamble to a 1726 law "for the Better Regulation of Negroes in this Province" grumbled that the emancipation of blacks too often led to their poverty.

By 1790 there were many more free blacks than slaves in the city and in the districts of Passyunk, Moyamensing, and Southwark. While some of the 2,102 listed in the 1790 Census under the heading "All Other Free Persons" were former white indentured servants, many were once slaves.

In 1814, 2,500 black men marched to Grays Ferry to build fortifications to protect the city from a British naval threat. But as the black community grew—24 percent of Moyamensing was black in 1830—so did the violence. From 1832 to 1849, riot after riot bloodied the city. More often than not, the violence was between blacks and whites, and, more often than not, the violence took place in South Philadelphia, from the wharves of Grays Ferry to the rural neighborhoods near Seventh and South.

Despite the Quaker influence and the virtual absence of slaves, Philadelphia was, in many ways, a Southern city—and in Southern cities blacks had their place. In South Philadelphia, many poor blacks and poor whites lived in the same unsanitary housing in the same dark alleys, but in communities that were separate. Those communities began to grate against one another as more and more poor, free black men came to Philadelphia and as the abolitionist movement continued to grow.

For many white residents, including the burgeoning number of Irish immigrants, these changes were a threat to the unskilled jobs they had or were trying to find, and a threat to the sanctity of their community. W. E. B. Du Bois called the city's nineteenth-century Irish population the "hereditary enemies" of blacks.

But the two groups shared more than they realized, as each scuffled to grab what lay on the bottom of the economic barrel. Both were rural people held back by a lack of education and job skills and an unfamiliarity with urban life. They were bumpkins in the big city, caricatures for others to mock. The continuing influx of Southern blacks and the prospect of even more free black men if slavery ended upset a teetering balance and unnerved the Irish American population. The Irish had little, but no one was going to take their jobs and overrun their neighborhood. And in early and mid-nineteenth-century Philadelphia, doing harm to blacks was, in the words of historian Sam Bass Warner, "socially acceptable violence."

One of the riots was in 1834. It lasted four days and Stephen James, "an honest, industrious colored man," was killed. Historians do not agree on the details of what happened on those summer nights, but there is consensus that the bulk of the violence occurred in Moyamensing between Seventh and Eighth Streets, South and Bainbridge, and that it all began on August 11.

On that Monday evening, whites and blacks had a free-for-all on South Street between Seventh and Eighth at a carousel that had been set up in a vacant lot on the southern edge of the black ghetto. The next night, a mob of whites destroyed the carousel and damaged a black church and some 20 homes

Agnes Moses, Jerry Moore's mother, and the family dog, King, outside the Manton Street house in 1931. She came from Atlanta to South Philadelphia in 1926 and originally lived on 17th Street near Washington Avenue. Courtesy of Jerry Moore

occupied by blacks. It was more of the same on Wednesday night, as whites marched south on Seventh, clubs in their hands, smashing windows, doors, and the heads of any blacks in their path. White residents protected their property with lighted candles in the windows. On the fourth night, another black church was defiled by white rioters. Mayor John Swift and two militia troops finally dispersed the mob.

It was not just the Irish in South Philadelphia who treated blacks badly. There were more blacks in Philadelphia than in any other northern city, but no northern city treated them worse. In 1862 Frederick Douglass said: "There is not, perhaps, anywhere to be found a city in which prejudice against color is more rampant than in Philadelphia." Blacks and whites still do harm to one another today, but the ferocity and hydra-like ugliness of the mob seem to have disappeared locally. But enmity's memory lingers; hatred is difficult to forget.

Jerry Moore came from Atlanta with his mother in 1926. He was 14 years old. They lived on the second floor of a house on 17th Street, between Carpenter and Washington.

"In those days, blacks was concentrated from Lombard Street to Washington Avenue, solid. And from Broad, I'd say, up to 20th Street, that was solid black. . . . We used to play ball on 16th Street and Washington. Mostly it was Italian boys I played with at that time. No, it wasn't tough being black, not in that section it wasn't. . . . I had more trouble with Irish boys, further up, going west, and on up to Grays Ferry. You had a lot of trouble. You had to run. They called you all kind of names."

61

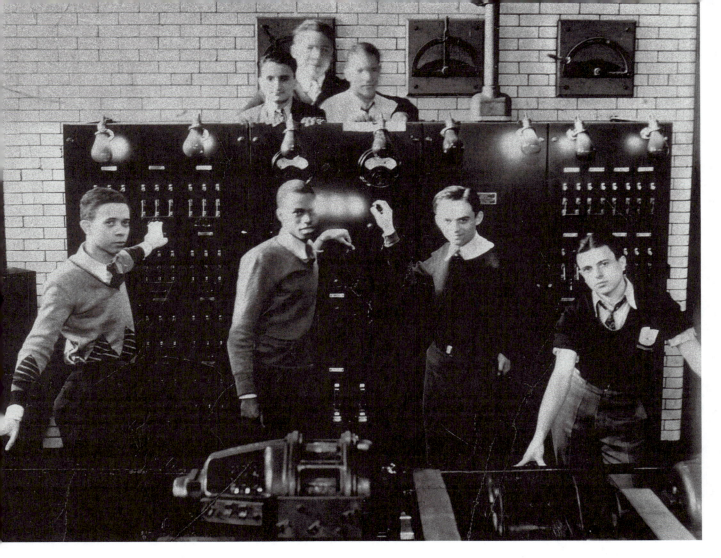

Electric shop at South Philadelphia High School in 1931. Jerry Moore is second from the left on the bottom row. Above him, right to left, with their appropriate nicknames, are Joseph Cusanno (Lefty), Alexander Mulholland (Mike), and Philip Pittore (Pit). On the bottom row, right to left, are Morris Rosen (Rose), Louis Latsion (Greek), Moore (Georgia Kid), and Harold Thomas (Tom or Fuzzy). Courtesy of Jerry Moore

Jerry Moore was actually more afraid of Irish neighborhoods than he was of Irish boys. Alexander "Mike" Mulholland was his friend. "He was a big kid. He lived about two blocks from me, on Oakford Street, and we walked to South Philadelphia High School together every day."

That was about 65 years ago. When Nick Cooper was born in 1958, Moore was already a married man with three children who had moved away from South Philadelphia the year before. Cooper grew up on Emily Street, near Sixth, just north of Snyder, a boy whose great-grandparents lived near 12th and Bainbridge behind the Standard Theater.

"When I was growing up, we were taught that there were no boundaries. If I wanted to go from down here to Broad Street, we would walk and go. Yeah, we would meet adversity on the way.

"We would walk through an Italian neighborhood, and these cats would come out the door with bats and chains. I'm about 12, I'd be walking up Snyder, Emily, Mifflin, those streets, and you'd find guys from my age to guys with beards and gray hair chasing blacks back into their own neighborhood.

"I'm not saying it's all Italians, or only Italians. But if we walked to the Broadway movies at Broad and Snyder, it was an adventure. You had a bunch of Italians on a corner. . . . If you walked by them and if you looked at them,

By 1934, Jerry Moore was married. His wife, Hura, pictured here looking west on Manton Street, is pregnant with their oldest, Geraldine. Courtesy of Jerry Moore

Jerry Moore's three children in 1943: Geraldine, Michael, and Acel (left to right), and their cousin, Doris Hill. Acel went on to be a reporter and an editor at The Philadelphia Inquirer *and a winner of the Pulitzer Prize. Courtesy of Jerry Moore*

it was, 'What are you looking at, nigger?' If you responded, it would be a big fight, or you would get chased. They expected you not to look. If you walked by and looked down, you were going to get a bottle upside the head for not even looking back. So most of the time, we looked straight where we was going. . . .

"You know, I went to the Key School, Eighth and Wolf, and it was predominantly Italian. And a lot of the kids were mobsters' kids, like [Sal] Testa. The mobsters' kids I got along with, no problem. Mafia kids didn't go through that thing with 'nigger this' or 'spearchucker that.' It was like, 'Yo, you come over my house.' We come down Eighth and Darien, we go to his house, I walk in his door, and, wham, sit down and eat just like they. We got treated like normal regular people. . . . It was the Italian kids outside of school we had problems with." He also had problems with other black kids because it was a time of turf and gangs. And, like blacks who feared walking in predominantly Irish Grays Ferry, Cooper had to watch himself at the Murphy Recreation center at Fourth and Shunk.

" . . . You took a chance staying until the pool closed, because . . . they would always let us out onto the playing field. . . . You got a whole gang of Irish kids out there waiting on you. So you had to picture in your mind a floor plan about how you were going to get home, . . . get from Murphy Field through their neighborhood."

Bill Lawson did not have to worry about navigating great distances. The problems were just outside his door. He lived in Tasker Homes.

Chairperson of the philosophy department today at the University of Delaware, Lawson was 12 years old when his parents moved from Sydenham Street, near 16th and Bainbridge, into the projects on the western edge of Grays Ferry in 1959. It was considered a step up.

"We lived in the PJs, that's what we called the projects. It was integrated. The people next door were white, and there weren't that many blacks in there. Tasker Homes was surrounded by whites on one side, oil refineries the other side. . . . You found a lot of young families in there. People were using it to raise their family and to accumulate enough capital to move someplace else. So it wasn't seen as a final resting place. . . . At that time, maintenance was good. They fixed things almost immediately. It was really a good place to live and grow up." Except for the racial and class differences.

"Animosity, fights. We had to deal with the blacks from Grays Ferry and their attitude towards people in the projects. They tended to look at the people in the projects as trying to be up and coming. And the whites looked at us as interlopers.

"My parents? No, they said little about racial animosity. You were on your own. And the whites in the projects? They knew the problems and everything, and some of them were pretty sympathetic to it. I remember one time we had a big snowball fight. It was blacks and whites in the projects against the whites who lived outside the projects."

Sometimes, the lines were that clear. They were for Frances L. Brown, who grew up on the 1700 block of Addison Street, just south of Pine. Born in 1931, she always felt that Addison, not South Street, was the northern end of South

Philadelphia. After she married, she changed her name and became nationally known for her work with black youths at the House of Umoja. Frances L. Brown is now Falaka Fattah.

"Addison was a black street. Pine Street began with the Caucasians. That was the dividing line then. You know the streets with the trees, Pine, Spruce, Walnut, Chestnut. They were all white. Go south, Lombard, South, Bainbridge, that was all black. Addison was the dividing line. I remember that because it was a matter of where we would play.

"We always went south, we didn't go to Pine Street. . . . How did I know? My grandmother told me, because she worked for white people. She was very clear where the line was."

It wasn't just young blacks who had problems with violence or boundaries. James Hill, Lillian Fauntleroy's father, was a trashman in the 1930s, and part of his route was in Grays Ferry. "The Irish didn't allow him to cross under the bridge on 25th Street to collect the trash," remembers his daughter. "He had to fight coming over and fight coming back. If you were black, you couldn't go under that bridge."

The movement of blacks into South Philadelphia encountered problems in the 1800s, too. The black ghetto of the early 1800s was on Pine and Lombard, just a street or two north of South Philadelphia. But as the century moved on, so did black residents, moving south, west, and southwest. By 1847, 866 black families lived in Moyamensing and 287 lived in Southwark, compared with just 202 families in the northern suburb of Spring Garden.

In 1848 the Crucifixion Episcopal Church opened in Moyamensing on Eighth Street near Bainbridge, offering clothing, food, and God's word to the poor blacks who lived in the alley housing nearby. On Sundays, church-going parishioners were often attacked by white residents. The attacks went on for years.

South Philadelphia was the city's most impoverished area, and blacks were the poorest of the poor. In Moyamensing, one of every eight black families received some sort of charitable assistance. Newspaper editorials decried the housing conditions of blacks and whites on a stretch of Fitzwater from Fifth to Eighth Streets. Agencies formed to help the poor, including the black poor. One, the Philadelphia Society for the Employment and Instruction of the Poor, described Lombard south to Fitzwater Streets, Ninth Street east to Fourth, as the "infected area" because of its unsanitary conditions.

The House of Industry opened in 1848 on Catharine Street between Seventh and Eighth to clothe, feed, bathe, and provide medical care to neighborhood youth. It had an industrial school for whites and provided space rent free for an industrial school for black youth. Black teachers taught calisthenics, shoemaking for boys, cooking for girls, and sewing for both. Though the House of Industry assisted adults too, not many were black—just 51 of the 1,073 given assistance in 1855–56. Blacks from Gettysburg, fleeing the advancing army of General Lee in 1863, found shelter at the House of Industry.

Blacks also streamed into Philadelphia from another direction during the Civil War, as more than 9,000 former slaves came north with the help of the Vigilance Committee of Philadelphia. One of the committee's leaders was

William Still, a black businessman who lived at 834 South and owned a coal yard at Ninth and Washington. Still also sold concessions at Camp William Penn in suburban Chelten Hills, where black Philadelphians began training to be Union soliders in 1863. Some blacks complained that he charged those young men too much money.

In 1864, as blacks and whites from South Philadelphia were risking their lives in the Civil War, an east–west streetcar line began serving Lombard and South Streets. The streetcar linked a black neighborhood to an Irish one, much to the consternation of the white community. But blacks were not permitted on the cars. Even soldiers from Camp William Penn could not return to their homes on streetcars.

Still and Octavius V. Catto, a schoolteacher, led a public campaign to desegregate the streetcars. That campaign made the color of passengers an electoral issue in the 1865 mayoral race. Republican candidate Morton McMichael ducked the issue, but the Democrat, Daniel Fox, insisted, "Races must be separate and distinct." If blacks could ride on the cars, Fox said, there would likely be "demands for political equality, including the right to hold office. . . ."

McMichael won, though it is doubtful that he carried South Philadelphia. State law desegregated streetcars in 1867. Fox was elected mayor in 1869. Catto was South Philadelphia's first black hero. Unlike Still, he was untouched by controversy. He was a civil rights leader and a political force in the community, a local boy who had made good and stayed in the neighborhood, teaching at the Institute for Colored Youth on the 900 block of Bainbridge Street. Many of the students trained there went to aid the South during Reconstruction. Years later, the institute would become Cheyney University.

The state legislature took the vote away from black men in Pennsylvania in 1837. It was forced to give the vote back in 1869 when it ratified—reluctantly—the Fifteenth Amendment. The following year, federal troops were sent to Philadelphia to protect blacks who cast their ballots. October 10, 1871, was Election Day in the city, but the biggest news in the papers that day was the great Chicago fire. In South Philadelphia's Fourth Ward, south and east of Seventh and South Streets, blacks had voted in 1870 and were prepared to vote again. But there were no federal troops to protect black voters this day. Despite violence that began in the early morning, Mayor Fox did not ask for federal help.

Blacks were overwhelmingly Republican; the police and white residents of South Philadelphia were overwhelmingly Democratic. New Republican voters would change life in South Philadelphia. Patronage jobs would be lost, power would shift. Early in the day, a black man named Levi Bolden was shot near Seventh and Lombard. He would die of his wounds three weeks later. The night before, a black Moyamensing shoemaker named Jacob Gordon was shot and killed on Eighth Street near Bainbridge.

Isaac Chase, a black man who lived behind Catto's house, was on his way to vote on Bainbridge Street when "Reddy" Dever and Frank Kelly split his head open with an ax. There was more violence that the police either could not, or would not, control. Angry blacks stood on rooftops and hurled stones at officers returning to the police station at Eighth and South. About 4 p.m. on

Election Day, Catto stood at Eighth and Lombard and could see the rioting to the south. He had already voted and wanted to avoid trouble. It would have been easier to walk down Eighth Street to his house at 814 South, but he chose a more prudent route, going up Lombard to Ninth, then south to South Street. As he walked the last half-block to his home, Frank Kelly saw him. Catto passed him. We do not know if words were spoken. Kelly shot him. A streetcar passed by. Catto stumbled and fell, not far from where Darien Street intersects with South today. He was dead.

Catto, once the community's hero, became its martyr. A black newspaper would write the next day: "Each home was in sorrow, and strong men wept like children when they realized how much had been lost in the untimely death of the gifted Catto." His body lay in state at the armory of the First Regiment, Broad and Race Streets, and was guarded by the military. City and state offices were closed. His funeral cortege on October 16 was the largest the city had ever seen for a black man, and the grandest since President Lincoln's death.

The Institute for Colored Youth would later become a public school named after local Congressman Samuel J. Randall. The name was given over the objections of black residents, who despised Randall because the Democrat had cast the deciding vote in Washington to bring federal troops home from the South during Reconstruction.

The Republicans won the 1871 election in Philadelphia. Ten years later, city schools were desegregated, though not without strong protest in South Philadelphia. And in 1881 the first blacks became policemen and postal workers in Philadelphia. South Philadelphia blacks worked as hod carriers (never masons) and ministers, in factories and in people's homes, as waiters and as small business owners, like Robert Adger, who owned a furniture and hardware store. *The Philadelphia Ledger* published this obituary in 1896: "Robert Adger, a colored Abolitionist, died Saturday at his home, 835 South St. He was born a slave in Charleston, S.C. in 1813. His mother, who was born in New York, went to South Carolina about 1810 with some of her relatives, and while there was detained as a slave.

"When his master died, Mr. Adger, together with his mother and other members of the family, were sold at an auction, but, through the assistance of friends, legal proceedings were instituted, and their release finally secured. Mr. Adger came to this city about 1845, and secured a position as a waiter. . . . Later he was employed as a nurse, and while working in that capacity, saved enough money to start in the furniture business on South Street, above Eighth, which he continued to conduct with success until his death. Mr. Adger always took an active interest in the welfare of the people of his race."

More and more blacks came to Philadelphia following the Civil War, and the movement north continued into the 1900s as part of the great nationwide migration into urban centers by Southern blacks. In 1870, blacks were just 3 percent of the population of South Philadelphia. Their numbers increased to 8 percent in 1910 and 11 percent in 1920, for a total of nearly 42,000 persons. No ethnic group experienced greater population growth in that decade.

When Ward 30, South Street to Washington Avenue, Broad Street west to the river, became 52 percent black in 1920, it was the city's first political ward with a black majority. The city's first black ghetto of the 1900s was in South Philadelphia, as was its first race riot of the new century. That occurred in 1918 when Mrs. Adelia Bond, a black woman who was a city court probation officer, bought a house on the 2900 block of Ellsworth Street. On July 26, she was sitting on her front steps when a crowd gathered and began to throw stones. She fired a shot into the air. It took four days and two deaths for the rioting to end.

Catherine Williams was born that year, 1918, in Orangeburg, South Carolina. Her parents, Jimmie and Bessie Bates, had relatives in Philadelphia and moved near 12th and Bainbridge in 1921 to find a better life. When Catherine was six, they moved to the 700 block of Hoffman Street, and several years later to 623 Hoffman, between Mifflin and McKean. Her father drove a truck; her mother worked as a domestic.

"Hoffman Street was mixed. We had everything. We had the Jews, we had Italians, we had the blacks, we even had a Portuguese family. You never knew there was a color thing back then. I was the only black in my class at Southwark, but you never knew. In the third, fourth grade, some of those Italian boys was big, but you would have thought they were brothers to me. I was a little thing and they protected me."

No geographical boundaries limited her, growing up in the 1920s and 1930s. Unlike her grandson, Nick Cooper, she was never terrorized when she left the neighborhood.

"We walked down to Pattison Avenue, which at that time was called the dumps, the Neck. There were people living back there with these white caps and aprons and long black dresses. On Saturdays, they would come up Seventh Street with pigs and chickens in their wagons. I guess they were on their way to the market around Second and South. That was our fun. We'd do it on Saturdays and after church on Sundays."

The Bates family were Methodists and went to Mount Olive, a black church on Clifton Street, near 11th and South. "The black churches in this vicinity were in houses and were around Marshall Street, Shunk, Howard. The first church I remember to move up near here in a church building was at Sixth and Mercy."

When she wasn't walking south to the dumps beyond Oregon Avenue, she might walk north, uptown, to the department stores, or east to the river. "It was fun. We'd take the ferry and go to Red Bank, New Jersey. The boat didn't cost nothing. They had a park in Red Bank with swings and things. We used to make french fried potato sandwiches and go."

She went to South Philadelphia High School. The girls' building was on Snyder Avenue, the boys' on Jackson Street. "There was nothing racial there. . . . Never was there a riot between whites and blacks. There was riots between the Italians and the Italians, but not with the blacks, never."

She married at 17 in 1935. Two years later they moved to the 600 block of Emily, and her first child was born, one of three who would be born on Emily Street. Catherine Williams shopped on Seventh Street, buying turnips at tables in the neighborhood. She danced to band music at block parties on McKean Street. She walked at midnight to a nightclub at 11th and Ellsworth and never thought twice about it. Years later, she would go back to school and

Catherine Williams' mother, Bessie Bates, is sitting second from the right in this circa 1925 picture of women at St. Martha's House at Eighth and Snyder. Judging from the fine clothes everyone is wearing, this is probably a formal picture of a club or social group. Courtesy of Catherine Williams

Christmas 1955. Catherine Williams (left) and her mother, Bessie Bates, are in the kitchen at 627 Emily. Courtesy of Catherine Williams

become a nurse. Today, there are no more block parties and no nightclubs nearby. Seventh Street is not the shopping mecca it once was, and neighbors don't keep the street clean the way they once did. But Catherine Williams says, "I'd never leave here to live anywhere else."

Philosophy professor Bill Lawson left and has no plans to go back. A few year ago he went back to attend the funeral of an old friend who lived at 29th and Morris. "They told me not to park on Morris Street because they still have fights and my car could get pelted with rocks from the playground when whites start throwing things at the black kids on the other side of the street."

The area around Tasker Homes was racially tense when he was there in the late 1950s and early 1960s, and it remains racially tense—though less so—today. "The funeral was at 33rd and Reed. As we drove around, we saw that the sons of the same people who were standing out there when we were kids were still standing on the same corner. The same families. . . . When I went to the funeral, it was like old home week. . . . I think people who had new ideas left and went someplace else . . . and that would just reinforce certain things about how you look at the world. It's amazing. To walk in this neighborhood and have them say the same things to me that they said 25 years ago about 'Don't park your car over there because it could be pelted with rocks.' Twenty-five years later, kids still can't go in the playground and play. It's like a little area in which the time stood still."

Time has not stood still for Lillian Fauntleroy, her daughter, Jean Branham, and Jean's daughter, Renee Branham—three generations of Grays Ferry residents. Each has viewed Grays Ferry and South Philadelphia through a different prism of time, but from the same vantage point, the 1300 block of Dover Street.

Renee Branham was born in 1954, the youngest girl of four children. She grew up seeing blacks and whites fight. "I had a lot of racial problems growing up in this neighborhood. There's always been a lot of gangs, and unfortunately I could fight, so I belonged to a gang, the Roads, 28th and Grays Ferry. I was 13, 14." She was the only one of her mother's children who joined a gang. "I just felt white people were prejudiced and didn't like me because I wasn't the same color."

She doesn't feel the same prejudice today and doesn't believe her daughter, who goes to a parochial school in the neighborhood, feels it either. She feels safe in Grays Ferry and South Philadelphia, safer than, say, North Philadelphia. The neighborhood has improved, and it has deteoriated. "I think it's for the worse, because of the drug situation. But everybody is friends now, everybody gets along. I mean, they speak to you, Hi, how you doing? . . . I don't think we have racial problems around here anymore."

Renee Branham has a nice house and a good job. Her mother, Jean, raised her without any job at all. Jean Branham was born in 1934 and grew up on the 1100 block of South Darien, near Federal. "My memories of that block are beautiful. I grew up in a house filled with music. We had an old piano. My oldest brother, Errol, played the drums, and my youngest brother, Luther, played the sax. What did I play? I danced, but my brothers could sing.

"And it was just a nice time growing up on Darien Street. We had block parties. We had a clean block at that time. All of South Philadelphia used to

have clean block streets, and we would win the prize. You would put your folding chairs out and beautiful fern plants, and we had the white stone steps, and we had to scrub the steps down. And you didn't just have to scrub your steps, you had to scrub your neighbor's steps. The children would pitch in."

And on Saturdays, she would walk to the Dixie movies at Point Breeze Avenue and Oakford. Unlike her daughter, no racial animosities marked her childhood. "I was never hassled. I guess I stayed on my side of the tracks." She dropped out of Southern at 17 and married Norris Branham. Their first apartment was at 21st and Dickinson. Later they moved to West Philadelphia. The marriage faltered several times over the years, and she would move back downtown with her children. In 1956, the marriage ended, and she and her children moved in permanently with her parents on Dover Street. She's still there.

"My mother didn't want me to come back, 'cause you have to try and make it. But my father told me I could come back and I came back. . . . I didn't have a hard time raising my children. My children didn't want for anything. I had a good father. And my mother-in-law was very good to me. . . . And I stayed right here with my mother, and she went to work and I took care of the house. And my children went to school, and all of my children graduated from school. . . . Now, like mother told you, it was no welfare when she came up, but I got welfare for my children."

The neighborhood changed over the years. The 1300 block of Dover had always been black. The 1200 block had always been white. That stayed the same, but the surroundings were different.

"When we first came here, we had all the little stores, drugstore, corner stores. . . . Get up Sunday morning and you didn't have the right socks, you always had a little store you could go to and buy socks, little hair ribbons. You don't have any of that now. You have to go out of the neighborhood. You really have to have a car because there's nothing around here anymore. . . ."

Racial problems have colored the neighborhood's history, but Jean Branham agrees with her daughter that those problems have lessened in a bittersweet fashion. "Now I see the blacks and whites are getting along very fine, because they all taking drugs together."

Like her daughter, Lillian Fauntleroy does not remember people treating her badly because she was black. She grew up on the 1000 block of South Chadwick Street, near 17th and Washington Avenue, a black street in a black neighborhod, and remembers the trains rumbling by on Washington Avenue, the backyard toilet, the coal stove, the account book in the grocery store that everyone used. It was about 1920.

"We played just like the children play now. There were a few white children lived around, Jewish children, and we all played together. And a few Italians was around. We had nice Italian people. They would call all the kids in and get a big loaf of bread and bake it, and give us all jelly and bread and peanut butter and things like that. They was bad off, too, but they was good to us. Whatever they had, they shared it. If they had a pot of stew or spaghetti, and they wasn't going to use it, they passed that on to us. 'Cause things were bad. It was no welfare. Before the soup lines come in, that's when it was really bad. They started giving away soup and stuff, but you had to go get in line. My father was working, so he didn't have to go to any lines."

Her father, James Hill, earned three dollars a day as a street cleaner and trash hauler.

"He worked for Vare, the politican; he had the street cleaning then. He did the city work and he hired my father. My father used to work out in the cold, lifting ashes. . . . People would put them out in tin tubs. . . . He had a team, two horses. And he used to bring them horses home lunchtime and put the bag, the baskets around, and the horses would eat. And then my father would eat his lunch. He liked nice hot meals, stews and a pot of greens and corn bread. . . . The horses would leave their dirty stuff there, and my father would clean it up before he went away."

The dump that Catherine Williams visited as a girl is where James Hill unloaded the ashes six and seven times a day. When he retired, he was a street cleaner working on a truck for the city.

Lillian Fauntleroy, whose grandparents came to South Philadelphia so they could farm nearby, married at 14 and had a baby the same year, the first of three children. "That's my baby, Jean. We lived in many little houses. The 1800 block of South Latona, the 1800 block of Titan, the 1100 block of South Dor-

rance, the 2200 block of Titan. I worked in clothing factory at 26th and Reed, and then it moved to 15th and Lehigh. . . .

"We had a nice little family. And whenever we had anything going on, we would make it to ourselves. Not that we didn't get along with people. But there was enough of us to have our own parties and our own good times and enjoy ourselves. We would get together, and, like, if you bring a ham and your wife, she would make a salad. And when you bring your little things, this table opens up, you put it all on the table. And the men would bring their bottle of wine and stuff, and you had a good time, you got along. The people wasn't fighting, killing, like they are now."

It is quiet now on Dover Street, but at her daughter's urging Lillian Fauntleroy recalls a time in the late 1970s when there were too many nights of broken glass.

"We used to get the windows broken out and everything. There was an old beer garden up at the corner where they would go and get drunk on Friday and Saturday night. Just go, 'Let's get some niggers tonight,' and coming through the streets and you in bed and break out the windows." It lasted a summer. Sometimes she saw the faces of the men who threw the bricks. They were neighborhood guys.

If anybody was throwing anything at Jerry Moore in Grays Ferry, he was running and too scared to look back. "They used to chase you with milk bottles, and you'd hear nothing but bottles breaking behind you. . . . The Irish despised black people in those days. I don't know why."

At Federal and Point Breeze was the Esquire, a popular corner bar with a black clientele. Note the pictures of Eddie "Rochester" Anderson, Joe Louis, and other black celebrities. Lillian Fauntleroy's husband, Irvin, known to friends as "Cready," is behind the bar in this 1948 photograph. Courtesy of Lillian Fauntleroy and Jean Branham

73

Who says in-line skating is the only way to go? Taken roughly 50 years ago, this picture, probably posed by the photographer, shows teens on a skating day in the Christian Street Y gym. Photo by John W. Mosley / Courtesy of Charles L. Blockson Afro-American Collection, Temple University

After he graduated from high school, he married in 1933 and moved from 17th Street to a home on the 1900 block of Manton Street, near the police and fire station. His three children were born on Manton Street. He lived there until 1957.

"I used to walk to the midnight movies on Sunday nights from 19th Street to 12th and South, me and my wife. Never had fear of anybody bothering you. Sometime people walk up at night, holler across the street, 'Hey, you got a match?' You wouldn't think nothing of it. You wouldn't do that somebody ask you for a light now. In fact, you wouldn't be out there walking that time of night. I know I wouldn't. . . ."

They often shopped on Point Breeze Avenue. The customers were primarily black. "It was all Jewish merchants. And the Roosevelt Bank was there, Point Breeze and Wharton. I don't know what kind of a bank you call it because you never knew how much interest you're going to get, never. And at the end of the year, you go in there, they would tell you. And the black people, I found this out later on, they only got a half a cent on the dollar, but the whites used to get up to two and a half cents. No black ever got over a half a cent and never worked a black in that bank at the time, never, not even cleaning the floors."

He worked in a cleaners and later as an electrician at the Navy Yard. He remembers playing pinochle outside on a table on Manton Street. And he remembers baseball.

"I was a great Philadelphia Athletics fan, but when Jackie Robinson come into Brooklyn, I changed over to the National League. I remember the first time he came here, black people was all up on the roof of Shibe Park. That was the biggest crowd they ever had. It was '47. . . . It was a racial thing, 'cause whites would be pulling for the Phillies, and all the blacks would be pulling for Brooklyn. In the seventh inning, all the blacks would stand up and the Philadelphia fans would holler, 'Go back to New York.' They didn't know we was all from Philadelphia."

Poverty is part of the heritage of most black South Philadelphians. Jerry Moore was poor. Lillian Fauntleroy was poor. So were Catherine Williams and Bill Lawson. They are not poor today, but growing up, their pockets were empty. Except for Falaka Fattah.

"No, I wasn't poor. I've never been poor. I guess you would say probably middle class. . . . My grandfather was the ice man. He had a horse and buggy and had routes all through South Philadelphia. . . . My father sold insurance. My father met my mother in college. He wanted to be an architect, but my grandmother told him that there were no black architects. She didn't know anything about black history, because there's been quite a few black architects. She told him that he should not be fooling around with something that he was not going to have a chance to do. He should take care of his family."

Percy Brown went to work in the post office, where a great many black

Wedding day for Falaka Fattah, born Frances Brown, and Russell Davenport at St. Philip's Episcopal Church, 19th and Lombard, on July 1, 1949. On the right are her parents, Percy and Lee Carlyle Summers Brown. Next to them is Walter Pendell, who would later marry Christine Hale, the woman standing next to the bride. The groom is in uniform. To the far left is the bride's brother, Carl. Next to him is the bride's aunt, Ann Summers. Courtesy of Falaka Fattah

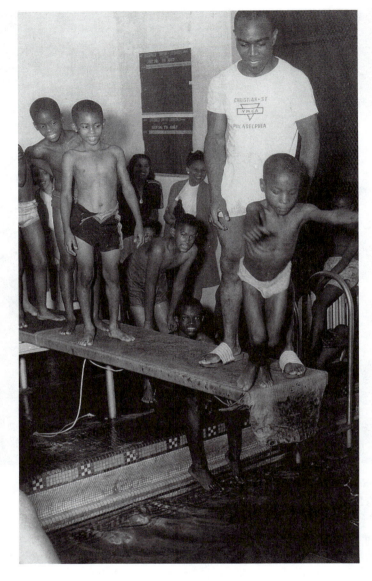

Black children have used the YMCA on the 1700 block of Christian Street since 1889. This picture is not that old. It was taken on a parents' visiting day in 1945 at the end of the summer camp program. Each of the youngsters, with the help of the youth director, Frank "Tic" Coleman, is trying to swim the length of the pool. Photo by John W. Mosley / Courtesy of Charles L. Blockson Afro-American Collection, Temple University

men with college degrees were employed, and later began selling insurance. Her mother's teaching degree was not accepted in Philadelphia, so Lee Carlyle Summers Brown cleaned homes before getting a job with the U.S. Treasury Department.

"No, there was no stigma attached to cleaning homes. That's what black women did then. . . . She knew she was getting out of it. She went into the government. And while she worked as a clerk in the Treasury, she took nursing courses and became a nurse. . . . She also, in her seventies, decided to go to beauty school, graduated, and had her own shop on South Street for a while and sold beauty products. My mother is still quite busy, always doing something. . . ." And still on the 1700 block of Addison.

"On our block, people were not badly off. For instance, the Mintess family, Lewis Mintess was the state representative. We were at 1727, he was, I think, 1730. So we had people who were in different professions. I remember people having cars. There were people around you that didn't have enough, but I don't remember it being a poor block.

"I looked up to Mrs. Mintess. . . . She was a milliner, made beautiful hats. And she also had a green thumb, she grew beautiful plants. She made my wedding headdress for me. You know, President Eisenhower came to Philadelphia, and the Mintesses were going to 30th Street Station to meet him. And they gave me the flowers to give to Mrs. Eisenhower. I don't remember the year, but they took me with them. That was a big thing. They were all Republicans. People on Addison Street were Republicans."

She grew up around relatives. "Our house was a way station. Everybody that came up from the South came to our house. It was mainly my father's family from Virginia. . . . Every time I turned around, somebody was coming, Move over, your cousin so and so is here. I saw so many cousins that I said when I grew up, I would never marry, and I would go to New York and live in an apartment by myself. I had enough of people.

"What they did was, they would come to our house until they were able to get a job. Once they got a job, they'd move and get their own place. In many ways, I think it's been helpful, because I'm able now to deal with a lot of different personalities. Maybe it was training for now. . . ."

Falaka Fattah has lived in West Philadelphia for more than 20 years now. She's been widowed, remarried, and raised six sons, including a Congressman. But home is still South Philadelphia.

"I have always loved Philadelphia, period. I've had the chance to travel many places, but I have never really considered living anyplace else. And when I think about what it is about Philadelphia that I love, it takes me to my roots, which is South Philly. It's not the history. It's not the beginning of the country or any of that. It is the way people treated each other on Addison Street, and people cared about each other. You talk about a kinship community. That kind of warmth and togetherness I have not experienced anyplace else. I have been here on Frazier Street around 20 some years. I've done a lot of work in this neighborhood. I still don't have the feeling that I had as a girl growing up in South Philly.

"I told you our house was a way station, but it wasn't just our house. There were other houses in South Philly like that. When people came up, when they migrated into Philadelphia, the saying was 'Walk South Street and find a friend.' Find somebody from home, a homeboy, and inevitably you would. You would connect up with somebody from home, whether home was Georgia or North Carolina or Virginia. And that's what I'm talking about. That's the essence of it. I don't know where you do that anyplace else."

Historians do not know whether anyone from home came looking for Robert Neverbegood. Home, wherever that was. In the seventeenth century, the Swedes did not believe in slavery, but it is naive to imagine that Robert Neverbegood was just a servant. Perhaps he was indentured, perhaps worse. While the history books do note the life of the man who employed him, Patrick Robinson, of Robert Neverbegood they tell us only that a black man with a first and a last name was alive in South Philadelphia in 1683.

4
Politics

The patronage boss of the city Democratic Party was first. Then a state senator, followed by a judge, a former state representative, a congressman, a city councilman, and his top assistant. The last one caught was the councilman elected to replace the first councilman. More were indicted and accused, but it was these eight political men who were convicted of crimes in the 1970s and 1980s.

All from South Philadelphia. All corrupt. All possessing a reputation that they were public servants who helped people.

Certainly other geographic locations in the city of Philadelphia can boast of their own politicians in trouble, but nowhere else has the quantity and diversity of downtown. Bribery. Tax fraud. Vote fraud. Cigarette smuggling. Ghost employees. Italians, Irish, blacks, Jews, a Lebanese, all caught. Why so many, and why from South Philadelphia?

Former State Senator Henry J. "Buddy" Cianfrani, one of the eight, offers an explanation: "I think because South Philadelphia, more than anyplace in the city, deals in services, and when you deal in service, you're more apt to get yourself in trouble. . . .

"For example, . . . to pick up the phone to say to a judge, 'I know Murray Dubin, he's a nice fellow, your Honor, and I certainly would appreciate it if you give him some consideration.' That's a crime today, whether you know it or not. Now, South Philly politicians think nothing of doing that. South Philly politicians think nothing of adjusting people's traffic tickets. South Philly politicians think it's nothing to go to Harrisburg and try to straighten out somebody's driver's license. Public servants don't do that in the other parts of the city, so South Philly people make themselves vulnerable. . . .

"I'll give you an example. You ever see a guy win the Golden Glove Award because he didn't make as many errors, because he didn't try for a lot of balls? Well, we try for everything down here, and that's why we get in trouble. Very easy to be an elected official, put your tie on, and say to your secretary, 'Let them get an appointment.' And when they come in, they ask you a favor, 'Well, I'll get back to you.' We don't operate like that. . . ."

Martin Weinberg, like Cianfrani, is the son of an elected official from South Philadelphia. Weinberg, an attorney, is the former head of the city Democratic Party and was the closest confidant of former Mayor Frank L. Rizzo.

"In the old days, you didn't take any money, the vote was the exchange. [But, then] people got to a point where they were saying, 'Hey, wait a minute, I'm not getting coal for people, I'm making money for people. If I'm making money for people, I'm going to get a piece of that money.' . . . Forget about the morality of the situation, that was bad enough, but . . . after having so many people caught, you would think that you would say, 'Hey, wait a minute.'"

Not downtown. For more than 150 years, politics has not changed much in South Philadelphia. Cianfrani is right—it is about service, not issues. Service-oriented, because that's the only way things would ever get done. This was Philadelphia's hindquarter, and residents did not expect help from city officials. The committeeman might help, but not the mayor. And politics wasn't a game to the committeeman. Service politics is business, and you worked at your business all year long. As ward leader Cianfrani still tells his committeepeople before Election Days, "You give me two days a year, I'll give you 365."

All politics is local, but nowhere is it more local than in South Philadelphia. Many South Philadelphia political figures have risen to wider power—Cianfrani, Rizzo, and former Congressman William A. Barrett, for example—but just one South Philadelphia political figure ever held high national office (more about him later). In both thought and deed, downtown politics is small and inward, conducted by committeemen who control three and four streets and deal in fixing potholes and finding jobs. It was that way for Republicans, and that way for Democrats. It was that way in the past, and it is, in many neighborhoods downtown, still that way now.

In the early 1800s, no political party was strong enough to control South Philadelphia, or, more precisely, the townships of Southwark, Moyamensing, and Passyunk. Not the Republicans. Not the Democrats or Whigs or Nativists or Know Nothings or the American Party. The Republicans would control the city and most of South Philadelphia at the end of the 1800s and well into the 1900s. But back in 1860, when their candidate for president had an anti-slavery plank in his platform, that issue was played down and the party name was changed. Republican Abraham Lincoln ran in Philadelphia as a People's Party candidate.

South Philadelphia's first real political boss was a Democrat, an Irish Catholic known affectionately, and out of fear, as the "Squire" and as "Bull." William McMullen ruled a slice of South Philadelphia, the Fourth Ward—South Street to Fitzwater, Broad Street east to the Delaware—from the early 1850s to his death in 1901. No one has ever held that much of downtown in his hands for as long.

McMullen was born in 1824 on Seventh Street, between Fitzwater and Bainbridge, in the Moyamensing District at a time when the land west of Seventh was woods and ponds and grazing cattle. As late as 1860, the police station at the southwest corner of Eighth and South was known as the Farm because of the open fields nearby. But land was cheap, and as McMullen was growing up, speculators built more and more narrow rowhouses on the streets west and south, and narrower trinities in the alleys behind.

As a young man, McMullen was a thug and a bully, a racist and a war hero. As an old man, he was an honored elder of the city's Select Council and a feisty pol who flew in hot-air balloons. He was canny, adaptable, and fierce.

Does this man look like a politician? This drawing shows "Squire" William McMullen, South Philadelphia's first local political strongman, as he returned home from the 1896 Democratic National Convention. The caricature appeared in The Record *on July 11 of that year.*

McMullen grew up in the poorest community outside Philadelphia. After the city and suburbs consolidated in 1854, it became the poorest and most violent community inside the city. Nearly half of the community were Irish immigrants who walked to low-paid, back-breaking jobs on the Federal Street wharves. Residents were uneducated, and their lack of municipal services was largely ignored by the city.

By the age of 20, McMullen had been in the Navy, had worked in his father's grocery store, and was a member of the rowdy volunteer Moyamensing Hose Company, known as the Moyas. On Election Day in 1844, probably because of his tough-guy reputation, he was chosen to examine residency requirements and distribute printed ballots in his district. Disputes about voting eligibility often ended in fights, with the winner controlling the vote. McMullen was good at his job. Two years later, arrested for stabbing a policeman, he escaped jail by enlisting to fight in the Mexican War. He was joined by his friends in the hose company. The men from Moyamensing were cited for bravery during the war.

Back home, the hose company fought with other fire companies and also with the police, none of whom were Irish because the city would not hire Irish policemen. Politics had the power to change that, and McMullen, a Democrat, wanted the Democrats in power. In 1850 he was elected president of the Keystone Club, a neighborhood Democratic Party workers' club above a saloon at Fourth and Bainbridge. His control of the community had unofficially begun and would last 51 more years. And he would see to it that Irishmen were hired as police officers.

In 1852 McMullen and the club supported Democratic candidate Horn R. Kneass for district attorney. Their hard work helped Kneass win, but the election was overturned because too many votes were cast by too many illegally naturalized Irishmen from Moyamensing. The state legislature tightened naturalization procedures and increased penalties for voter fraud, but McMullen now had a reputation as a politician who could deliver votes.

While he may have been an unprincipled scoundrel, politics in Moyamensing was the business of scoundrels. Consider this description of a pre–Civil War Election Day in the neighborhood:

"The Whigs and the Democrats would line the curb on either side of the street, to be counted as most numerous, the majority to . . . receive the votes, count them and make the returns. These lines . . . would be made up, not only of legal voters, but grown up lads, and after being counted once, would go to the far end to be counted again, so . . . there could be no reliance on the count. Then a rush would be made for . . . the polls and the best fighters would get possession." Under those conditions, McMullen did very well.

He was against the 1854 consolidation because he thought that the city would control Moyamensing. He lost that political battle, but he never relinquished control of the community. He opened a saloon in the neighborhood, and it soon became a voting place. In 1856 the Democrats and Mayor Richard Vaux took control of the city and McMullen was rewarded with his first political job—on the Board of Prison Inspectors at Moyamensing Prison, a role enabling him to shorten the prison sentences of friends and supporters. In 1857 he ran for alderman and won. Aldermen received a fee each time a case was heard and functioned like magistrates, able to fine, imprison, and make financial settlements. Today, lawyers are accused of shopping for the right judge. In McMullen's time, the accused could shop for the right alderman. So in an era with very few lawyers, McMullen controlled entry into and exit from the justice system, and was clearly the community's most important man, the "Squire."

He enlisted for three months when the Civil War began in 1861, but did not support the principles behind the war. He did not want a larger federal government imposing its will in Moyamensing, and he certainly did not want more black men taking jobs and voting Republican, for Lincoln's party. Local blacks in trouble with the law rarely chose him as their alderman.

McMullen did what he could to keep blacks out of Moyamensing. In 1863, a campaign to desegregate the streetcars influenced the mayoral election. In 1864, the Lombard–South Street streetcar line opened. Lombard Street was the home of the black community, while South Street was predominantly white, Irish, and McMullen territory. The line was not yet desegregated, but the Fifth Street–Sixth Street route had stopped excluding blacks. So McMullen hired two unsuspecting black men who had been cleaning cesspools, paid their fares, and told them to ride the car from one end to the other. When passengers objected to their odor, the two men were arrested but later released. Black churches criticized McMullen and called for his ouster as alderman, but his Moyamensing neighbors saw him as a protector of their rights.

In 1866, he tried again to protect his neighbors from outside influence. A cholera epidemic was killing people citywide. City Council voted to make Moyamensing Hall, the community's pre-consolidation seat of government, into a hospital. The building, on Christian Street west of Ninth, had been used as a hospital during the Civil War.

Residents saw the city dumping a dangerous institution, one that would spread disease, in their community. There were threats that the building would be burned before it opened. On the day that the hospital bedding arrived, the word spread about the fire to come. Neighbors put buckets of water on roofs to protect their own houses. Two night watchmen left the building early that night. The fire was visible by 11 p.m. McMullen and the volunteer firemen were there quickly, with the shortest hoses they had. They used hatchets to cut the longer hoses that other fire companies tried to use. The hall burned to the ground.

The next day Alderman McMullen cleared the two watchmen of charges that they had left their post.

The prospect of blacks voting in 1871 was another change McMullen did not want to see. The exact role he played in the violence of that Election Day— and in the killing of black civil rights leader Octavius Catto—is not certain, but little happened in the Fourth Ward without his approval. And Frank Kelly and "Reddy" Dever, accused in two of the killings, were both members of Moyamensing Hose.

Time after time, McMullen fought to keep outside forces from changing South Philadelphia. His actions have been repeated often over the years by political figures downtown. One of the more blatant examples was Mayor Rizzo's effort in the 1970s to keep Whitman Park, a federally mandated low-cost housing development, from being built in South Philadelphia. Rizzo,

Most people will recognize Frank Rizzo in this Evening Bulletin *picture, but who is the second man on the left? The date is early January 1972, and the event is the swearing in of the city's first Italian mayor, Frank L. Rizzo. Judge Leo Weinrott is on the right. Next to him is the new mayor, then the new First Lady, Carmella Rizzo. Next to her are the two Rizzo children, JoAnna and Frank Jr. The next gentleman is one who was rarely photographed—Ralph Rizzo, the mayor's father. Next is the outgoing mayor, James H. J. Tate. Courtesy of Frank Rizzo, Jr.*

82

like McMullen, delayed change and played on the mindset of South Philadelphia against the world, downtown versus uptown. But in the end, blacks in South Philadelphia rode the streetcars, voted, and even moved into Whitman Park.

In his last 25 years, McMullen—with Republican help because the Democratic Party was a shambles and no longer supported him—was elected to council and became one of its distinguished elder members. With his ties to Congressman Samuel J. Randall, he continued to control federal jobs, including those at the Navy Yard, and he continued to provide service. Even though his community had become more black and much more Republican—the Republicans controlled the city from 1884 until the 1940s—McMullen stayed in power.

Over the years McMullen worked with Gilbert Ball, a saloonkeeper-politician like himself. McMullen was a racist, but he may have been more anti-elite than anti-black. In Ball, he had a friend with similar biases who also did not like uppity blacks or whites. Ball was black and a Republican. Black involvement in South Philadelphia politics dates back to the 1800s and to men like Catto, the reformer, and Ball, the politician. Today, that tradition appears to be ebbing.

"The reason why I stayed in politics as long as I have is because the committeemen in my ward, they really don't know the game, and so they're like babies in the woods. Who's coming up in South Philly politics that's black? No one."

Speaking is Alfred Ford, a black man born in 1912 who has been either a Democratic or a Republican committeeman in the 36th Ward for more than 60 years. In that time, 12 men have been mayor, including two from South Philadelphia, Bernard Samuel and Frank Rizzo.

"I became a committeeman when I was either 22 or 23 years old. There used to be a lot of black committeemen, but they were all Republican back then. The Democrats didn't have no party."

Ford grew up on the 1300 block of South Opal Street, between Wharton and Reed, a black street with one white family. He was raised by his mother, who cleaned houses in West Philadelphia, and an uncle.

"It was nice for me growing up on that block because me and Georgie Cassano—he was the Italian kid—we didn't allow nobody to come in the street. We beat them up. Black, white, didn't make no difference, we just didn't let them on the block."

He did odd jobs and gambled a little after quitting high school, and then landed in politics because he needed a job. He helped secure the reelection of Ben Lynch, a committeeman in the 36th Ward, and was rewarded with a laborer's job in City Hall and a committeeman's job in the Republican Party.

"I never had another job that you could call a job. I've been in politics all my life. I kept that job until the Democrats began to get powerful."

He sought and followed the advice of Leon Blundon, a black committeeman from the neighboring 26th Ward who had little formal education. "Because he wasn't educated to the point where they could make him a magistrate or put him in office, they told him, 'You go ahead and make some money for yourself.' So he got into the numbers game and into selling whiskey, and he made a lot of money. But he spent his money wisely, because he turned around and made a couple of white fellas magistrates. So that made him a pretty powerful fella in that ward.

"And I remember going into their headquarters on Broad Street . . . how big those houses were on Broad Street and how far they ran back. . . . He showed me how to make contacts and things. One magistrate was named Brady. He carried me into his office and said, 'Mr. Brady, anything that Mr. Ford wants, I want you to serve him.' And he carried me into another magistrate's office, Tommy Connors. And he said, 'Tommy, whatever he wants, help him out.' . . . At that time, you really had to learn all the tricks in order to stay a committeeman, because the Republican Party had a policy—when you lose, that's it, you go. If you got beaten on a Monday, Tuesday the person that beat you had your job."

Those magistrates, latter-day Squire McMullens, could put people in jail and get them out. "When . . . somebody got locked up, well then, you'd go and get what they call a copy discharge. The magistrate would sign it. Yeah, he'd sign because I asked him to. Well, some of them would get a little greedy, and they want you to give them five dollars, and you have to pay them. . . . Then you had some that were very nice. . . . I could walk in and say, 'Sign this.' They'd say, 'Okay, Al.'"

In the 1940s, Ford was already a political veteran. "I was becoming kind of strong in this division. I learned my way around, and I wasn't a little boy no more. I was a man in the game, but I was a young man because I had learned

South Philadelphia's first mayor, Bernard Samuel, casting a ballot in his run for City Treasurer in 1933. Used with permission of the Temple University Urban Archives

Win or Lose, He Tried!
Jessie Jackson Lever #103

Alfred and Dorothy Ford

Dear Voter's:

Mr. Alfred and Mrs. Dorothy Ford, your Committeeperson's, are asking for your support to be re-elected in the up coming Primary Election, April 10th, 1984.

Our Lever Numbers on the voting machine are **#229** and **#230.**

Some of us are perfect. Few of us reach the stage of extra ordinary ability, but we try to do the best we can by everybody.

We thank you for your support in advance.

ALFRED and DOROTHY FORD

36th ward, 9th Division

Phone 462-7468

This 1984 campaign flyer was handed out to voters by the Fords, Alfred and Dorothy. Both were reelected. Courtesy of Alfred Ford

from Mr. Blundon how to get things done. Both parties are set up so that the committeeman is the person that serves the people of the area.

"When a committeeman gets elected, he has no job and he has no office in order to serve the people. So the only way that he can get money in order to serve the people is to get a political job. Once he gets a political job, then he got a little extra money to run the division with."

Ford switched to the Democratic Party as it began to flex its muscles in the early 1950s and win elections. Congressman and South Philadelphia ward leader William Barrett encouraged him. "Barrett said, 'Al, I want you with us.' I just went on and switched my party." He respected and admired Barrett, but the party's two elected leaders, Richardson Dilworth and Joseph S. Clark, were reformers, not politicians, not Ford's kind of people.

"I think Bill Barrett was one of the best ward leaders that the black people had. . . . He was able to get jobs by doing little favors. . . . Let's assume that a person had a store that could employ two or three people, and they needed some type of political favor. Barrett would never charge anybody. All he would do is say, 'Well, give me a job for whatever favor I've done.' So when somebody comes to him and says, 'Mr. Barrett, can you get me a job?' he'd look around. . . . It didn't have to be a political job, but it was a job. So that person

84

would tell his family, 'Whatever Mr. Barrett wants, that's it.' And if I say, 'I'm one of Barrett's committeemen,' that's it. . . .

"What Dilworth and Clark did, they destroyed the committeemen's setup. They tried to build an organization without accepting the ward leaders and the committeemen. That's where the community people would begin to take over and where you get people coming from everywhere running, because there was no organization. . . . [They] tried to build a party that would be free of politics, and be more better for the people. They tried to have a different type of party. . . . The charter said everything must be under Civil Service. That meant that the committeeman who works for the party wouldn't get no jobs."

In the long run, the committeemen survived and so did Ford, who managed to keep his job and then got a better one, with Barrett's help, as a crier in the criminal courts. He sent two children to college and worked 35 years before he retired. Today, he is still in the neighborhood, still a committeeman.

"Politics is like any other business. You got to be able to know how to run it. The difference in South Philadelphia . . . is, the majority of politicians down here know how to build an organization."

McMullen may have single-handedly controlled and organized a slice of South Philadelphia the longest, but three Republican brothers had the whole loaf in their hands. They grew up in the second half of the nineteenth century on a pig and produce farm at the southwest corner of Fourth and Snyder.

Their name was Vare, and the boys, George, Edwin, and William, sold cabbage and potatoes door to door. Unlike many local political figures, the Vares had no ethnic ties to neighbors or constituents because not many folks

World War I had its share of parades. In this 1918 spectacle on the east side of Broad Street near Cherry, Edwin H. Vare promotes his contracting and street cleaning business. Courtesy of Henry Vare

downtown had emigrated, as their grandfather had, from the Isle of Jersey. But by the early 1900s, the land south of South Street was known as Varesville.

George, the oldest, was born in 1859, son of Augustus and Abigail. Edwin was born three years later, and William was born in 1867. Frank Rizzo would graduate in 1936 from a junior high school named after Edwin H. Vare, and his father worked for a police department overseen by William S. Vare. Today, there is a playground in South Philadelphia named after George and a school named after Abigail.

The three brothers were close, with Edwin and William marrying sisters, Flora and Ida Morris. The three of them put together what they called "the largest street cleaning business in the world." Their beginnings were more humble. George A. Vare started out leasing wagons to hucksters on the waterfront. He got involved in First Ward politics with Republican ward leader Amos Slack. He ran for the state legislature in 1890 and won. The next year,

Edwin Vare, known as the "Easy Boss," was the middle brother and the most powerful of the three. Here he is riding on his country estate in Ambler in 1922. Used with permission of the Temple University Urban Archives

he and Edwin began a small contracting and street cleaning business. In 1896 he dethroned Slack as ward leader and won election as a state senator. The business grew and the Vares began to get city contracts and control hundreds of jobs. In 1907 George Vare paid $150,000 for a country estate in the northwest end of the city, at Allens Lane and McCallum Street. He didn't have much time to enjoy it—he died in 1908.

Edwin, not George, was the political mastermind of the family. Known as the "Easy Boss," because of his penchant for charity, and as the "Little Fellow," because of his size (U.S. Senator Boise Penrose, a large, rotund Republican who frequently differed with Vare, was known as the "Big Fellow"), Edwin Vare led the city Republican Party for two decades, controlled thousands of jobs, and helped the Vare family earn more than $20 million in city and suburban contracts. The "Easy Boss" was not an easy man. He was a contractor-politician who used his power to control men and votes, and to enrich himself. City Council, Congress, the state House and Senate, the city row offices—just about all answered to the "Little Fellow." As a state senator and leader of the 39th Ward, his only political failure was an inability to get Republican bosses like Penrose to support his younger brother's effort to be mayor and U.S. senator.

Like his older brother, George, Edwin had a country estate. In 1920, the reformist Committee of 70 challenged his right to vote from his official residence at 2009 South Broad Street because of all the time he spent in his Ambler mansion. Vare was unable to describe how the dining room in the Broad Street home was furnished, but the Committee of 70 still lost its case. After Edwin died in 1922, William took over the reins of the party, which was so

William S. Vare relaxing near his Ventnor summer home in August 1928. Soon after, he suffered a stroke whose effects lingered for years. Used with permission of the Temple University Urban Archives

powerful that John O'Donnell, the head of the Democratic City Committee, was on the Republican payroll. William continued Edwin's largess, giving the needy coal, clothes, food, and even scholarships in exchange for votes.

William Vare was the leader of the 26th Ward and was elected to Congress. All the Vares believed that the way to continued political success was "to give people something they can see." And Vare made sure that South Philadelphia had electric lights, new sewers, and improved public squares and parks. He continued a tradition of constituent service, not issues. And, like his brothers, he controlled jobs.

One way he consolidated his power was by offering work to new immigrants through middlemen—ethnic leaders downtown. For example, Charles C. A. Baldi, Sr., was an important go-between and power broker for the Republicans in the Italian American community in South Philadelphia. The immigrants were both eager to find work and distrustful of government. It was not difficult to persuade these new Americans to become Republicans.

The city Republican machine, controlled by the brothers Vare for so many years, began to lose its power with the rise of Franklin D. Roosevelt. Its reign ended in the late 1940s and early 1950s. William Scott Stewart Vare did not live long enough to see the end. He died in 1934.

Most Italian Americans in South Philadelphia were Republican during the first half of the 1900s—in fact, just about everyone was.

"You had to be out of your mind to be Democrat," says Henry J. Cianfrani, whose father, Henry B. Cianfrani, was a ward leader and then a Democratic legislator from 1952 to 1962. "If you were a businessman and you had a grocery store and you voted Democrat, you'd have eight or nine inspectors in there. So my father was all alone down here. Then I came in for the gravy later on what he built, . . . but he did all the hard work."

The elder Cianfrani asked his son to run for his seat. "He said, 'Don't put your picture up. Everybody is going to think it's me running again.' We had the same names. I ran and I won."

Neither father nor son wanted to get into politics. Henry B. Cianfrani was a successful man who had his own fleet of cabs on the 500 block of Fitzwater Street.

"My father was a bootlegger. He was in the bootlegging business even before Prohibition. He made a lot of money, and [the cabs] were, more or less, a front for him. In those days, it was an honored profession. It was no disgrace because every other businessman in South Philly was a bootlegger. . . . Bill Barrett was in the bootlegging business in those days, worked for my father. . . . I remember going in the garage as a little kid and they'd let me put corks in the bottles. I remember going into Jersey with the truck drivers, riding the back roads."

His father entered politics at the request of a World War I Army buddy.

"My father played on the Army basketball team with Jack Kelly," of the Princess Grace, Philadelphia brick-laying Kellys, "and they became close friends. When my father got out of the Army, Jack Kelly became chairman of the city Democratic Party. He was just starting up and he was looking for people."

Kelly would have called Cianfrani, but he couldn't find him. That's understandable. Downtown, where Cianfrani was well known, he wasn't known as Henry Cianfrani. He was known as Henry Brown.

"Our family is known as Brown in South Philadelphia. My grandfather, when he came from Italy, his name was Pietro, Pete. When he got off the boat at Ellis Island, or wherever they got off, they were giving them work. So they all reported to the paymaster, and the paymaster explained to them: 'You give me your name, then you go to work, and then you come here and you get your pay.' When they asked his name, he said, 'Pietro Chun-frani.' And the paymaster said, 'No, no.' Now, he knew Pietro, what that meant. He said, 'Now look, you're Pete Brown. When you come here to get your pay, you're Pete Brown.' And through the years, he became known as Pete Brown. My father was Henry Brown and I was Buddy Brown. I'm known as Buddy Brown up and down South Philly."

Kelly forgot about Cianfrani when he heard about an influential fellow downtown with some money named Henry Brown.

"He sent for him and was surprised when he saw my father. . . . He asked my father to get involved in politics. My father said okay, and gave up the bootlegging business and became one of the first Democrats in those days. . . . It was just to keep a second party going. You have to remember. There were no Democrats."

Besides becoming Democrats, the Cianfranis also did not fit another downtown Italian stereotype—they weren't poor.

"There's nothing I love better than when they write these stories about me, like how I came up from the gutter and all. I didn't. I was born with a silver spoon. Everything was given to me, even politics to a certain degree. . . ."

He was born March 19, 1923. Both his grandfathers were successful in the rag business on Marshall Street. "My mother really pampered me and my brother. We used to wear Peter Pan collars when the other kids had regular shirts. A lot of times I had to fight them because they made fun of me. And my mother would say, 'Well, they made fun of you because you dress better than them.' I would let my knickers hang down 'cause I wanted to look like the other kids, and my mother would hit me 'cause she wanted them buckled up. . . ."

He couldn't go under the fire hydrant with the rest of the kids, and he couldn't go to the local swimming pool on Montrose Street. "She said, 'No, no, you don't have to go under the fire hydrant. What do you need it for? They have nowhere else to go.' " The Cianfranis had a summer house at the New Jersey shore. "And we used to say the fish gang went to the pool 'cause all the kids whose families worked on Ninth Street would go there. . . ."

His mother was Vincenza Mardello, but everyone called her Chinzi. She was a bank clerk at the Baldi Bank on Eighth Street—an impressive job for the times—and played the piano at a Christian Street silent movie theater before she married in 1922. Her two sons were born on Marshall Street, but the family soon moved to the 700 block of Fulton Street.

"It was all Italian. People slept outside in the summer on hot nights, on the steps, on beach chairs. No one locked their doors, no such thing as burglary or drugs in those days. They didn't do that in the neighborhood, they didn't do that to one another. . . ."

Henry J. "Buddy" Cianfrani, being held by his father, Henry B. Cianfrani, in 1923. The elder Cianfrani was a bootlegger, cab company owner, ward leader, state legislator, and one of the early influential Democrats in South Philadelphia. Courtesy of Henry J. "Buddy" Cianfrani

Buddy Cianfrani poses with "Teens for Cianfrani" in 1967 during his reelection campaign for the state Senate. On his right is his daughter, Mary Ellen. Next to her, wearing a tie, is Cianfrani's cousin, Joseph Vignola, who would later become the city controller and a member of City Council. Courtesy of Henry J. "Buddy" Cianfrani

But for Cianfrani and his friends, the good feeling was toward Italians only. He is embarrassed about what happened.

"Bainbridge Street was like the line. Jewish kids didn't come over our side, south of Bainbridge. We punched them if they did. Black kids didn't come over the line. The black guys would be coming from the other side of Broad Street. And it was like territorial rights. . . . It was a disgrace when you stop to think of it, but, yeah, it was that way."

He played basketball at South Philadelphia High and at South Catholic, then at Seventh and Christian. Both schools had great teams in the late 1930s. "There was a Jewish clique at Southern and I couldn't break into it, and there was an Irish clique at South Catholic. Either way I was middled, if you follow me."

Cianfrani had worked in his uncle's coal yard at 13th and Washington and was selling tablecloths and aprons to restaurants when his father talked to him about getting into politics.

"I didn't want to. . . . All my friends' fathers . . . were Republican committeemen. I felt funny. My father said, 'You're going to get involved. Look, I put my sweat and my blood into this thing. You could get the advantage of it, because this city is going to change over.' And I got involved. Then, a couple of years later, he said to me, 'I'm going to run you for ward leader.'

"I was married at the time to my first wife, my childhood sweetheart, Rita Marano. Her family had King Midas Macaroni on 11th Street. . . . I got married in 1946 when I returned home from the Army. I was in Merrill's Marauders. I had a rotten marriage because I was unsettled. During those days, I was notorious. I was a gambler. I liked the horses and a fast life. I didn't come up to snuff. I was not doing what was right, and I was separated."

As a ward leader, state representative, state senator, and chairman of the Senate Appropriations Committee, Cianfrani had many friends, including the two best-known Italians downtown: Cosa Nostra boss Angelo Bruno and Frank Rizzo.

"Angelo was from the neighborhood, and he occasionally would intervene on behalf of people. . . . The first time, I think it was when I got into the House of Representatives around 1964, 1963. I got this phone call. He introduced himself and said that earlier that day, a woman had come to see me. She was having trouble getting a permit to put a bay window in her house or something. He asked if I would intervene, see what I could do."

A call from the head of the local crime family might make the average guy nervous. Shiver, even.

"I don't shiver that easy. I make people shiver. I said to him, 'I would be most happy to look into it.' And we were successful. Now time passed, and I got involved in an argument at a polling place with the judge of elections . . . and his nephew, and I punched him, the nephew.

"This was shortly after that. And they went home, and they threatened that they were going to do certain things to me. People heard that. And friends of mine, whose names I don't care to mention, . . . ordinary neighbors, well, before anyone went looking for me, they—my people—went looking for them. Angelo Bruno apparently got wind of it, and he sends someone and said he would like to talk to me, he would be at Ninth and Fitzwater Street, waiting. So I went and he said he heard about the argument, and he would hope that I could calm these people down. He was going to calm those people down. . . . I said, 'All right, I'll talk to my people.' He said, 'It's bygones, bygones.' . . .

"And we became dear, close friends. Many a time, I would sit with him and discuss things, like what he thought was a buying market, with homes and all. I felt the warmth with him, I enjoyed his company. . . . He spoke very well. . . . Angelo Bruno was a mild-mannered man that was knowledgeable in any subject. You want to talk about Broadway plays, he knew the backers, what was going on. You want to talk about stocks and bonds, he knew the market. You want to talk politics, he had a good ear for politics. He would have made a good politician. He always let me feel like he was listening to me, when I think he probably knew what the hell I was talking about before I said it. . . .

"I was very attached to his wife, Sue, a nice person. I had the privilege, which very few people had, to knock on his door. His wife was a registered Democrat who voted for me and put my picture in her window. So that automatically entitles them to my service, the way I count.

"I think he got votes for me. . . . Not through threats or anything. People considered him an intelligent man, and he . . . said Cianfrani is for the people. And it really meant something among the Italians. He spread the gospel, so did his followers. No, he never made no contribution to me, 'cause he knew that I would have to report it and it might embarrass me. I never asked, he never offered. I did him big favors. I did him little favors.

"The big favors? He had trouble when he had the cigarette vending company, and I intervened and helped him to get the state stamp. Legally, perfectly legal. I felt that unless you got something against him, I think they're entitled to get the stamp. Trying people on rumors and all? I was very adamant about it."

Cianfrani was criticized for his visits to Bruno's Snyder Avenue home. "The crime commission wrote that I was consorting with characters. And my answer was that every other person in South Philadelphia, at one time or another, might have had a problem, and I wasn't going to walk around with a sign on my back: Don't say hello to me if you were ever arrested, 'cause I couldn't survive here as the senator. . . .

"I live by my standard. When I get up in the morning, I can look myself in the mirror even 'til today, just like when I went away. I didn't have to go away. I made a deal to make sure that all those people who went before the grand jury who might have lied to try to help me would not be punished for it. I said, 'I'll plead, just let them alone.' . . . When I walk down the street today, people tip their hat to me. I go places, I don't have to pay for anything. I didn't get that reputation because of the way I part my hair. I was good to people. I stayed by them. That is what South Philly is all about. That's Buddy Cianfrani. And I think I'm South Philly. I'm your typical South Philadelphian, barring my problem. . . ."

Another man thought to be a "typical South Philadelphian" was former police chief and two-term mayor Frank Rizzo—even though Rizzo lived downtown for just 19 years. Rizzo died of a heart attack on July 16, 1991, two months after he had won the Republican mayoral primary.

"I don't think he knew the real intricacies of being the mayor, but nobody could deny that he loved the job," says Cianfrani, who was both his friend and his foe. "He loved the city and he was a pussy as far as helping people. You could stop him on the street, give him a sad story and he'd give you a job. That used to be my argument with him. 'You give this guy a job? Who is he? He probably voted against you.' 'His wife is having a baby, Senator, guy needs to make a living.' I said, 'You don't even know him.' 'Yeah, but he stopped me. How could I say no?' That's the other side of Rizzo. . . .

"I screamed at him. 'Give me a list,' I said. 'I'm going to fire 25 people and I'm going to give these jobs to people that mean something.' 'All right, go ahead.' So he gave me the books. I wrote down 25 names and come back three hours later. I read him a name. He said, 'Now wait a minute, you can't do that.' Why? 'That guy's father broke me in on a red car.' All right. I went to the next name. 'That's Carmella's hairdresser's nephew.' The next one. 'This guy wrote a song about me, Senator.' I did about eight of them. Then I said, 'hey, do me a favor, drop dead.' . . ."

When Cianfrani was in prison, Rizzo quietly sent him $50 a month. When he was freed, Rizzo gave him $500. "I don't think he knew how to be a phony. He was not a good liar. . . . One on one, he was the greatest, . . . never a dull moment. Anybody says they were with him and they didn't enjoy himself, got to be crazy."

James P. McGranery, a South Philadelphian, served as U.S. attorney general. Note the picture of President Truman and McGranery on his desk. Courtesy of The Philadelphia Inquirer and Philadelphia Daily News Photo Library

Although Rizzo was the best-known South Philadelphia political figure of the past 50 years, neither he nor Cianfrani nor Barrett nor the current legislative strongman, State Senator Vincent Fumo, is the highest-ranking elected official from downtown.

That title belongs to James Patrick McGranery, a little-remembered Irish American politician and leader of the 36th Ward who was U. S. attorney general during the last eight months of Harry Truman's presidency in 1952.

McGranery grew up on the 1100 block of South 23rd Street and was a four-time congressman, first elected in 1936. Later, he became an assistant U.S. attorney general and, in 1946, a federal judge, but he gave up that lifetime appointment when President Truman asked him in 1952 to succeed Attorney General J. Howard McGrath. No other South Philadelphian has served in all three branches of government—legislative, judicial, and executive. McGranery was 67 when he died during a Christmas vacation in Palm Beach, Florida, in 1962.

In the hundred years or so from McMullen to McGranery, other Irish Americans have made their names known in politics downtown. Besides William Barrett, there is former Congressman Michael J. "Ozzie" Myers, who was one of the eight South Philadelphia politicians found guilty of crimes in the 1970s and 1980s. Not as well known is Thomas J. Kelly, who has deftly kept the spotlight pointed elsewhere.

Kelly, who headed the Board of Revision of Taxes from 1984 to 1991, and the Philadelphia Housing Authority from 1973 to 1984, is a Democrat who has never been elected to any office higher than committeeman, and that was many years ago. The Democratic Party has been good to him, and he is a loyal functionary who will not speak ill of anyone.

"Ozzie Myers was a good guy. When he drank whiskey, he'd say anything, but he has a good heart. Lee Beloff?" (Leland Beloff is a former city councilman and one of the eight.) "I always liked him, I still like him. Nice wife, nice kids, and all. He just got, I guess, in the wrong company."

His family moved around South Philadelphia, but Kelly, born in 1935, spent most of his early years on the 2500 block of South Hicks Street. He lives near 18th and Shunk now, not too far from where he grew up.

"I remember down the Lakes, League Island Park, there was a place called The Rocks where the Walt Whitman Bridge approach is now. We used to go there, play, ride bikes. I can remember wooden bridges over Broad Street at Packer, three of them. . . .

"And there was a stadium, they used to have fights there. That would be between Broad and 15th on Packer, in the early '50s. Then you had the South City Drive-In movie where the Vet Stadium is. Before the drive-in, there were farms and dumps there. . . . I can remember my mother's aunt saying that when she was young . . . the entrance to her uncle's farm was at 18th and Shunk, before these homes were built. . . . I can remember as a kid when Oregon Avenue ended at 18th Street. . . . And I remember when the Girard Estates tenants had a private tennis court at 19th and Oregon. Girard Estates was special in those days. . . ."

In the early 1950s, after high school, he went to work in the real estate office of the local state representative, whose mother knew Kelly's mother. Kelly's father was a Democrat who worked at the Navy Yard.

"He wasn't political, but he was active. In those days, you had a Democrat or Republican club every couple of blocks, and they had one on Porter Street. It was like $50 a year to get a liquor license. Every ethnic group, political group, had a little club to play cards. . . . I think [political clubs] were more prevalent in deep ethnic areas."

Kelly worked for the legislator and a Democratic state senator as well until 1965. That year, he took his services to the city housing authority, a party patronage haven. He became its executive director eight years later. Today, he is a real estate broker, without any official ties to the party. But political figures still seek his counsel.

"Who were the political powerhouses in South Philadelphia? Barrett. Manny Weinberg. Beloff [Lee Beloff's father] and Lou Menna were the Republicans. Menna was the Republican leader of the 26th Ward. He was strong. The guy who really was the big Republican downtown, even though he wasn't in office, was Frank Palumbo. He had the big restaurant, everybody ran there, he would do all kinds of favors for everybody, and he really held sway over most of the Republican ward leaders in South Philly. Palumbo's would always give you good veal, always had a good show.

"Manny Weinberg was very powerful. . . . I used to go over there, and Marty would be playing basketball outside. Manny would hold court in his house. He'd be in the kitchen. He had a big ward, and he had some powerhouse committeemen . . . who would win their division by 600.

"Your strength depended upon your ability to turn out and take care of people, and Weinberg was good at that. Barrett was good at it, too. . . . They were both powerhouses. Barrett was on one end, Weinberg was on the other, . . . you had everybody else in between. You couldn't do anything citywide without those guys."

Kelly, like many other downtown pols, was an admirer of Barrett, who was in Congress for 30 years until his death in 1976. (He died just before Election Day, and it was too late to take his name off the ballot. Barrett won.) While in Congress, Barrett returned to his South Philadelphia ward headquarters at 24th and Wharton nightly.

"Barrett controlled the Republican ward leader in his ward, because not only did Democratic committeemen have jobs under Barrett, but the Republicans did also. He controlled both sides and he elected the Republican ward leader. . . . Barrett's theory was, one meant three. If I got Murray Dubin to register Democrat, that meant that I had him, they couldn't get him, and they had to get one to get even. "

Kelly says that South Philadelphia politics is unique because it is passed down from father to son in the same way that dads teach their boys to throw and catch. "Other parts of the city don't have the tradition in politics. Downtown, there's family tradition, there's loyalty." U.S. Representative Thomas Foglietta and his father. Former Judge Louis Vignola and his city councilman son, Joseph. Beloff and his father, Cianfrani and his. And Marty Weinberg and his father, Emanuel.

That's Frank Palumbo in the suit in the left foreground attending a picnic in Willow Grove in 1957. Also eating watermelon are a host of local politicians and elected officials, including (left to right) City Council member Benjamin Curcuruto (behind Palumbo); Judge Adrian Bonnelly (with bowtie); County Commissioner Louis Menna; Sheriff Austin Meehan, eating from the hand of Council member Thomas Foglietta; Judge Samuel Clark, looking on; Council member Louis Schwartz, with watermelon and watch; and seated in the right foreground, Court officer Edward Veneziale. All the Italians are from South Philadelphia. Used with permission of the Balch Institute for Ethnic Studies Library, Edward Veneziale Collection

William A. Barrett in 1973, bad toupee notwithstanding, was the top South Philadelphia politician for decades. The Philadelphia Inquirer / William Steinmetz

"I was a participant from the time I was seven years old," says Weinberg, who was born in 1937 and grew up on Mildred Street, near Ninth and Porter. His father was a ward leader from 1932, the year Roosevelt took office, until he died in 1966.

" . . . My father had been in World War I and was wounded. He came back, went to college, and went into the life insurance business. When he lost his job in the insurance business, he decided to go into politics because what else would a good Jewish boy do? He was an aggressive guy. Immigrants went into politics. . . . That was the way to advance. So he became a committeeman. . . . We lived in the 39th Ward, which at that time was one ward. Now it's 39A and 39B. It went from the Delaware River to Broad Street, the southernmost part of the city until McKean Street."

The southernmost part of the city had as few Democrats as where the Cianfranis lived, two miles to the north. There were just no Democrats downtown in the 1930s.

Weinberg says: "The Republican party was so strong in the '20s and '30s that they . . . would elect the Democrat committee people as well as the Republicans. . . . But my father led a group of . . . committee people who knocked out the Republican [selected] Democratic committee people. And then they knocked out . . . the Democratic ward leader, and my father became the ward leader. They were a group of Jewish and Irish politicians. . . . In that ward, you had some of the toughest Republican politicians in the city—Barney Samuel, he was the council president [and later mayor]; Magistrate [John] O'Malley, who was the chief of the magistrates, and you had Manny Beloff. . . . My father fought them. . . . So he was a pretty tough guy in a tough area.

"My dad was always a guy they tried to get to become a Republican. They tried to persuade him. I remember growing up with paint bombs. A paint bomb is where they would . . . open a can of paint, take the lid off, then put it back on, but not real tight, and then they throw it through the window of your living room. When it bounced and hit something, the top would come off, the paint would go every possible place, all over the downstairs. We had that happen a half a dozen times in our house."

When he was seven, Marty Weinberg handed out pamphlets. Not too much later, he was knocking on doors. "You know the wooden cardboard things on shirts. [My father] pulled out the cardboard, and he had these street lists, and he would cut them up. Instead of by the whole division, you do it by street. Say it's the 2600 block of Mildred Street. You have your workers at the division who would check off people as they came to vote. And then around 3 p.m., when I came home from school, I would go out, get the cardboard thing, and go to the houses that hadn't voted yet and knock on doors. Then I'd go out again at six.

"And then the big boss, my mother, would come out about 7 o'clock and make sure they came out to vote. Each street had somebody like myself to make sure that everybody who could came out to vote on Election Day. That's one of the reasons why the percentage of voters were so much higher in those days. You don't have that kind of organization now."

One of the reasons that the Weinbergs and Cianfranis and Barretts and, before them, the Vares stayed in power in South Philadelphia was because of the immigrant population and the committeeman structure.

"In those days, if you had any kinds of needs with the city, . . . the committeeman was the guy who took care of you. In exchange for that, he would say, 'Look, if you need anything, you can always come to me. On Election Day, the only way I can help you is if I stay in office and I am strong enough to do the things for you that you need done, so I need your vote. And no matter who the candidates are, you're really voting for me. If you're Republican and Franklin Delano Roosevelt is running, I'm asking you to vote for me. [If you're Democrat], I'm asking you to vote for me. . . . You might like Roosevelt, but what's he going to do for you? I'm the guy you're going to have to come and see.'

"In an area like South Philadelphia, there were so many immigrants. That's why it became the hotbed of machine politics. Those immigrants really needed the help of their committeepeople to exist. If you were in Wynnefield, where you had a big home and a car and you worked in town, you didn't have a need. The poorer the people are, the more you're part of machine politics. Not because you're ignorant or because there's something wrong with you, but because there's a closer relationship, because of need, between you and the committeeperson.

" . . . You didn't knock on the door two weeks before the election and discuss abortion, or issues. . . . Nobody really gave a shit about people's positions. It was a very, very service-oriented job. You voted for your committeeman."

Election Day, Weinberg knocked on doors to make sure people voted. Election Night, he counted those votes on a blackboard.

"We had our headquarters at Eighth and Oregon, and I was in charge of writing the division results down. I was 11, 12, . . . and the deal was that all the committeemen would come in . . . they'd have to stand in front of everybody and announce the results of their division, and hand in the official return to my father so they couldn't phony it up. . . . After you were done, you would sit there and wait because everybody who came in had to announce in front of everybody, and nobody could leave until everybody was through. . . ."

The community that Marty Weinberg grew up in was divided in ways other than political. There were boundaries.

"You can't help but know that South Philadelphia was a distinct community religiously. Basically, it was divided by about 10th Street west, which was Italian. And from east of 10th Street to probably Fifth or Third or so, it was Jewish, and then from Third Street east was Irish, Polish. And then there were some groups of blacks north of Snyder Avenue, and a few streets south of Oregon Avenue around Fifth Street. So you were venturing into the Italian area or the Irish area when you went out of your boundaries.

" . . . I think there was more of a problem between Jews and the Irish than between Jews and the Italians. You never went into the Irish areas, you just never did. . . . [And] you never walked past a group of boys on the corner, Irish or Italian.

"I rarely went out at night. If I would walk in the daytime, I would always walk toward the curb, . . . far away from where somebody might be hiding in an alley or in a building. When there were groups of people on corners, I would

Marty Weinberg, son of Manny Weinberg, is best known for his political acumen as city Democratic Party chief and the closest confidant of Mayor Frank Rizzo. But before his political star rose, he was a star basketball player at South Philadelphia High School and team captain in 1955. Weinberg is in the middle. Courtesy of Martin Weinberg

either go up another street, or across the street, or walk in the middle of the street through the cars. . . ."

Weinberg says he is not talking about growing up with fear. No, it was growing up with survival skills. "I graduated Southern, January of '55. I was captain of the basketball team. I was a leader there. I was Jewish. I was able to work and play with Italian and Irish and blacks and Polish, both in basketball and baseball. It was like the United Nations down there, and you just learn to live with all kinds of people."

Good training for politics, even for a behind-the-scenes operative like Weinberg. But what of politics downtown today? Most residents are not immigrants anymore. Those who are—from Southeast Asia—are often not voting. The Republican and Democratic machines that once routinely found jobs and fixed alley lights cannot do that anymore.

Service is still important, but voters are more likely to have seen the candidates on television and read about the issues. The ethnic mix is changing. Jews have left, but the Italians and blacks and Irish are still there, and are, Weinberg says, "the children of the original people, and they have that family [political] tradition. . . . A lot of them are still serviced by the same committeemen that were there back . . . when they were kids."

The loss of power for committeepeople can be viewed as a sign of progress, a needed dilution of political machine power. Al Ford would disagree. So would Marty Weinberg and just about every other pol from downtown. They would argue that the committeeman gave people power. What is certain is this: If committeemen are still solving people's problems anywhere in Philadelphia today, it's a good bet that it happens on the streets of South Philadelphia. Politics hasn't changed that much.

As if to prove that point, the Democratic committee members of South Philadelphia's Ward 39B elected Lee Beloff ward chairman in June 1994—just four months after his parole. He had spent six years in a federal penitentiary for plotting with a Mafia boss to extort a million dollars from a developer. He had also pleaded guilty to forging absentee ballots. Two days after the ward election, in the face of criticism from the mayor and other party leaders, Beloff resigned. Ward leader Joseph Howlett said he did not understand all the fuss: "I don't see that the committeepeople did anything wrong."

5

Italians

More than two hundred years after the Swedes first settled near the Delaware River, Italians were still not a blip on the immigrant map. Today, South Philadelphia is often described as an Italian neighborhood, but only about 300 Italians lived in the community in the early 1850s—and that figure may be high. With thousands of Irish, German, and English residents, it is unlikely that anyone paid attention to a few hundred more foreigners. But in 1852, the Catholic Church paid attention.

Italians in the city and surrounding townships and districts worshipped at area churches, but those churches were not often in South Philadelphia. There were just two Catholic churches south of South Street—St. Philip De Neri, founded in 1840, and St. Paul's, founded in 1847—and neither made neighborhood Italians feel welcome.

With the assistance and counsel of two Italian-born Jesuit priests, Italians asked Bishop John Neumann for their own place of worship. On September 24, 1852, he purchased a small black Methodist church and cemetery on Mariott Street (Montrose Street today) between Seventh and Eighth Streets and created the first Italian church in the nation. The Reverend Gaetano Mariani, a Florence-born priest who had been teaching music at St. Charles Seminary, then at 18th and Race Streets, was named the pastor. He called the new church Saint Mary Magdalen de Pazzi, after the 16th-century Florentine saint.

St. Mary's, as it would come to be known, was the first local church established because of the national origin of its parishioners, but many more—including St. Stanislaus for the Polish and St. Casimir for the Lithuanians—would be built in South Philadelphia as Catholic immigrants continued to arrive.

The Italian history of the city began before St. Mary's, but how far back is unclear. Italian wine merchant Giovanni Gualdo sold madeira, claret, and beer in 1767 from a store on Walnut Street west of Front, where he also composed music. Five miles west, across the Schuylkill, lived Milan native Paul Busti, one of the few residents of that undeveloped area in 1798 and maybe the first Italian in West Philadelphia.

Back in South Philadelphia in 1800, drinkers at the Sign of the Two Brother Sailors, 144 South Street, were treated to the extraordinary sight of an

11-foot ostrich, courtesy of an Italian named Secundo Bosio. Little else is known about the ostrich or its exhibitor. Captain Joseph Lametti, who arrived in Philadelphia in the 1790s, distinguished himself in the War of 1812. Vito Vitti, a Genoese marble importer, settled in Philadelphia in 1815, but he did not live in South Philadelphia. Nor is there any reason to believe that Lametti, Gualdo, or Bosio lived there.

In fact, no one is certain who was the first Italian to live downtown. Early Italian surnames in South Philadelphia included Raggio, Malatesta, Romano, Fabiani, Cuneo, Conti, and Bonavitacola. Cuneo was Andrew Cuneo, who arrived in 1845 from Genoa. With immigrant enterprise, he provided the organs that local organ grinders played. In 1865, Lorenzo Nardi arrived in Philadelphia from Italy. St. Mary's had been open for 13 years, but Nardi said it took him two days to find another Italian. Two years after his arrival, he founded the city's first Italian society, Union Fratellanza.

There was no distinct Italian neighborhood in the 1850s and 1860s in South Philadelphia. People lived here and there, south of South Street and east of Broad. If the neighborhood had an ethnic tinge, it was the green of Ireland. Ninth Street, where the Italian Market is today, was an Irish residential row; St. Paul's, known now as the Italian Market Church, was an Irish church in the middle of a neighborhood called Irishtown. As late as 1890, newcomer Carmillo Erminio was the first Italian to move into the 700 block of Fitzwater Street.

The Italian parishioners at St. Mary's came from the center and north of Italy, from cities like Genoa. As Italians from the south, from Calabria, Abruzzi, Campana, and Sicily, began to stream into Philadelphia from the 1880s on, the regional differences that had marked Italy historically were felt here.

Unwelcome at St. Mary's because they were from the south, and unwelcome at St. Paul's because they were Italian, many of the newcomers turned to Nostra Signora del Buon Consiglio—Our Lady of Good Counsel—which was founded in 1898 by three Italian Augustinians who bought St. Paul's school for $15,000 and turned it into a church located between St. Paul's and St. Mary's on the 800 block of Christian.

"The Irish pastors were rather belligerent toward the Italians. They considered them . . . a different genre than they were used to seeing in South Philly and they made a big stink," says Father Michael Gambone, a South Philadelphia native and the pastor of St. Paul's since 1976. Of St. Mary's and St. Paul's back then, he explains, "You can't lock the church to anybody, but you can make it difficult."

Our Lady of Good Counsel, which closed in 1933, was probably the busiest Catholic church in Philadelphia. "In the 35 years that parish was in existence," says Father Gambone, "there were more baptisms than there were at St. Paul in 150 years. As a matter of fact, 10 times as many. One Sunday, there were 84 baptisms, which is remarkable. Average that out."

The discomfort that so many Italians experienced in Irish-run churches in South Philadelphia had much to do with the difference between Irish and Italian Catholicism. Italians were both more emotional and more indifferent to the

Three altar boys from St. Mary Magdalene walk north on Seventh Street on a feast day in June 1940. The boy on the left is Michael Gambone. Courtesy of the Reverend Michael Gambone.

Church than the Irish were. Theirs was a warmer, more superstitious, laissez-faire view of religion, and it did not mesh well with the formal, structured church that the Irish had successfully built in Philadelphia.

The Italians' unease extended well into the 1900s, concedes Father Gambone, who attended St. Mary's as a boy. "People would be told, You don't belong here, go to the Italian church down the street. Like King of Peace, that was the Italian church at 26th and Wharton, or go to Good Counsel over here. It's unfortunate. It should never have happened, 'cause we have to take everybody. But the attitude, you could tell. In the '30s, there might have been still a lot of tension. I heard stories about the pastor at St. Edmond's. Some of the people still talk about Father Duffy and how mean he was."

Father Gambone served in four churches before he came to St. Paul's. One of them was in South Philadelphia.

"It had an Irish pastor who was there through all this, and they loved him. St. Monica's. His name was Farrell. He was at that parish 50 years or something like that. . . . If you go out and show the people that you want to work with them and appreciate them, they will do you double. . . . St. Monica's is Italian now, but at one time it was half and half, and was mostly Irish to begin with. But this Irish priest who was there had the wisdom. . . . People started calling him Father Farrelli."

Arlene Notoro Morgan did not grow up hearing about priests like that when she was growing up. Born in 1945, she lived on the 1400 block of Dickinson.

"At one time, you know you couldn't get in front of the church at St. Thomas," she says of the Morris Street church. "They had this chapel in the back. The Italian Americans went to the chapel, and the Irish people went to the main church. My Aunt Clara remembers that 'cause she grew up in St. Thomas parish. She wasn't allowed in the front church until maybe sometime in the '30s."

Dorothy Marcucci doesn't personally remember discrimination like that in the church. Born in 1921, she is the daughter of two South Philadelphians, James Francis Mullen and Agata Quintieri. She does remember ignorance and sadness.

"My mother's family was absolutely Italian, Calabrese, the whole thing.

. . . When my mother eloped with my father, my aunt told me that one of her brothers, who was 12 or 14, ran out into the middle of Federal Street screaming, 'My sister married a Irishman.' . . . They said that Grandmom screamed. My grandfather put his head on the table and cried. His reaction was great pain that she left the family." It was 1915.

As a girl, she understood there was a tension between the church and her family.

"One of the problems, and this was very strong in my head, was money. The Italian attitude, because of Italy, was they [the church] don't need any money. But the Irish attitude is that they have no money, and please give us money, and it was money, money, money. . . . When my family was contributing, there was a lot of money. And then suddenly there was [the Depression and] no money. There was hardly any food. And the priests were not understanding. My Italian mother-in-law said the priest would come and say, 'Well, if you don't go to church, I need your five dollars.' And she threw him out. She's a widow. She has nine kids, and the guy's saying, I want your five dollars. I think the priests were under pressure because they had no money."

Like her mother-in-law, Marcucci once threw an Irish priest out of her home.

"I had my first child and I was pregnant with my second, and the priest from St. Monica's came to collect money. They called it the house visit, and I'm thrilled because he can bless me. But he . . . started a philosophical discussion in my apartment. 'Oh, I'm so happy to see you're having more children.'

"I said, 'Well, Father, it's sad to say this is my last child.' I'm talking about that I'm not going to be able to have more. He said, 'Oh, no. God wants you to have more children.' I said, 'Father, sad to say, I'm not going to have more children because I cannot.' I started going into this discussion, but he said, 'You have no choice.' And I told him why. So he said again, 'You have no choice.'

"I said, 'Father, you're not the person to tell me what choices I have.' I'm really angry that he's saying this to me. . . . And then he said, 'You do that and you're excommunicated.' Well, I said, 'Father, leave my house!' I was furious that this man is throwing me out of the church. I got upset. What I did was, I talked to a Jesuit. God bless them. They're bright, they research, they do everything. He said, No, you're right, it's a medical choice.

"I learned after a while not to even discuss with the parish priest the fact that I thought God was in my heart. I said that to a priest one time, and he said, That has nothing to do with your going to Mass."

Finding a church and going to Mass was not the sole preoccupation of the new Italian residents in South Philadelphia. Like the Irish and blacks who had come before them, they needed work, they needed housing. They needed to start a new life.

Most of the rural southern Italians were unskilled workers, a phrase heard again and again when describing South Philadelphia residents who had no specific job training when they arrived in the neighborhood. They had not apprenticed as anything. But they needed to work, and a booming city and region needed them. The railroad—through a system of employment brokers called padrones—contracted for their work in Italy and used their muscle to lay the

The 800 block of Christian in about 1920. Luigi Fiorella's Meat Market is on the left, V. DiPietro Watchmaker and Jeweler in the center, and the Ingenito Realty Company on the right. The meat market is still on Christian Street, and DiPietros and Ingenitos are still at South Philadelphia addresses. Used with permission of the Balch Institute for Ethnic Studies Library, Fiorella Brothers Sausage Co. Collection

tracks that lined the region. Italians built the Broad Street subway and the Market–Frankford elevated lines, City Hall and the Reading Terminal. Italians paved streets, built sewers, and collected trash. They were also hucksters and barbers, masons and factory workers, stone cutters, plasterers and shoemakers.

Italian women worked as well, though usually in the home. It was common to see them carrying bundles of clothes to subcontractors, who were also Italian. The women sewed on their kitchen tables. Angelina Valdi sewed for 13 years, beginning in 1917, inside a 12-family apartment house. Her pay for finishing a dozen pairs of trousers was 24 cents. She was the mother of 10.

The subcontractors preferred Italian women, who were plentiful and worked cheaply, earning perhaps $99 a year. Said one: "I go out on Christian Street and pick up a couple of Italian women that know how to finish trousers. I do not know their names or where they live. With each new order, I get a new worker for these Italian families move place to place."

They kept moving because so many were poor. A 1904 study of the dwellings between Eighth and Ninth, Carpenter and Christian—by then an Italian enclave—found that 41 of the 167 residences were occupied by three or more families. Twenty-eight percent of the families lived, cooked, and slept in one-room apartments. Most of the toilets were outdoors and shared.

The poor were from southern Italy, and many were from Sicily. By the late

1800s, some of those Sicilians had set up sidewalk pushcarts and stands selling fruit and vegetables. Genoese merchants had stores on Eighth Street by this time, but they did not sell fruit and vegetables. Most Italians walked east to Dock Street, near the Delaware River, to buy fruit. The Eighth Street store owners complained about the sidewalk stands, and about the Sicilians. So the Sicilians moved to the east–west streets, like Christian. Soon, they spread to Ninth Street, and now it was the Irish residents who were complaining. Police were called to move the vendors away. But as more and more Italians moved in, the Irish began to leave, moving west and south. No one knew it then, but the Italian Market had begun.

So at the turn of the century, a collection of Sicilian and southern Italian merchants began selling everything from live chickens to green peppers on Ninth Street from about Wharton to Christian Streets. Jews were there soon as well, selling clothing and dry goods. Today, the Ninth Street Market still sells everything from live chickens to peppers. But the Jews have been replaced by Koreans, the customers are no longer just neighbors, and third- and fourth-generation Italians are behind the storefronts and stands. Behind the counter at Claudio's, a cheese store at 924 South Ninth, are the three sons and daughter of the founder.

Sal, Claudio Auriemma's oldest son, began working on the street in first grade. His father was working then at the Maggio Food Company, Ninth and Montrose. Everyone called the store "Magic Food." It was 1963.

"I was on jobs . . . like sorting beans. People would mix beans together, I

Claudio Auriemma, the King of Cheese, in his Ninth Street store in 1975. Jars of mushrooms, artichokes, and marinated eggplants sit behind him while provolone and bread hang above. Claudio was the first modern store owner on Ninth Street to hang food from the ceiling, but Antonio Bucchieri did it on Fitzwater Street in 1922. Courtesy of the Auriemma family

would sort them out. I became pretty handy grating cheese. It was more a grocery. This is before supermarkets really kicked in. It had things like Maxwell House coffee, beans, some cheese, nothing like what we have now, boxes of tea, canned orange juice."

A couple of years later, Claudio Auriemma and his wife, Sally, decided to open their own little store at 902 South Ninth Street, a cheese store, one of the street's earliest.

"My family had no money," says Sal of his father. "People were just going to give him merchandise on his word, say, Yeah, I think you can pay me. He didn't have the money you would need today to open a business. . . . But he did it somehow."

Claudio's wife remembers that first day: "I didn't know if we were going to make it. We didn't have all the cheeses in there because we didn't have much money to start. We had Stella D'Oro cookies and some cheeses. . . . We used to go in six in the morning and come home 11:30 at night. Everybody would be closed, but my husband would still be hanging cheeses and salamis. We didn't advertise. Good stuff sells without advertising."

Sally Auriemma was born in Naples in 1939 and came to South Philadelphia—alone—when she was 16. "My mother was born in Haddonfield, New Jersey. My grandfather used to work on the train tracks, but he got run over by a train and wasn't able to work anymore, so he took all the kids back to Italy."

Filomena Giamone was only seven when she returned to Italy. In her early twenties she married Salvatore Russo, a shoemaker from Montella, near Naples. After she began voting in Italian elections, she lost her right to return to the United States. At least, that's what the letter from the American consul seemed to say. It also said that any of her children under 16 could go to Amer-

106

ica under her citizenship. "I was the youngest, so I came. I had to do it to help the family and send money back."

The day before she left, she married her sweetheart, Claudio Auriemma, and then sailed without him.

"I had to leave . . . and then send for him. He came 11 months later. If the American consul knew that I got married, I wouldn't have rights anymore, so I came under my maiden name. Then after you come over, they forget all about it, and you can send for your husband. I'll never forget that day I left my mother. As I was saying goodbye to her, I just got in the car. I couldn't turn back, 'cause she was crying. I was just a kid."

She came over on the *Andrea Doria* in 1955 and moved in with Joseph and Margaret Basile, her husband's aunt and uncle, on the 700 block of Fitzwater. Carmillo Erminio may have been the first Italian on the block in 1890, but by 1955 just about everyone was Italian, which was fortunate because Sally Auriemma spoke no English.

"I was too young to go to work. My aunt took me to school to register, but they wouldn't take me. . . . I had the wedding band on, and they said I couldn't be with the other girls. I went to school at night twice a week at the House of Industry. I didn't learn English there. I learned it on Fitzwater Street."

Soon after her husband arrived in 1956, they moved to 746 Fitzwater and he went to work with his uncle at Maggio. Sal was born in 1957, and four more children followed. She and Claudio moved to Norristown in the early 1980s. Her husband died in 1991.

David Auriemma, born in 1964, is the youngest son. He grew up in the store, just like his brothers, Sal and Claudio. As a teenager, he had no intention of making the store his life. "I guess when my father passed away, I changed my mind. . . . I feel it's mine. It belongs to me, and I don't have to work for nobody."

The street has changed since he was little. "People were warmer and friendlier. You worked together. It isn't the same anymore. Before it was like a little Italy. If you weren't Italian, you weren't on that street. Today, there's a lot of trouble on that street. People don't want to pay for the trash [collection] and it's dirty."

But business is better. So good that Claudio's now packs and sells its own olive oil. "We ship it to Puerto Rico, California, Texas. Twenty years ago, the feta cheese we sold was from Greece. Now we sell French, Italian, Bulgarian, Hungarian, feta from Israel."

Sal, like David, did not believe he'd go into the family business. "After high school, after Neumann, I had decided I wanted to go to college. I sort of had the idea of being a lawyer. It didn't sit too good with my father. He wasn't thrilled. Once he accepted the idea, I changed my mind."

Four of the five Auriemma children now run the store, and some of the grandchildren work on weekends. "Now that we import from Italy and all that, I buy everything," says Sal. "My brother Claudio is a great salesman. He can sell anything. David has his own niche. He takes care of deliveries. You could send him to Hong Kong, no problem. He makes sure things bought are delivered. And he also works the counter."

Inside the photograph:
A BENEFICIO DELLA
CROCE ROSSA ITALIANA
E DELLE OPERA ASSISTENZIALI
IN ISPIRITO PURISSIMO D' ITALIANITA'
AD INIZIATIVA DELLA
SOCIETA' UNIONE ABRUZZESE
DOMENICA 19 APRILE 1936-XIV E. F.
HOTEL PALUMBO PHILADELPHIA, PA.

VERNA ART PHOTO STUDIO
806 CHRISTIAN STREET
PHILADELPHIA, PENNA.

It wasn't all provolone and pepperoni for the Italians of South Philadelphia. These gowned and tuxedoed partygoers are at a benefit for the Italian Red Cross at Palumbo's in 1936. Used with permission of the Balch Institute for Ethnic Studies Library

Yvonne also works in the store, but her younger sister, Lana, does not. "My brother Claudio never wanted to do anything else," says Sal. "David, I think he had his moments. I mean, I have moments. Some days, I can think of a thousand other things I would rather be doing than this. But realistically, this is what we do best."

The fact that Sal's father initially did not want his oldest son to go to college is not suprising. The Italian immigrant tradition was focused toward work, not education.

It was not uncommon for Italians to come to the United States, earn money working, and then return to their hometowns in Italy. In 1904, 10 percent of the Italians entering the country had been here before. By the 1920s, the percentage was even higher. Education was not emphasized. An Italian youth was typically not pushed to finish high school. In 1918, just 5 percent of the Italian students at South Philadelphia High School completed 12th grade. It was not until 1949 that nearly half—49 percent—graduated.

One reason so few Italians graduated is that they worked. In 1930, more Italian teenagers, ages 14 to 16, worked than any other white ethnic group in the city. And most of those Italian youths lived in South Philadelphia. The children who went to college were, for the most part, from the middle and professional classes. Like Marie Mobilio Stapinski. Of course, children of some working-class parents went to college, too. Like Mobilio's childhood friend, Arlene Notoro Morgan.

Morgan was the only child of James Notoro and Mary Actis-Grande. Stapinski was the second of three children, born in 1946 to two pharmacists, Marie and Joseph Mobilio. Her father's father arrived at Ellis Island in 1914 from Rocco Imperiale, near Calabria, and opened a shoemaker shop on Carlisle Street between Morris and Tasker.

"In our family, I don't know why, but it was always very important that the children be educated into a profession. You never even thought about doing anything else. My father wanted to go to med school, but they could not

Joseph and Marie Mobilio vacationing in Atlantic City in the late 1930s. Courtesy of Marie Mobilio Stapinski

Pharmacist Joseph Mobilio showing his new line of Whitman Chocolates in his Broad Street store in the late 1940s. Courtesy of Marie Mobilio Stapinski

afford that. The next best thing in the family's mind was to go into pharmacy, which was a three-year program that they were able to afford. . . ."

Both her parents graduated from the Philadelphia College of Pharmacy in 1931.

"That's where they met, which I think was more of an exception for her, a woman, to be in college. They didn't marry until '38. Even though my mother's family was Italian, my mother was not first-generation. Her parents lived in Hammonton, New Jersey, and were born in this country. . . . My father's family was from the old country. My mother's parents were not enthusiastic about the marriage, so they went together for seven years, more than that. They went together a long time."

After working in a pharmacy at 22nd and Federal, her parents moved in 1944 to a home and pharmacy at Broad and Dickinson. The move was considered a step up.

"That was considered an elite neighborhood," says Morgan, who lived around the corner from the pharmacy. "My mother bought there specifically because it was an elite neighborhood, where the doctors lived, the lawyers, members of the Philadelphia Orchestra, the teachers."

Stapinksi is a pharmacist today; Morgan is a top editor at *The Philadelphia Inquirer*. Neither lives in South Philadelphia anymore, and they see each other about once a year. But they have been friends for more than 35 years, and the two women still finish each other's sentences. Asked exactly what part of South Philadelphia made up their "elite neighborhood":

Stapinski: "From 17th to 13th and to Dickinson, maybe Morris. I don't know if we wandered that far away. You think we did?"

Morgan: "I'd say it was the Strolli [restaurant] neighborhood. Broad Street seemed to be fine for us. . . . Passyunk Avenue, I think of that as our neighborhood, but I don't think of, say, . . ."

Stapinski: "Above 15th Street, except to go to church or, like you, to go to your grandmother's, and you had a couple of friends that lived that way. But outside of that, we didn't really go two or three blocks in either direction."

Morgan went to the neighborhood parochial school, St. Thomas, and then to St. Maria Goretti, while Stapinski went to the Notre Dame Academy on Rittenhouse Square.

"Quite a few of our neighbors' children went there. . . . Dr. Diodati, his daughter went. . . . And there was a dentist, Dr. DiPietro. And then Pelosi. And then Cuccionata, his children went there also. They were all doctors."

Morgan spent lots of time in her friend's house, some of it arguing with Stapinski's father about politics. "He had a good time doing it," says Stapinski. "I think he egged her on."

"He was the quintessential Nixon Republican," says Morgan. "He was an Italian. He came here off the boat. He made something of himself. Nobody gave him anything. . . . You got what you got through your own hard work. Affirmative action is not something he believed in. Yet, when he met people . . . it didn't matter what the color of your skin was. He was a gentleman to everybody and treated people very courteously, very professionally. But as far as his politics went, he could get really wild. He was absolute rock-bed supporter of things Italian, Italian Americans, and the fact that he remembered growing up being discriminated against."

Stapinski grew up with a father in the pharmacy. Morgan grew up with a father in the hospital.

"My mother was basically a single parent, because my father was very sick at an early age. He was in and out of hospitals. . . . I didn't really know that it was much different, between my mother and Marie's parents. I wasn't deprived of anything. Marie went to private school and I went to St. Thomas, and maybe that was the only difference. Her parents never acted like I was any different, and my mother certainly never acted like they were any different. Marie's parents were the pharmacists, and my mother was a tailor. It was the neighborhood, I think. If you lived in that neighborhood, you were all sort of equal. . . ."

And if you lived in the neighborhood and you were a teenage Catholic, you went to the Bishop Neumann dances.

"It was for Goretti and Neumann," remembers Morgan, but she always got Marie in. "They were typical high school dances where the boys stood on the one wall, the girls sat on the other side, and maybe someone would ask you to dance. Sometimes they had a lady's choice. I always remembered the Bishop Neumann dance, Johnny Mathis singing "Misty," Father Cox screaming at everybody. He was the disciplinarian and in charge of the dance. He'd get up and make these announcements, and everybody would be throwing spitballs and hooting and hollering and he'd be going, 'Yo, yo, listen up.' And I don't know what the hell he had to say to us, . . . but he was tough and everybody was scared to death of him."

In the summers, Stapinksi and her family and her best friend went down the shore. "Longport is where we grew up, Longport and Margate. Everyone else went to Wildwood," says Morgan.

"Wildwood was for the tailors. Even though my mother was one, we still didn't do that. . . . I never had a [family] vacation, because my father was sick. We didn't have the money. But she was not one to go with the Wildwood crowd. She would look more toward the things like the opera, theater, cultural things."

Those "cultural things" did not include the Mafia. Both women say their parents did not discuss the Mafia. "My father was very adamant about the word 'Mafia,'" says Stapinski. "He always felt that it was a defamation of the Italian name. Call it 'organized crime' because there were other people involved. There were Irish and Jewish and everybody else involved in it."

Only Italians, however, were involved in the Graduate Club, a social group of Italian male college graduates formed in the early 1930s on South Broad Street. A Depression-era version of networking, the Graduate Club may have also been a reaction of white-collar professionals to the image of Italians as uneducated and as mobsters. The club still exists today. Back in the 1950s, Joseph and Marie Mobilio (though a college graduate, she was relegated to the ladies' auxiliary) were very active.

"It really promoted the Italian professionals," says Stapinski. "There were a lot of doctors and lawyers. They had dinner dances, parties, card nights. One thing that sticks in my mind is they would have dance lessons. Professionals would come in, and they would go and learn how to tango and rumba."

Nicholas Cipriani did not participate in the dancing lessons when he joined the Graduate Club after World War II. "It was a way to work with everybody who had achieved and to . . . do things on a higher level, a cultural level, without being snobbish but to say, we have made it and we have a club."

He was not nearly as active as Mobilio or some of the founding members, men like Robert Sebastian, Dr. Charles DeLuca, Jack Ianucci, Dr. Albert Cietto, Edward Furia, and Americo Cortese. "I've not been active for the last 20 years. They honored me after I became a judge and gave me a beautiful gold chain for a pocket watch I had."

He was born on July 1, 1919, on 12th Street between Morris and Moore, just about the time Italians became the largest single ethnic group in South Philadelphia. In 1850 there were about 300 Italians, but by 1920 more than 44,000 South Philadelphia residents had been born in Italy. Four years later, the goverment turned off the immigration spigot. Never again would so many fresh-off-the-boat Italians (and Jews and others) arrive in South Philadelphia.

Cipriani's parents were both born in San Marco La Catola, a small town just east of Naples. The first family member to come to South Philadelphia was his mother's father, Michael Bozzuto. He opened a barber shop on the northwest corner of 12th and Moore at a time when very few Italians lived that far south. In 1903 Bozzuto moved less than a half a block north to a larger, five-chair shop at 12th and Pierce. The family would live there for the next 76 years.

"My grandfather was very enterprising. He got involved in community activities. I believe he was the first Republican committeeman of Italian extraction in the First Ward. Grandpop was part of the William S. Vare organization. He took his first job with the city in 1919. He ended up in the tax office, when he retired in 1944. He had given up the barbering business."

It was the good heart of his grandfather that made it possible for Cipriani's father to come to the United States.

"My maternal and my paternal grandfathers were friends in their hometown. So much so that when grandfather came here, he brought with him my father's oldest brother, Joseph Cipriani. . . . In 1910 my paternal grandfather had gone completely blind in Italy. He wrote and asked if my maternal grandfather could care for his youngest son, who was my father. My dad came over, 16, 17 years old, with a tag around his neck, all alone."

In 1917 Cipriani's father, already a barber and now called Gene, not Giacinto, married Michael Bozzuto's eldest daughter.

Nicholas Cipriani, the oldest of three children, grew up at 12th and Pierce in the 1920s and 1930s. "People gathered together from the same hometown. The 1100 block of Pierce Street and Watkins Street, 95 percent of the people came from a town in Sicily called Caronia, in the province of Messina."

His family went to St. Nicholas of Tolentine Church, an Italian parish at Ninth and Watkins. It is where his mother married and where he was baptized. The family was never discriminated against there until years later, when reverse discrimination occurred.

Cipriani's sister married an Irishman. "When he went to enroll his boy at St. Nick's, they refused to accept the boy because his father was Irish. Said he would have to go to Annunciation Church, the archdiocese parish. Still had those rules then."

Cipriani was graduated from South Philadephia High School in 1935 and wanted to go to college. "Going to college and professional school in the '20s and '30s was a big event. My wife's brother became a doctor in 1935 and people in the community gave him a banquet at Palumbo's. . . ."

His father believed in education but, at 25 cents a haircut, could not afford to send his son to college. Cipriani worked in the South Philadelphia law office of Robert Sebastian after high school. With Sebastian's help—tuition and two dollars a week—he went to college and law school, finishing in 1943.

He married in 1947 and moved to Wolf Street near Broad in 1949. He was elected a Common Pleas Court judge in 1969, retired in 1989, and works part time now as a senior judge. And still lives on Wolf Street.

"In the early 1960s I was looking to move because all my maternal relatives had gone. I had an uncle in Doylestown, an aunt in Horsham, an uncle in Ambler. My sister is in Oreland; my other sister moved up near Doylestown. The only ones left down here are myself and a brother of my mother." His mother-in-law lived two blocks away, but she died in 1963.

"We looked around and didn't find a home that was as comfortable as this was. And I could go to work. If it snowed or rained, I didn't have to worry about transportation. And let me say, I was not wealthy. . . . We grew out of the Depression, didn't believe in loans. When we bought the dining room set, we couldn't get a bank loan because we had no credit. . . .

"It's a beautiful neighborhood, convenient to Center City. Since '49 I don't think there's been four new families in the whole block. Next door, the mother and father died, the daughter moved in. The neighborhood remains constant. And very frankly, where are we going to go? We live here very comfortably.

We enjoy the people. People call me Nick, they don't call me Judge. . . . We just go about our business, so that's why we're here."

Sal Auriemma, on the other hand, got away from South Philadelphia as quickly as he could. He works on Ninth Street seven days a week, but he lives near Norristown. He moved there at first because it was a place to keep the horses he has ridden since he was 19. He has no horses now, but he is still out in the country with his wife and children.

"I don't want to live in South Philly. There's nothing for me here. . . . South Philly, you don't . . . have any space. Where I live, I can sit outside all day long in my underwear if I wanted to; there's nobody there. In South Philly, you don't have privacy. I can turn up the stereo as loud as I want, nobody is going to bother me. In South Philly, someone will knock on the door and say, 'You want to lower that?'"

Noise or the need for privacy did not make Gabriella LaBella move away. It was values.

"The people in South Philly are satisfied with what they have and where they are. That's a positive in a way, but for me, it's a negative. . . . The ultimate in South Philly is you own your row home, you rent a house in Wildwood for the summer, drive a nice car, . . . order out when you feel like it, and you've made it in life. And if your kids can live as well as you, that's okay. There isn't that drive to get out, and maybe there doesn't have to be, but for me there needed to be."

She was born in Miranda, a region of Abruzzi, and came to Philadelphia in 1966 when she was 11. The route was circuitous.

Her grandmother was born in Oklahoma, but left as a young girl when her own parents returned to Italy. Santa Borrelli grew up in Italy, married, and had three children, including LaBella's mother. "In the early '50s, she decided she wanted to be back in the States. My mother opted not to come, because she wanted to marry my father and my grandmother could only bring her unmarried children. My mother married and had four children, but she always wanted to be reunited with her family."

LaBella's grandparents settled near 10th and Porter Streets, while her parents agonized about whether to leave Italy.

"As soon as grandmother came to the U.S., she petitioned for my mother, but the immigration quotas were difficult then. . . . So it wasn't until almost 15 years later that my parents actually had to make the decision, do we go to America?

"My father had his own construction business. He built houses, but it was a struggle. My mother had just bought the machines to start her own business, a little knitting factory."

At the time, Italy was not doing well economically, and Santa Borrelli was sending money home to her daughter. "We were living comfortably versus others, but it was a struggle. My older sister was in boarding school. My parents' goals were to . . . keep us in private boarding schools, ultimately send us to the universities. . . . Their issues were, we have lots of things we want to give our children. Are we going to be able to?"

Maria and Nicola LaBella decided to leave. "They're ambivalent now

(*above left*)
In the basement of Gabriella LaBella's home in the late 1960s, the family gathers to make salami and sausage. On the left is her uncle, Angelo Barile. To the right, her aunt, Sandra Cifolelli. Seated in the center is Gabe's father, Nicola. Courtesy of Gabriella LaBella

(*above right*)
Girlfriends born in Italy help Gabe LaBella celebrate her 15th birthday in 1970. The birthday girl is about to blow out the candles. Courtesy of Gabriella LaBella

(*left*)
High school senior Gabriella LaBella in her physics class at St. Maria Goretti in 1973. She had just put streaks in her hair. She was in a class for bright girls. "It was okay to be smart in those classes." Courtesy of Gabriella LaBella

about whether they made the right decision, because the people my father sold his equipment to are millionaires now. There was a construction boom after we left."

The 11-year-old girl was excited about leaving. "I had this vision of America . . . where everything is wonderful. . . . And when people talk about the Statue of Liberty, it really is true. We were seven days on this ship, and we were all on the decks. It really is an incredible feeling when you see that statue in the harbor. People were crying. "

Life in South Philadelphia started out so well. The family lived at 10th and Daly. She had a wonderful teacher in a class for foreign-born students at the

Prom night at Goretti, 1973. Gabriella LaBella, left, is ready to party. Her date is Italian-born Lucio Varanese, and her father is in the center. She paid $150 for the dress at the Mansion House. Courtesy of Gabriella LaBella

McCall School. But in less than two years, she was mainstreamed and sent to seventh grade in the Church of the Epiphany school on Jackson Street.

She was bright, but she was in immediate trouble. "In Italy, they don't teach penmanship, so I had a problem writing. . . . I wasn't comfortable asking questions, because I wasn't sure if I was stupid or if it was okay if everybody doesn't know this. Part of it was the age, too, but when I did try to answer, speaking with an accent or maybe asking a stupid question and being made fun of, I pretty much retreated.

" . . . I remember being called wop and greaseball by the Italian kids. They called me names because I spoke differently, I looked differently. And there wasn't the connection I had expected in terms of being Italian. That wasn't even an issue in their lives. . . . It's just the way things were. We're the people from South Philly, you're the foreigner.

"I thought America was going to be this wonderful place, and it was horrible. My father got very sick shortly after we came, so he couldn't work. And my mother, who really had never worked outside the home, had to go and work two jobs because she had to support a family. She went to a factory. . . ."

After two painful years, LaBella entered Goretti and found that she was not alone—Italian-born girls from other parishes were there as well.

"We would eat lunch together; we would walk to Passyunk Avenue after school together to get a water ice, whatever. And we spoke English, interestingly enough. We were all from Italy and we had this bond. . . .

"And that's the time we discovered the Italian dances 'cause we were just starting to be old enough to go. . . . Dances every week, and everybody who went was from Italy. They used to be sometimes at the Fiesta Hall, 20th and Snyder, any kind of wedding-type hall. Caribe Gardens, I remember. Saturday night."

At Goretti, she also made friends for the first time with non-Italians.

"Sheila Hewitt, she's Irish. We became friends in ninth grade. She's an assistant district attorney now. I would eat at her house on Lawrence Street. It was such a neat experience. First, her mom was a single parent, and second, the food they ate. That was my first experience of how people other than Italians lived. I had pierogis at her house. Cream chipped beef, that was just wonderful. Then I would go home and tell my mother, and we would try to make the stuff. It was my first peep inside an American house."

She became more acclimated, but her mother never did. Her parents had not intended to stay downtown, but her father's illness forced them to remain. Her mother was never comfortable with the neighborhood's strange customs.

"She thought that it was bizarre that people would sit on the steps. She never sat on her steps. And she felt uncomfortable with neighbors saying to her, 'Oh, I saw people leaving your house last night. What was going on?' We came from a little town where everybody knows everybody, but people wouldn't ask . . . personal questions in the street."

One thing people did not ask about was the Mafia. "It was a fact of life. It was just there," says LaBella, who found herself in a curious relationship with some organized crime members.

"I used to babysit for them. My parents didn't know. I babysat for Salvatore Merlino. For his kids, Joey and Maria. . . . I found Italian American children were cruel and mean, but the adults were very nice to me, and very kind. They thought I was a nice girl from Italy, so I wasn't corrupt and they could trust me with their kids. Sonny's wife, Rita, she's a lovely woman. I started out by tutoring little Maria. And then I would babysit. I remember babysitting for another family. I forget the name. I think he and Sonny were kind of associated. I started babysitting for the other family first, 'cause they used to live on my street; then they moved. That's how I met Rita and Sonny.

" . . . The first family I babysat for, I remember a man came in. No big deal. I knew he was a friend of the husband, whatever. He comes in, says he got to get something. I saw him get a gun out of the closet and just leave. And that was real okay for me, because I thought this is how it is in South Philly. I never questioned things that I would have questioned normally, because there were so many things that were new to me. . . .

"By the way, this is something no one talks about. I knew because I knew, but you don't talk to them about what they do. You just don't. I still wouldn't. I babysat for them; I got to know them. . . . When I would run into someone in a nightclub, at the Melrose Diner, the tab was always paid . . . because I knew them."

LaBella worked for many years helping other immigrants as coordinator of Migration Services at Nationalities Service Center. She lives in suburban Philadelphia, as do her parents. Sheila, her childhood friend, lives in LaBella's old house in South Philadelphia.

While Gabriella LaBella and Sal Auriemma consciously moved away, the Reverend Michael Gambone was delighted to return.

He had been a pastor in Coatesville, Pennsylvania, for seven years. "I'm a city boy. I don't know if you have lived anyplace outside of Philadelphia. You expect the nights to be quiet, but when the days are as quiet as the nights, you begin to wonder. I'd walk out the rectory. I'd see a car, I'd wave at them, and that would be about it. You saw nobody, except on Sunday, when they would all come to church. Nobody was in walking distance, because the church was not located right in Coatesville. . . . I was very happy there. I had four acres of ground. The people of the parish cut the grass, did the plumbing. It was really a great parish. . . .

"But I was kind of lonely. How many times do I go to the hospital? How many times do I do this or that? When I got the change, I was sort of shocked at first, 'cause I was just settling down. But I wasn't that depressed. . . . I said, 'St. Paul's, holy mackerel.'"

He was born in 1928, the youngest of four boys and three girls of Michael and Angelina Gambone, who lived on the 500 block of Queen Street. His father had an iron shop on Bainbridge Street and built many of the awnings in the Italian Market in the 1930s.

"Directly across of our house, there was a clothing store, Goldstein's. It's still there. It's run now by a couple of Italians, who are about my age, but as boys they worked in the store and helped deliver, carry packages. Mr. Goldstein had two sons, David and Paul, and both of them died. And the result was that the boys took over the store. They kept the name Goldstein."

It was a time of trolleys on every numbered street and playgrounds around every corner. "The neighborhood center was on Fifth and Christian, that was all Jewish. The Weccacoe Playground was at Fifth and Queen. Spent many, many days there playing ball. Around the corner on Christian Street, there was another playground called Sunshine, between Fifth and Sixth. There was a House of Industry too, where we used to play ball."

Most of the neighborhood Italian children went to public school. The Gambones went to St. Mary Magdalen.

"I think it was because my parents were religious. I have to admire my father, because men, men in general, did not practice the faith then. . . . In those days, for a man to go to church every Sunday was unusual. . . . And that's the way my mother was also, and all the children just followed automatically."

He didn't like working in the iron shop and toyed with the idea of becoming a doctor before entering the seminary in 1946, after being encouraged by a priest at St. Mary's. He had just graduated from high school. "My friends said I ought to have my head examined. They couldn't figure it out."

He was ordained and sent to churches in Bethlehem and Reading, to St. Monica's in South Philadelphia and St. Donato's in West Philadelphia, and to the church in Coatesville before coming back to St. Paul's and South Philadelphia in 1976.

"Everything was the same. This is what fascinated me most. It was just as I left it, as far as the people were concerned. Maybe they don't come to the church the way I would like them to, but they were friendly and gracious and they'll do anything for you. I walked along Ninth Street, they all knew my father, they knew me. It's quite comfortable here."

But the community mix was changing. Professional people were moving in and renovating old homes, which was good for the church. Many of them were not Catholic, and those that were Catholic were often elderly, and that was not so good. A parish needs children to remain viable. Today, there's a growing Puerto Rican population, but even newer are the people from Southeast Asia. "When they practice the faith, they are very good at it, but most are not Catholic. We are starting programs in our parish, inviting them in, letting them be aware of what we have."

Father Gambone is not just comfortable, he is proud of where he grew up. He is describing a place, but it is as if he is talking about the teacher who made you work so hard, the teacher you will never forget, the one who changed your life.

"What is the expression? You can take a person out of South Philly, but you can never take South Philly out of the person. It's true. If I go anywhere and someone asks, Where are you from? I say, 'South Philly.' I just don't say Philadelphia. You had to really go through a process down here. You came from big families; it was a struggle. Get yourself educated and move up.

"The only other Philadelphia neighborhood I've lived in was West Philly, around 65th and Callowhill. And I can easily say there is a difference. They're Italians, same type people. But somehow or other, you don't get the same warmth there as I get over here. You can't describe it any other way."

Dorothy Marcucci returned downtown under less pleasant circumstances than Father Gambone. She had just become a widow.

She and her husband had lived in Broomall for 30 years when he died suddenly in 1977. She just couldn't mourn there. "I would see people I knew, and six months later they'd say, 'How are you Dorothy?' I'd say, 'Terrible.' I didn't especially want their sympathy; I just wanted to be honest. When I would say, 'Terrible,' some people turned around and walked away from me. Some would say, 'That's too bad,' and leave.

"And I thought, you're a person that I have known a long time. . . . Why are you walking away from me? People have since said, and I have a hard time with this, that they're upset too, and they don't really want to deal with what's happened to you. In South Philly, they'd say to me, 'Oh, Dorothy, we heard about your trouble.' And they'd say, 'I'm so sorry.'

"You don't get that in the suburbs. What you got was, 'How are you doing?' If you're asked a question by someone you know, they should be able to accept, 'I feel terrible,' but they wouldn't. . . . So I said, 'I don't need this. I don't want this. I'm leaving this.' "

The second of four children, she grew up on Passyunk Avenue near Mifflin, above her father's electrical appliance store. Both her parents grew up near 10th and Christian.

"My grandfather, from what I can gather, had a pushcart and sold bananas. I'm sure my mother's family would be very upset with my saying that. He went to Dock Street and bought bananas, and then he pushed the pushcart through the neighborhoods and sold them. He became ill. He didn't survive the change in America. My aunts have told me that he sang the song 'Oh, Calabria, how I miss you. *Bella Calabria.*' . . . My aunts tell me that he cried a great deal.

"My mother's mother was the person we called *pazzi*, crazy lady. She was

119

the person they called to funerals to express grief. She was paid for that. . . . But my memory of her was during the Saint Cosmas and Damian Festivals in Conshohocken. She would dance, and the dancing was insane, violent. As a little child, I was terrified. I saw this woman so excited and dancing furiously. . . . But I realized later, when I read about the tarantella, that it's a way of getting rid of the poison from the tarantula. They actually did that in the fields."

Marcucci was a five-year-old during the Sesquicentennial, but she remembers the celebration in South Philadelphia.

"My father was an electrician, and he was contracted to do work there. . . . I remember he would put us in the truck and we would go with him. . . . And we used League Island Park when the Sesqui was done. A lot of the things that were built just stayed there.

"One of my most vivid memories is . . . my mother screaming one day in the store. We all ran down. Some Indians had come in full regalia. They were from the Sesqui. And my mother is like out of her mind. We're little kids. 'Mom, Mom, what is it?' She said, 'Go next door. Call Mr. Green.' Mr. Green was a Norwegian who had a deli. We run in, 'Mr. Green, there's some crazy people in the store.' They couldn't speak, these Indians. Well, Mr. Green ushered them out of the store. . . . It was very exciting."

She was Dorothy Mullen then, and she looked Irish and ate more Irish stew at home than pasta. But she felt Italian and married one, Philip Marcucci, when she was 22. They saved, bought a car, and moved to the country, to Broomall.

"The thing was, I wanted my children to see the earth, to see the trees. I think that's very Italian. They spent their childhood digging up worms, going fishing, things like that. None of that was possible in the city."

She paid her own way through the University of Pennsylvania, but marriage interrupted her education in literature. She was to become a lecturer and teacher about Italian food and Italian life, but that did not happen until her sons left for college.

She and her husband had been to Italy and elsewhere in Europe many times and had joined the Council for International Visitors. They hosted foreign guests and attended receptions for visiting ambassadors, learning about foreign food and culture. She became an even better cook, and he knew how to eat. "I'd say, 'Now we're going to try a dish, mole, that the nuns made in Mexico for a visiting bishop.' And he'd say, 'Okay, I'll tell you if it's any good.' You know, that kind of thing."

When the boys left, a Reading Terminal merchant suggested that she teach foreign cooking. And she did for two years, until a friend said that what she should really teach was Italian cooking. It was the early 1970s. The Marcuccis went to Italy again.

"What we knew was the kind of food we ate in South Philly. But we began to see why there were so many different ways of making tomato sauce. . . . If you're Sicilian, you make it differently from a Neapolitan."

She returned and began to talk to Italian Americans about cooking Italian. "What I'd say is, 'Who's Abruzzese?' And they put up hands. 'And who is Calabrese?' See, you're not Italian. You're telling me you're Neapolitan. You're Abruzzese. You're whatever. The point is that Italy was not a country when

A wedding day kiss outside the Annunciation Church for the new couple, Dorothy and Philip Marcucci, on May 25, 1946. Courtesy of Dorothy Marcucci

Outside the car of the smooching couple are friends and family. Check out the hats and the hair styles. Courtesy of Dorothy Marcucci

your family came here, and for centuries you were always Abruzzese. . . . We have a different history of a different culture.

" . . . I began participating in festivals, . . . and I was exploring the food of Italy. I was making pizzas made with pie crust that had ricotta, eggs, cream, nutmeg, and spinach that were from . . . Tuscany. The pizza we knew was Neapolitan pizza."

Italian American food is wonderful, but it is based on southern Italian cooking, which is "basically a Greek cooking, because we use olive oil, use garlic. And so what we know of Italian food has little to do with the rest of Italy. It has only to do with the part of Italy that belonged to Greece."

She cooks, she lectures, she feeds friends. And she will not leave South Philadelphia again.

"How people feel and react to where they are has to do with holding on to identity. I really feel that way. That's the reason I came back. . . . My kids live down the street. That's true all over South Philly. . . .

"South Philly represents a kind of naturalness. That's why I came back. . . . In the suburbs, what you get is people rejecting you or not speaking to you. In South Philly . . . people will talk to you. They may insult you, but they'll talk to you. I once had a woman say, Why do I like shopping on Ninth Street when a supermarket has the same thing? I said, 'Because in a supermarket, nobody speaks to you. You pick up the tomato and you leave. You're a nobody.' But in South Philly, he says, 'Put the tomato down, lady.' You're alive."

6
Sports

Two stories from two former South Philadelphia schoolyard ballplayers. First, Samuel "Leaden" Bernstein:

"I went into the Army in 1941. I was stationed in El Paso, Texas, and I got into a tournament—basketball. Baseball was my better game. Our Army team played against St. Louis University. We lost in double overtime and I had like 30 points. I never played college ball, I never played high school, only baseball. The St. Louis University coach came over to me. He said, 'Wow, where the hell do you play, kid? You look terrific. You're the most valuable player in that tournament.'

"Pepperdine College was in the tournament, Arizona, too. So I say, 'I'm from South Philadelphia.' He called his team over. He says, 'You know why this kid is so good? He's from South Philadelphia. Nobody plays basketball like the kids in South Philadelphia.' This was 1941 in El Paso."

And now one from Bob Vetrone, former sports writer for *The Evening Bulletin* who later wrote the Buck the Bartender sports column that appeared in *The Daily News*.

It was 1981 and Mafia member Phil Testa had just been killed by a bomb that destroyed his house. "I was coming back from a trip, and a guy I knew from South Philly said to me, 'Did you hear about who got blown up on Porter Street? Testa's house blew up.' I said, 'Oh my god, that's first base foul territory for our softball game.' "

Ethnicity and economics define communities, but in South Philadelphia sports did as well. Reputations and nicknames—identities—came from the basketball court and the football field and the boxing ring. It was a chunk of the culture, part of what it was all about. Guys hung on the corner, ate water ice, played ball.

For most of the twentieth century, the neighborhood—not the city, the neighborhood—has had a national reputation for its basketball players and its boxers. World-famous athletes—pool shooter Willie Mosconi, light-heavyweight boxing champion Tommy Loughran, and Hall of Fame basketball player Earl Monroe, just to name three—hail from South Philadelphia. As do nationally known sports figures like former Temple University basketball coach Harry Litwack, boxing trainer Angelo Dundee (born Mirena), and basketball mogul Eddie Gottlieb.

123

But it is the status given to the little-known players, not the big shots, that reveals just how important athletes were. For they were celebrities too, no matter how long ago, or how briefly, they competed. Eddie "Itzy" Feinberg, an infielder who played 16 games for the Phillies in 1938 and 1939, owned a candy store on the northeast corner of Fifth and Wolf Streets in the 1940s and early 1950s. It was my corner. I was a little boy and I will never forget how all the men—my father included—looked up to Itzy. He was a ballplayer.

Sports has always been important downtown. On one level, it was what kids did on weekends and when they came home from school. If no one was around, it was wire ball or step ball. With a friend or two, half ball or chink. With six, the game was basketball in the schoolyard or box ball in the street, and with a ton of guys, football or softball in the park. As a young comedian, Bill Cosby did routines about playing street football in North Philadelphia, cutting left at the manhole, down and out in front of the Chevy. Those manholes were not a joke in South Philadelphia, because they were the down markers in football and third base in box ball. That's how we played.

On another level, for those who were truly talented, sport could be a way out of the alleys and tiny rowhouses, a way for the children of immigrants to be "treated like a kingpin," says former pro basketball player Alexander "Petey" Rosenberg.

On both levels, athletes were supported and encouraged. Ballfields, boxing rings, basketball courts—the places to play were everywhere. And if they were crowded, there was always the street. You were expected to play. Coaches in schools, community centers, and athletic clubs taught youngsters how while friends, neighbors, and family watched.

No effort will be made here to say that there were more great athletes in South Philadelphia than in other city neighborhoods. Not even in other Philadelphia neighborhoods. That would be foolish—correct, but foolish nonetheless. But it would not be foolish to look back once again in time and see how deeply steeped sports is in the South Philadelphia psyche. For instance, South Philadelphia High School was a nationally known basketball center in 1914; men were sparring in large South Philadelphia boxing gymnasiums in 1911, gyms so big that they seated more than four thousand paying customers in one of the city's poorest neighborhoods; men were playing baseball in organized leagues in the 1860s and racing horses at a modern, newly built track in Point Breeze in the 1850s.

Before anyone raced a horse or put a bat to a ball in South Philadelphia, people hunted and fished. In the late 1600s, there were herring and oysters in the water, deer and wild turkeys in the forests, wild pigeons and geese in the air. Near the Blue House Tavern at Ninth and South Streets, there were swamps, a forest, a pond, a creek, and game aplenty. The year was 1726.

Horse racing was nothing new in Philadelphia—that's how Race Street got its name—but for 30 years in the mid- and late 1800s, Point Breeze Park, just east of the Schuylkill River, was one of the city's favorite places to enjoy the pastime. *The Public Ledger* announced in 1855: "The trotting course belonging to this association on the Penrose Ferry Road . . . has been completed and

The skaters were on the rink at Second and Mifflin in 1865, and the trotters were on the track to the west at Point Breeze Park in 1870. Used with permission of the Library Company of Philadelphia

enclosed with a substantial fence. Clubhouse to be completed is of brick, two-stories high. . . . No betting allowed upon races." One wonders how well that rule was enforced.

At the same time that men and women were watching the trotters at Point Breeze, further east people were playing baseball in the warm weather and skating in the cold. Ice skating rinks at Third and Morris and at Second and Mifflin were popular in the 1860s. And baseball was played on the field at 11th and Wharton, near the Moyamensing Prison. Among the players was an infielder and team captain who is better known today for his oratory, his teaching, and his leadership in the campaigns for voting and civil rights. Octavius V. Catto was a martyr, a hero, and a ballplayer as well.

Organized black baseball began just after the Civil War. The Excelsiors were the first team in the city, beginning play in 1866. The Pythians, captained by Catto, began a few months later. Blacks played baseball in other cities as well: Albany had the Bachelors; Washington had the Mutuals and the Alerts; Harrisburg had the Monrovia club; and Chicago had the Uniques.

Sometimes clubs were afraid to journey as far south as the Wharton Street field, concerned about the "contention" that they might experience from white residents. So the Excelsiors and Pythians would take the ferry and play visiting teams across the river in Camden. Church Sunday schools would hold picnics by the field, and hundreds of people would watch the games. If the game was played in South Philadelphia, the enclosed stands and bleacher seats would fill quickly. The Pythians' games were a social as well as an athletic event.

The influx of Italians and Jews into South Philadelphia in the late 1800s and early 1900s led to the growth of two sports—boxing and basketball.

"Everyone at Southern High School wanted to be a boxer," says Dave Dabrow, who boxed but is better known as a longtime basketball coach at Southern and as one of the leaders of the Jewish Basketball League.

"Why? Because we had a local kid by the name of Harry "Kid" Brown, who was a good boxer. You ever hear of Joe Brown, who was a sculptor? That was Harry's brother. You had a guy like Lou Tendler from South Philly. A southpaw, terrific. How he never became the world's champion when he fought Benny Leonard twice is very hard to understand. Leonard was too smart for him. Everybody wanted to be a boxer because the way to riches would be through boxing in those days. So I boxed a couple rounds."

Dabrow was born in 1905, six years before the opening of the Olympia, South Philadelphia's first boxing arena, seating 4,200 at Broad and Bainbridge. The National, at 11th and Catharine, opened in 1918 and was even bigger.

"One of my bouts was at the Gaiety Burlesque House, about 1920, 1921. It was at Eighth and Vine. I was to receive $25. I won, beat some Italian boy. I boxed under the name of Joe Benjamin. No one used their real names in those days. Anyway, my manager took half, which left me $12.50. I had two seconds, who I had to give $5 apiece, so I finished with $2.50. I quit boxing."

Adolph Ritacco quit boxing because shrapnel tore his body apart. Not

126

much else would have stopped him. He was fighting as a little boy and still fighting as an old man.

At the age of 77, Ritacco, perhaps five-foot-two, walked into a South Philadelphia taproom one day in 1991. "I go in this bar 'cause they have the horses. I don't have to go to the track. I bet them horses over here, and get paid track prices.

"Well, I walk in there to see a friend of mine. He's about 63. There's a guy bothering him. I say to the guy, 'Why don't you leave the poor man alone?' And he's jabbing him with his finger.

"I said to my friend, 'This guy's hurting you. Take a punch at him. What are you worried about? I'll back you up.' So my friend went to throw a punch. The guy gets up to hit him, and I hit the guy with a left hook. . . . When he went down, he hit the bar thing. Bang, boom. I say, 'Gee, this is where I go to jail.'

"I knocked him out. He must have been 28, 29 years old. I thought he was dead. I'm hollering for ice. I put it on his neck and down his pants. When he come out, he was like in another world. Just got up, walked out, and I never seen him again. What a shot I hit him. He wanted to throw a right hand, . . . I moved to a side, and wham, I hit with that hook."

Ritacco was a flyweight, a little guy who wanted to parlay an uppercut into some money, but he received more acclaim as a cut man than as a fighter. His fingers are gnarled for the trying. Born in 1914, Ritacco grew up on the 1900 block of South Iseminger Street, between Moore and Morris, and on the 1000 block of Emily Street. His parents, Marietta and Emilio, were from Calabria. She took care of five children while he worked in local sales.

"I'm not gonna kid you. He was a bootlegger. When he first came to the United States, he was in with the racketeers. He met a few people. They told him, 'Why don't you get into politics? You're smart, you're learning how to speak good English.' And it's just what he did. But before he did that, they made a pinch and he and his two brothers did time."

Ritacco says his father was in jail with the brother of Barney Samuel, a local Republican who would later became mayor. "My dad took care of him in there. My dad was a tough potato." In return, the elder Ritacco was offered a job as a deputy sheriff. "He was a sheriff for 18 years and he was a committeeman. . . . I never got involved in politics because he wouldn't let me. He said politics was a rotten, rotten thing and everybody was a double crosser. 'They made me go to jail 'cause I was a bootlegger. They're the biggest crooks in the world,' he used to tell me."

As a child living at 1019 Emily, Ritacco was always fighting. He went to the elementary school at 10th and Snyder.

"See where the big gas station is? That used to be a public school. I was in a fight every day over there. They hated me. Called me, You dago, your father's a jailbird. Irish kids. A few Italians, but mostly Irish. I was always in the Passyunk Gym, even when I was 12 years old. I was small, and everybody picked on me. I said, 'I'm going to learn to fight, and I'm going to knock a lot of guys dead,' which I did. When I was 19 years old, I had over 90 amateur

Adolph Rittaco, ready to punch your lights out, in 1939. Courtesy of Adolph Rittaco

Names That Come Up When You Talk About Great South Philadelphia Fighters

- **Tim Witherspoon** *played football for Southern, was heavyweight champion twice in the 1980s.*
- **Joltin' Jeff Chandler** *was bantamweight champ.*
- **Moses "Buster" Drayton,** *from Seventh and Snyder, was junior middleweight champ in 1986.*
- **Johnny Jadick** *was junior welterweight champion in 1932.*
- **Tommy Loughran** *was light-heavyweight champ in the late 1920s.*
- **Midget Wolgast** *was flyweight champ in the 1920s*
- **Ad Wolgast** *(no relation) was lightweight champion in 1910.*

By the way, Rocky Balboa, the boxer played by Sylvester Stallone in the Rocky *films, was not from South Philadelphia. He may have run through the Italian Market, but the Rock was a pug from Kensington.*

---

fights. I was 91–1 as an amateur." And 18–0 as a professional. Impressive, but Ritacco isn't a name that comes up when you talk about great South Philadelphia fighters.

Remembering the names of the local fighters whose reputations live on is a reminder of the neighborhood's poverty and its ethnic diversity. Hundreds from South Philadelphia filled boxing posters and gymnasiums. Mike Rossman. Al Fisher. Leland Beloff (yes, that Beloff). Tony and Frankie Cocco. Dan Bucceroni. Ernie Petrone. Jews and Italians early on, then everybody, then primarily black boxers and now not many at all, but you can still hear the plop of gloves against the heavy bag in gyms downtown. Dreams die hard.

After wounds from World War II took him out of the ring, Ritacco began working outside the ropes.

"I was a trainer, a cut man, and I really knew how to tape a guy's hands. Nobody ever hurt their hands with me in 20 years, and nobody ever lost a fight because of a cut. Giardello used to cut every time he fought. I had him for 12 years. I was one of the best. I really mean it. I was involved in 29 championship bouts. Maybe it was 35. Who the hell can remember?

"I trained Wallace Buck Smith, a black kid from Boston, 1955 to 1960. He held the lightweight title. A world champion, not a Pennsylvania or a New York, or that crap. I learned how to close a cut. Some chemist showed me how, with tea leaves.

"Nineteen sixty-three, I trained Joey Giardello; he was the middleweight champion, beat Dick Tiger for the title. In 1982, I had Matthew Saad Muhammad. His name used to be Matt Franklin. He come over my house. He said, we won the light-heavyweight championship. I was making money. When he lost

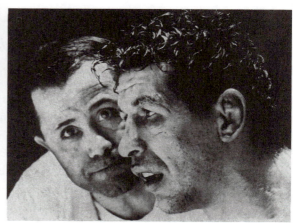

the title, in one fight I made $46,000. Who the hell makes $46,000 in one night? Paid my house off, bought a car, put money in the bank."

His friends were fighters, Tommy and Johnny Forte, Joe Maffei. People respected him.

"You know who my manager was when I turned professional?" Restaurateur and night club owner Frank Palumbo. "Nicest man in the world, loved him. He loved me like a son. . . . He was a straight shooter. See, the mob ran boxing then. Say you were a good fighter, just like Tommy Forte when he was coming up. They'd try to nail you. They wanted a piece of you. They come to me. I said, 'Talk to Frank.' Frank was like the law. Frank was a powerful, powerful man in this city. He said no, and they wouldn't fool with him. . . . He wasn't afraid of nobody. . . . And he was a good man with it."

Adolph Ritacco is semi-retired. He has a pension and makes a little money taking bets. He uses his "tea leaves" to stop the blood of local children who have fallen off their bicycles. He hasn't hit anyone since that night in the bar.

"I tell you, I hit that guy a shot right on the button. It couldn't have been a better shot. It reminded me of Joe Louis throwing a left hook."

Some kids who fought grew up to become boxers, like Ritacco. Other fighters grew up to become ballplayers, especially basketball players, like Dave Dabrow and Petey Rosenberg. It was a tough game that used to be played inside a metal cage. Elbows were as important as a two-hand set shot. And South Philadelphia was where the best players came from.

(above left)
Rittaco the trainer, with fighter Bud Smith when he won the lightweight title in Boston in 1955. Courtesy of Adolph Rittaco

(above right)
Rittaco talking to his fighter, Joey Giardello, in the 1963 title fight for the middleweight crown with Dick Tiger. Courtesy of Adolph Rittaco

Former pro basketball player Petey Rosenberg used to fight, though never professionally. Born in 1918, he grew up near Ninth and Shunk, and on Sheridan Street near Oregon Avenue.

"My neighborhood was all Jewish. From 10th Street west, it was Italian and Irish, and from Fifth Street down, all Irish. When I was in grammar school, I couldn't go past 11th Street because of the Irish kids. They'd pick on you. But as I got older, after 13, maybe, I beat the shit out of those kids. Most of the Jewish kids in those days were timid; they wouldn't fight. I was born to fight, believe me."

Everyone Fought

Everyone fought. Blacks, Jews, Italians, Irish, Poles, everyone:

- **Bobbie Wolgast**
- **Solomon "Young King Solomon" Tabakin**
- **Nayon Padlo**
- **Willie Curry** *(born Louis Molinari)*
- **The Carto brothers, Nunzio, Joe, and Frankie**
- **Babe Kaufman**
- **Joe Flocco**
- **Joe Belfiore**
- **Jimmy Soo**
- **Marty Collins** *(born Collucci)*
- **Battling Dundee**
- **Mike Evans** *(born Evancich)*
- **The Reed brothers, Calvin, Tiger, and Vincent**
- **Robert Adams**
- **"Irish Abe" Kauffman**
- **Teddy Baldwin** *(born Joseph Bologna)*
- **Tony Morgano,** *who defeated six champions in the 1930s, but none of the bouts were title fights*
- *and one of boxing's more unforgettable names,* **Yi Yi Erne**

He was the only son of David and Elsie Rosenberg, who came to South Philadelphia in the early 1900s from Russia. As a little boy, he regularly followed Peaches, one of the men on the ash wagon who collected the coal ashes that people put out. Neighbors called the little boy "Peaches" and then "Petey."

He was at Southern from 1932 to 1936 and played as a guard for the varsity basketball team immediately. "As a freshman, I remember we played Roman Catholic at the Palace Royal, Broad and Bainbridge. Used to be a fight club. I was the high scorer for the team, but very few points got made. I might have [averaged] seven, eight points."

He wasn't fighting much anymore. He was too busy playing basketball and

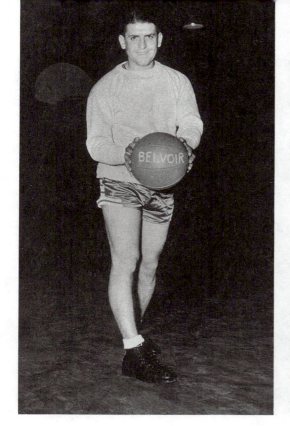

Petey Rosenberg excelled in two sports. Here is the basketball player in 1942 and the baseball player (with Phillies owner Bob Carpenter) in 1946. Courtesy of Bill Esher

baseball. Southern won the 1936 Public League basketball and baseball championships. Rosenberg, on both teams, was a neighborhood celebrity.

"Yeh, everybody would look out for you, and all the kids would sit down with you and want to talk with you. . . ." He was even permitted to operate the scoreboard for the SPHAs—the South Philadelphia Hebrew Association, a basketball team formed in 1918. After a year of prep school and college at St. Joe's, he joined the SPHAs in 1939. "The SPHAs were a big thing in those days. One of the best independent basketball teams in the world. We used to play against the Baltimore Bullets, Wilmington Clippers, New York Wrens, Brooklyn Jewels, Brooklyn Visitations, Kate Smith Celtics. She owned the team. It was in New York."

In 1940 the fans gave him a car for his play in a game against the New York Renaissance. "I'll never forget the day. I threw in 10 baskets, my first 10 shots. I never shot that much against them. We beat them. And Magistrate O'Malley presented the car to me, a 1940 Chevy. My father never had a car."

In 1946 he joined the Philadelphia Warriors in the Basketball Association of America, the precursor to today's National Basketball Association. That 1946–47 team won the championship, and two of the players, Rosenberg and his roommate, Jerry Rullo, were from downtown.

His pro career lasted just two years. "The money wasn't there. I could've played another two or three years, but I ain't going to go play for no $5,000 a year. I figured that I can do better on the outside, people I knew. In my first year with the Warriors, each team was limited to $50,000 with ten players. Some guys got less, some guys got more. You weren't going nowhere.

"After the second season, they traded me to Baltimore, but they wanted to

131

The South Philadelphia Hebrew Association, the SPHAs, were the best independent basketball team in the nation. Here they are in the late 1920s. That's Eddie Gottlieb in the suit; next to him is Harry Litwack, later the basketball coach of Temple University. Gottlieb and Litwack, like most of the players, were from South Philadelphia. Courtesy of Bill Esher

One of the most famous SPHAs was South Philadelphia's Reds Klotz, shown here in 1941. Klotz was known for his two-hand set shot. Courtesy of Bill Esher

The Mount Sinai Hospital women's basketball team competed in the Nurse's Basketball League in 1934. Used with permission of the Balch Institute for Ethnic Studies Library, Albert Einstein Medical Center Collection

pay me the same, so I quit. I opened a hoagie place downtown, 10th and Moyamensing."

He has never thought much about why so many basketball players came from downtown. "The guys all used to play basketball in the schoolyard, day and night. Me, I loved it, and I had nothing else to do. I would come home from Thomas Junior High, and my grandfather would give me a piece of bread and some butter and a piece of raw garlic. 'All right, go play.' That was every day.

"I was actually a better baseball player, but all the guys played basketball. I played semi-pro later with Warnerville; that's a little place above Reading. And I had a tryout with the Phils in 1946. They wanted to send me down to Wilmington, but I was a little old then. I was 28."

And he played professionally for one month in North Carolina while he was still in high school. "Tarboro, in the Coastal Plain League. A guy from Philly, he played there, and he said they needed another ballplayer. It was racist down there. In those days, colored people, they walked on the opposite side of the street. You weren't allowed to walk with them. It was tough even for Jewish men. I played under a different name. I was Pete Rossi."

He quit in a month, even after the team said they might move up to Milwaukee in Triple A ball. "I played good, but I didn't like the food and all. And we lived in a home with people. It was hard on Jewish ballplayers."

He remembers Oregon Avenue when it was laced with railroad tracks, when he stole ice and coal from the railroad cars and went swimming in the river at Delaware and Oregon. "You weren't a man unless you came out greasy."

Professional Baseball Players from South Philadelphia

- **Al Brancato**
- **Frank DiMichele**
- **Harry Marnie**
- **John Marzano,** *a catcher on the 1984 Olympic team*
- **George Riley**
- **Joe Rullo,** *brother of basketball player Jerry Rullo*
- **Eddie Silber**
- **Ad Swigler**

Grays Ferry was too far away from the Delaware River, so swimming greasy was not something Jerry Rullo thought much about. He just played ball.

"There used to be empty baseball fields. The older guys would play and the little guys would watch them and then we played. We followed the older guys. Every neighborhood had their own team, but they also had a club behind them that was able to sponsor these guys and organize them. Sunday afternoon, you try and pick the best game to see. And we would walk, and we wouldn't have to worry about getting jumped. Kids today can't do that.

"We had a lot of athletic clubs around here, the Kaywood Club, the Welcome Club, Stanzione, Mitchell AA, Pontiac, Arcadia, Grays Ferry AA. Lot of them were drinking clubs, but they all sponsored an athletic team. When football season came, it was a football team. It was a great tradition, really. They don't have it much today."

Generoso "Jerry" Rullo was born in 1923, second-youngest of the eight sons born to Theresa Carbonara and Generoso Rullo. They had married in their hometown of Nusco, near Naples, and came to the United States about 1913.

The family had friends and relatives in New York, and the Rullos stayed there until after World War I. He did track work for the Long Island Railroad. But the word was that life was better in Philadelphia, and they headed south.

"They lived in what they called the Bottom in Grays Ferry. Down on the 1200 block of Harmony Street, between 35th and 36th, off of Wharton Street. After a few more years, they moved to the 1200 block of 33rd, between Oakford and Wharton. That's where I was born and raised.

"Our house was nice. It was big, a two-story brick building. We had a large yard, which extended from 33rd Street all the way back to the next small street, Spangler Street. We had three bedrooms. . . . The yard was large enough for my parents to have a garden where they grew their own vegetables. It had a fig tree."

His father, known as Joe, worked for the B&O Railroad. He didn't make much money, but no one in the neighborhood did. "My mother would make her own bread, get flour, wash out the flour bags, steam them with hot water to get out all of the stencil and the printing, and make pillowcases out of them."

It was a predominantly Irish neighborhood, but it was okay being Italian. "Where we lived, we had all kind of ethnic groups there, and believe it or not, it was beautiful, and everybody got along, plus we got to know each other's life, holidays and all.

"For instance, on the Jewish holiday, their stores would be closed and the Jewish people would come out all dressed up and walk to 23rd and Wharton, where the synagogue was. Happy holidays, whatever it may be, we would extend it to them. And when it came Eastertime or Christmas, it was done in reverse. . . . We had Greeks. We had Polish, predominantly down at the Bottom. Italians and blacks, Negroes. It was great. We went to school; everyone knew one another. And believe me, we even got to know the Presbyterians. When they went to their church on Sunday, we would go to Mass at the King of Peace on 26th Street. We got along.

"When that [Schuylkill] expressway went through [in 1959], it disintegrated our whole neighborhood, just tore it apart. The highway took away rows of homes, like it did away with 34th Street, did away with Spangler Street, did away with part of our block, took half of our house. People were uprooted, and they had to go their separate ways."

But there were still the fields and the gyms. He played basketball at the Webster House, Napa and Wharton Streets, at Vare Recreation Center, and then at Bartram High School, where he was second-team All-Public under Coach Menchie Goldblatt, who was also from downton. Rullo was a six-foot guard.

"From there, I went to Temple University. Before that, I played with Passon AA Sporting Goods. Nat Passon was very helpful teaching me the real fine art of basketball, like the tough part, the aggressiveness. We played in a South Philly league. Hard, tough-nosed basketball. A lot of great teams. Every neighborhood had an outstanding player. Every corner had its pride."

He was the first of the Rullos to go to college. One of his older brothers, Amato, was a fighter, a promising light heavyweight. "He . . . almost had a scholarship to Villanova, but as he was ready to go, Villanova discontinued boxing. So he lost his opportunity. My younger brother went to Temple, too."

He idolized basketball coaches Harry Litwack and Menchie Goldblatt and wanted to be a physical education teacher and a coach, too. But by his senior year he was a starter and a star for Temple. So he tried out with the Philadelphia Warriors, a team he used to sneak into Convention Hall to see. He made the 1946–47 squad. "I guess I was doing all right. A lot of people came over to watch me play. I lived at home on 33rd Street. I wasn't making the money they do today. Then I went to Baltimore. I played for them about 16 games, but I didn't want to fly, so I left and went with the SPHAs. I played for a while. Then Eddie Gottlieb, the Warriors' owner, called me, and I went back to the Warriors for the '48–'49 season."

He played for the SPHAs again and then in the Eastern League for another seven or eight years.

"I realized that I can't be playing basketball all my life. I got into recreation because I was able to fit in my ball playing with my recreation job. . . . I started

135

Before there was an NBA, there was the BAA. The Philadelphia Warriors were the champions of the Basketball Association of America in 1946–47. Jerry Rullo is number 7 on the left. Petey Rosenberg is number 15 on the same row. Eddie Gottlieb is in the suit on the right. Courtesy of Jerry Rullo

refereeing, working high school and college games, Big 5, in the mid- and late '50s. I refereed baseball, soccer, softball. I would travel wherever the game was."

He married late, in 1968. He met Eileen Rafferty at a local recreation center. She would come and ask questions about basketball. She was a good high school player, and he helped her get a job at RCA. He thought that was the end of it, but it wasn't. "We've got two sons and I was fortunate to get these two guys." One went to Notre Dame, the other to Drexel, and, like his father, was a starting guard on the basketball team.

Jerry Rullo has worked with kids in athletics for more than forty years now, and he says the adults who helped him and thousands more are not out there in South Philadelphia anymore. No more like Howard Cull, Bill Connors, Bill Berry, Shooie Sissman.

"These guys organized teams, sponsored teams. We don't have guys like that today. Kids don't have nobody showing them the way. Kids now, they missed . . . being part of a team."

Professional Basketball Players from South Philadelphia

- **Hall-of-Famer Paul Arizin**
- **Nate Blackwell**
- **Stan Brown**

- John Chaney
- Larry Foust
- Reds Furey
- Bob Gainey
- Ollie Johnson
- Herman "Reds" Klotz
- Sonny Lloyd
- Andre McCarter
- Dave Riddick
- Ray "Chink" Scott
- Lionel Simmons
- Bozo Walker
- Kevin Washington
- Isaiah "Bunny" Wilson
- Jim Wilson

I've left out the SPHAs, because they are too numerous to mention.

Dave Dabrow spent most of his childhood in a Sixth and Lombard Street playground still known today as Starr Garden, about four miles away from Jerry Rullo's neighborhood.

"The kids that I hung around with on the playground . . . came from poor families, but we didn't know any different because at nine in the morning, we went over to Starr Garden and played baseball, soccer, basketball. Would have our lunch across the way at Levis', where we would buy a hot dog or a fish cake for two cents and a soda for one penny. About 4 or 5 o'clock, my rabbi would come after me. My mother insisted I take Hebrew lessons. My rabbi would pick me up at Starr Garden, take me home, get my Hebrew instruction for a half hour or so, and then when he was through, I'd go back to Starr Garden and stay there till 9 o'clock."

Dabrow played there with Jewish and Italian boys. "Very few black boys at that time. On Lombard Street, there were a number of black children, but they didn't come to Starr Garden. They were leery of the white boy. I'm going back to 1914, '15, '16."

He was born at home at 534 South Street, the second of three children of Benjamin and Cecilia Dabrow. His father was a railroad policeman.

"My house was what we would call today an apartment house, but I call it a tenement. It was a four-story building. The downstairs was a hardware store. The second floor had people living in there, and one of the women had a restaurant there. We lived on the third floor with one bathroom for the two tenants on the floor. It was a toilet only. On the fourth floor were some other tenants. It was all walk up, a very, very poor type of living.

"Our apartment had three rooms. We had the bedroom, another bedroom, and a kitchen. No dining room. In the kitchen was a coal stove. It's the same building today, but the third and fourth floors have been destroyed. Today, there's a clothing store.

South Philly has been a hotbed of great basketball for a long, long time. This is the Southern High basketball team, Public League champs, in 1914–15. Courtesy of Bill Esher

"The 500 block of South Street then was entirely business. The street was very busy. The Number 40 trolley ran on the street to 44th and Parkside. On Saturdays there were pushcarts on the street. The farmers would come Friday night, sleep over in their wagons, and sell their wares Saturday morning."

He played at the Shot Tower playground on Carpenter Street, and at the Young Women's Union building at Fifth and Bainbridge. From 1918 to 1922, he went to South Philadelphia High for Boys. "I loved going to Southern. At the age of 15, my family moved to West Philadelphia, 38th and Wyalusing. I refused a transfer to West Philadelphia High School. For three years, I traveled from 38th and Girard to Southern every day.

"I was into athletics. In 1916, Southern High won the Public League football championship. . . . Southern was also known as the basketball center. In 1914, we had the Public League championship team. . . . Then in 1916, we had Mockie Bunin, the greatest foul shooter in the country. He could shoot fouls nine out of 10 with his eyes shut. . . . The reputation of Southern went all over the country. Look at the scholarships the kids got to various colleges. Menschie Goldblatt to Penn, Lou Sherr to Penn, Petey Rosenberg to St. Joe's, but he never continued with it. Moie Weinstein to Lehigh, Albie Weiner, Billy Freedman, Chickie Passon, the Dessen brothers. The reputation goes back to 1910, when the school had its first graduating class."

He played on the 1920 and 1921 varsity teams, a five-foot-seven-inch forward. Dabrow says basketball was popular at Southern because it "was a sport which didn't need much space. All you needed was a little piece of ground and you put up a basket. Baseball, you needed a field. Football, you needed a field. So it was normal for Jewish kids to get in an activity that didn't need much space, because they all lived in the city. All you needed was a round ball. If you didn't have a basketball, you stuffed something with rags and made a basketball out of that."

After Southern, Dabrow went to the Philadelphia Normal School at 13th and Spring Garden for two years to prepare for a teaching career. But he did not stop playing basketball. He played in the Jewish Basketball League until 1930 and later became a referee, a coach, and its president. In 1928, he found time to marry Eleanor Simon, a West Philadelphia girl.

The JBL was founded in 1902 and had teams from North Philadelphia, South Philadelphia, and Germantown and two from Center City. "You had to be Jewish in order to play on those teams, and we were very stringent. There were always only five teams, and it was very desirous of being a player in the league because your chances of getting a scholarship to a college was very great. I played for Germantown. The boys on the team were friends of mine. But the South Philadelphia team was usually the best. The kids practiced more there."

Dabrow taught physical education in junior high schools until 1940. He wanted to teach at Southern, but no Jew taught physical education or coached a major sport in city high schools then. Dabrow said he talked to a local congressman, Ben Golder, who was Jewish, and the school policy was quickly changed. Men like Dabrow, Goldblatt, and Litwack soon began working in high schools.

"I started at Southern in 1941. I became the basketball coach in 1942, until 1960. We won championships in 1944–45 and 1945–46. We didn't win another for 40 more years."

Dabrow coached hundreds and hundreds of basketball games in his career, but the one he remembers best is one against Southeast Catholic, then Southern's biggest rival. "In 1944–45, we won the Public High Championship. We met at Convention Hall to play for the City Championship, and we were somewhat a favorite. In the last minute, we were ahead 37–36. Jocko Collins, an outstanding official, was the referee. We thought the game was over. Jocko Collins said, 'Hold it, somebody asked for a time out. You got 10 more seconds to go.'

"We thought we had won the City Championship. I brought my boys back on the court, and we played the extra 10 seconds. Larry Foust, who later played for LaSalle and went to the NBA, tapped the ball up with about a second to go. It went around the circle and went in, and they won 38 to 37. My kids started to cry and carry on, and the fans carried on, but we got more publicity by losing that ball game than if we had won. All over the city, Southern High School, they were the great sports."

He left Southern in 1960, worked for the board of education for a couple of years, retired, went back to Southern at the school's request in the 1960s to teach again, and finally called it quits in 1972. "The only place I ever taught after 1941 was Southern. I wouldn't teach anywhere else."

*P*rofessional Football Players from South Philadelphia

- *Four Philadelphia Eagles:* **Dan DiRenzo, "Black" Jack Ferrante, Bob Oristaglio,** *and* **Steve "Nut" Sader**
- **Ray Abruzzee,** *who played for the Buffalo Bills*
- **Ed Cook,** *a lineman for the St. Louis Cardinals and the Atlanta Falcons*
- **Jack Del Bello,** *who played for the Baltimore Colts*
- **Bob Petrella,** *who played for the Miami Dolphins*
- **John Sandusky,** *who played for the Cleveland Browns and the Green Bay Packers*

The most recent players are two offensive linemen: Pro Bowler Erik Williams of the Dallas Cowboys and Dwayne White of the St. Louis Rams.

Pearl Perkins Nightingale may be the most talented South Philadelphia athlete of all, and probably the least well known.

She was the number-one woman selected for the 1936 Olympic gymnastics team and a three-time AAU all-around champion. She was the Mary Lou Retton of her day, but it was a day without television and without much popular interest in women's gymnastics.

"I was good, but what the kids do today is unbelievable. The balance beam we didn't have as competition. They do their floor exercises on a mat. It's really nothing more than a little trampoline, because they do unbelievable stuff as far as tumbling is concerned."

Pearl Perkins Nightingale did her floor exercises on the floor—no mat.

She was born in 1914 on the northwest corner of Camac and Oregon in her parents' home and store, Barney's Deli. Her father was Benjamin, her mother Sadie. His name was changed from Perkofsky to Perkins. He wanted to be more American.

"All the customers were on credit. It wasn't a five and dime. It was a penny and a nickel store. It wasn't a Jewish delicatessen, because it was a Catholic neighborhood. Irish, Italians, Polish. We were the only Jewish in the neighborhood."

She used to walk to St. Martha's, a settlement house at Eighth and Snyder, and to the swimming pool at 10th and Mifflin, where she was a lifeguard. She joined the gymnastics team at Thomas Junior High, encouraged by gym teacher Ruth Huxley, who got her a scholarship to the Philadelphia Turngermeinde, a national German American group with a gym and a pool at Broad and Columbia. She practiced three evenings a week at the Philadelphia Turners. Unlike the basketball or baseball players of her day, she had little or no neighborhood support and even less recognition initially.

"My parents encouraged me. My father used to be a wrestler in Russia. He encouraged athletics. It wasn't just gymnastics then for me; it was track and field, too, shotput and running broad jump, and step up step jump."

The woman flying around on the horse is Pearl Perkins Nightingale, the U.S. all-around gymnastics champion in 1937, 1941, and 1943. Her friends called her "Perky." Courtesy of Pearl Perkins Nightingale

She practiced in junior high, but she began to win championships at the South Philadelphia High School for Girls, 13th and Snyder. "I excelled in swimming and diving first. I won a city championship in diving."

The girls' gymnastics team was the best in the city while she was there. She graduated in 1932, but colleges did not offer athletic scholarships for women then. "I never pushed myself to say, 'Why am I not on a scholarship?' I didn't know any better. I took the academic courses at Southern so I could go to college. It was the Depression. My parents couldn't afford to send me."

So she worked in the store and kept practicing and competing for the Philadelphia Turners, the only South Philadelphia woman gymnast in the organization. Known as Perky to her friends, she was national champion in side horse and vault in 1941 and 1943, and national all-around AAU champion in 1937, 1941, and 1943.

Before those championships, her goal was the 1936 Olympics. She competed all over the country for a spot on the team. She was becoming better known. Winning does that. "Yes, I was well known in the neighborhood, but I never bragged. I didn't emphasize the fact that I was a gymnastics champion. I never talked about it."

She competed for the Turners in the rings, side horse, even parallel bars and the floor exercises to make the Olympic team. The Turners kept beating other gymnastics clubs, and she came in first on the team. The wins in 1935 put her on the Olympic team. "We had six girls and one alternate, and I was number one. We had all worked toward that goal—the Olympics."

The 1936 Olympics were to be held in Berlin. "And then when the time came to go and my parents found out it was Germany, they said no. They didn't know it was Berlin initially. . . . I was the only Jewish one on the gymnastics team."

She had gone through six months of practice. "Sure, it was painful. My father said no, and that was it. If it's going to be Germany, and Hitler was supposed to be there and be the presenter, he said no. I said okay. It wasn't that traumatic. It was in my house and my mother and my sisters and brother were there. It was their decision. I was under their jurisdiction and I never questioned it, period. I never took it personally."

The women's gymnastics team finished fifth in the 1936 Olympics. She doesn't remember the name of her replacement.

Pearl Perkins married Robert Nightingale in 1938, moved away to Olney and then to Feltonville, both neighborhoods in the northern end of the city. She continued to compete for a few years, then coached gymnastics at area recreation centers and schools. But during the war years, she needed some money and used her gymnastic ability to earn it.

"I was a hand-balancing act. High hand stands. I had a wonderful partner who taught me the ropes. We were Rixford and Gale. I was Gale and he was Otis Rixford. He was in show business before, and he saw my potential and then we put an act together. We did it for four or five years. We appeared in Elks and Moose halls on weekends, in firehouses."

She is a widow now and responds easily to questions about her youth and her preoccupation with gymnastics. No one has asked her about these things in a long time. "My life was centered around athletics, gymnastics primarily. . . . I was very religious about practice. We had to practice, practice, practice, perfect ourselves. . . . I have no regrets."

South Philadelphians in the Olympics

Two South Philadelphia High School graduates who competed in the Olympics:

- *Wrestler* **Sam Gerson** *(1920)*
- *Gymnast* **Lou Bordo** *(1948)*

Wisdom and gracious assistance with the athletic lists were provided by Bill Esher, Mike Goffredo, Sonny Hill, Harvey Pollack, Bob Sensky, and Elmer Smith.

7
Jews

In 1852, the same year that St. Mary Magdalen de Pazzi opened in South Philadelphia as the first Italian church in the nation, the first synagogue opened in South Philadelphia.

Jews had been living in the city for 150 years before that. In fact, a few Jews were probably living in Philadelphia in the 1680s and 1690s, and at least six Jews were residents in 1706. Being Jewish in early eighteenth-century Philadelphia could not have been easy. For those Sephardic Jews from Spain and Portugal, there were no kosher meat, no synagogues, and often not the ten men needed to begin Sabbath prayers.

In the 1730s the Levy brothers, Nathan and Isaac, arrived from New York and became part of the Jewish community's growth. Just north of the Moyamensing district, Nathan Levy buried his tiny daughter in a small plot that he had purchased on Spruce Street just east of Ninth. That plot would become the city's first Jewish cemetery. By the 1740s, the Levys were attending services with other Jews in a house between Cherry and Race, Third and Fourth Streets. By 1765, there were about a hundred Jews in the city, and perhaps as many as three hundred at the time of the Revolution.

That house on Stirling Alley where the Levys and other Jews prayed in the 1740s was the beginning of Mikveh Israel Synagogue. A new synagogue building—the city's first—was completed in 1782.

It would be another 70 years and three more synagogues before a Jewish house of worship opened in South Philadelphia. While Jews probably date back to the 1690s in the city, they may have ventured into South Philadelphia before that. The evidence is circumstantial, but inviting.

In 1655, two Jews from New York, Isaac Israel and Isaac Cardoso, came south to trade in what is now Newcastle, Delaware. They were in the area again a year later with another Jewish trader and may, quite possibly, have gone further up the South River (the Delaware) to trade in the little Swedish settlement known as Wicaco. This is more than supposition. In 1663 the man running the trading post in Passyunk was known as the "Honourable Concillor Israel." No other identification exists for him.

When Mikveh Israel opened in its own building in 1782, there was no Jewish neighborhood in the city, but there was a Jewish presence. There were already stores, most of them north of Market Street and east of Fourth, run by Jews—hatters, coopers, embroiderers, watchmakers, haberdashers. Four Jews were among the early subscribers to the new Chestnut Street Theater in 1792. And in the late 1700s, a small number of Dutch, Polish, German, and English Jews began arriving in Philadelphia. Some of them began praying apart from the Jews of Mikveh Israel. And so, about 1795, Rodeph Shalom, the oldest Ashkenazi synagogue in the United States, was begun in a small room near Third and Dock Streets.

The city's tiny Jewish population grew in the 1800s, and there were clearly a few Jews who worked in South Philadelphia. A widow named Frances Solomon made and repaired umbrellas on the 100 block of South Street in 1825. Just west of her on the same block, A. B. Cohen was a carver and a gilder. But there were not enough Jews to form a synagogue until 1852.

Jews from Holland had arrived and wanted to pray among their own kind. Neither Mikveh Israel nor Rodeph Shalom suited them; nor did they join the city's two other synagogues, Knesset Israel and Beth Israel, the latter just outside the city in Northern Liberties, near Fourth and Wood Streets.

So, in 1852, they began praying in a house on South Street between Second and Third. Five years later they moved to a building at the southeast corner of Fifth and Catharine and called it Bene (or Bnai) Israel. That synagogue, in a rural area, lasted just one generation. By 1880, the Dutch Jews had assimilated, and the synagogue was gone. But many more synagogues would come. By 1930, Jews seemed to have synagogues on every corner south of South Street, and all but one—at 23rd and Wharton—was east of Broad. In 1930 still another house of worship, the Kreminitzer Synagogue, opened at 1908 E. Moyamensing Avenue. It was the 155th synagogue south of South, and the last to open downtown. Just three remained in 1995.

When Allen Meyers was born in 1953, the decline in the Jewish population was already well under way, and the abandonment of the synagogues in South Philadelphia had begun. Meyers grew up in Strawberry Mansion, but he spent a lot of time at his grandparents' house in South Philadelphia.

"As a little kid in the late 1950s, riding the Route 9 trolley car, I would see these boarded-up synagogues. I'd ask my mother, 'What are these places? There's a Star of David on it.' And she'd tell me that a lot of the Jewish people are moving away and resettling in different parts of the city. . . .

"When my grandparents were in their dying days in the '70s, they were in the Mount Sinai Hospital. As their cases grew worse, they kept on moving them up in the hospital—my grandmother in particular. By the time she was near death, she was near the top. . . . I was about 22, and I had to look out the window, and guess what stared at me down from the streets—boarded-up synagogues. I wanted to tell the story about what these places of worship were really like. . . ."

Meyers has spent years studying the synagogues of South Philadelphia. Some were created to provide pulpits for influential rabbis from Europe. Townspeople from the same shtetl formed others. Synagogues also grew out of political beliefs, like Zionism, while other *shuls* were formed by Socialists more concerned with cultural traditions and education than religion. One of the syn-

The Jewish star was visible on the building at Fifth and Dudley Streets in 1981, but the name could barely be made out—Congregation Kehilas Kodesh Anshei Sodo Lovon. Once it was the synagogue for the "Holy Community of Men from the White Fields of Russia." Courtesy of Allen Meyers

agogues that Meyers knows well was Shari Zedek, on the northwest corner of Third and Manton. Russian Jews, from the town of Zitomer about 50 miles north of Kiev, transformed a Presbyterian church into a synagogue in 1903. His father's mother prayed there.

"They built a staircase with two entrances in front of the synagogue. . . . The Jewish tradition is you come into this world one way and leave the other way. It's like an enter and an exit. People in South Philadelphia believed that if you went in one way, you would never come down the way you came in."

As the synagogue and its members prospered, additions were built—a mikvah (ritual bath), a school. It became a sort of Jewish community center, but strictly Orthodox. "The building was one of the largest synagogues in South Philadelphia. . . . Probably about 120 families were members, but membership wasn't equated in terms of families. It was only about how many men belonged to the congregation. Only men paid dues, and it wasn't really a dues system. If you could afford a hundred dollars as a donation on a special occasion, that's what you gave. If you could only afford five dollars, that's what you gave."

By the early 1970s, Shari Zedek was no longer active, its members having either died or moved away. A fire damaged it in the early 1980s, and the building was demolished soon after.

Despite their numbers, synagogues never held the religious sway that the churches did in South Philadelphia.

"There was a million synagogues," each its own little fiefdom, recalls

145

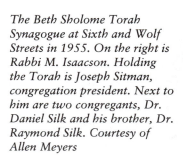

The Beth Sholome Torah Synagogue at Sixth and Wolf Streets in 1955. On the right is Rabbi M. Isaacson. Holding the Torah is Joseph Sitman, congregation president. Next to him are two congregants, Dr. Daniel Silk and his brother, Dr. Raymond Silk. Courtesy of Allen Meyers

Sanford "Sandy" Wizov, who was born in 1930 and lived in a half dozen South Philadelphia houses, most of them within a half ball stick of Fourth and Ritner.

Each had its governing body, a "group of men, never willing to relinquish" power and not willing to "combine forces with other synagogues to survive. They wouldn't do that. The only ones who did were the big synagogues . . . out on the Main Line, where you push a button and glass doors slide open to see the Torah. God wasn't in there. He was in South Philly, where you smell the sweat of these little old guys standing in their *talises*"—prayer shawls.

Of course, the number of synagogues had swelled to 155 because the Jewish population had swelled as well.

In 1870, the population of South Philadelphia was nearly 133,000. No one is certain about the exact number of Jews, because the Census does not count religious groups. At the time, the largest group of foreign-born residents were the Irish, numbering more than 24,000. Next were about 5,000 German-born. Just 26 residents were Russian-born.

In February 1882, 200 years after William Penn arrived on a ship with no Jews, the *S.S. Illinois* landed at the foot of Federal Street with 225 Russian Jewish refugees. The city did not routinely greet immigrant ships, but an official municipal delegation, together with a large crowd, greeted the Jews. Philadelphia knew about the czar's atrocities and had raised $20,000 for the newcomers. More Russian Jews would follow.

Between 1870 and 1910 South Philadelphia's population more than doubled to 336,000, and the Irish were no longer the largest group of foreign-born residents. That mantle fell on the Russian-born—Jews, for the most part—who exceeded 45,000. Second were the Italian-born, who numbered nearly 33,000.

South Fourth Street was a
Hebrew highway in the early
1900s. Merchants with
pushcarts sold everything from
lettuce to lace. This 1914
picture was taken at Fourth
and Fitzwater. Courtesy of the
Philadelphia City Archives

Immigrants, many of them Jews, had also arrived from Austria, Rumania, and
Hungary, but the bulk of the new Jews had come from the Russian Pale. So in
the 1910 Census, for the first and last time, South Philadelphia had more Jews
than any other foreign-born immigrant group.

One reason so many of the newcomers started in South Philadelphia is simple—that was where the ship docked. And for those whose ship docked elsewhere—New York, for instance—the Jewish neighborhood near the river was
well known. And Jews were not searching for land to farm or own. Historically, European Jews had not been permitted to own land. No, they were
tradesmen, merchants, and skilled workers, and they needed to be in a city to
find jobs. The nearby eastern end of South Street was already a merchant strip
of German and Dutch Jews, a thoroughfare of new and used goods. Also, less
than a mile from their landing spot, at Fourth and Lombard, lived a Jewish
community of Lithuanians, Ukrainians, Poles, and Hungarians.

Those who did not peddle or sell found work in clothing and cigar factories. Women worked in these factories as well. The community around South
and Bainbridge Streets, Fourth to Sixth Street, became a transplanted shtetl, a
compound of pickle barrels and pushcarts and the sounds of Yiddish.

Jewish organizations flourished. A few benevolent groups had been around
since the early 1800s, but new ones formed to serve the new community.

The Joseph Levine funeral wagon, circa 1910. The office of the Jewish funeral home was downtown at 1022 South Fifth Street. Courtesy of Allen Myers

Helping the immigrants were the Young Women's Union, which evolved into the Neighborhood Center, and the Federation of Jewish Charities.

Some Jews prospered and quickly left South Philadelphia for Strawberry Mansion, East and West Oak Lane, West Philadelphia, and Wynnefield. Unlike the Italian newcomers, who, for the most part, stayed in South Philadelphia, Jews had little connection to territory, to a neighborhood. They left to buy a bigger house with a nicer yard in a little better neighborhood. But as some left, more arrived, and they, too, settled close to the crowded eastern end of South Street. Still others began moving further south. In the 1900s, arriving Jews, poor Jews, kept moving south.

"We were supposed to be poor, but we weren't really poor. I can't tell it to you any better than that."

That is the recollection of Sam Bernstein, known as "Leaden" to his friends, a South Philadelphian who left in 1970 and has missed it every day since. He lives in the Northeast today.

"I've been on this block 15 years year now, and I don't know anybody around here. Isn't that awful? Me, I could make friends with a rat, and I don't know anybody around here. People are different today. Those people in South Philadelphia were perfect. Nobody was jealous. Everybody was equal, everybody was in the same predicament. We all had to struggle for a living. Nobody had it real good. Sure, you had slobs here and there, but most of us were real hard-working people. . . ."

He grew up on the 100 block of Roseberry Street, and lived as a married man on Fifth Street between Wolf and Jackson.

"Italians, Irish, Jews, Polish, blacks, I grew up in a real melting pot. We all went to Southern High. Only problem we had was that we were Jews. Don't know how you can put that down in your book, but it was always there. Sometimes, people would throw stuff at us. But when we all started going to high school together, it became a democracy. We all learned to live together. It's unbelievable how we all grew up in this poor section, 54 houses to a street, maybe five people to a house, 80 kids on one block, so many blocks.

"Remember [the distillery] Publickers? Municipal Stadium. You had Martin Village, right near the river. It was near Wolf and Jackson, little houses, shacks. Then you had Stone House Lane in the Neck, where the food distributors are now. Everybody lived there for nothing. Didn't pay no taxes. Rats all around, and swamps. We used to go to the Neck to play ball, and you had to pass 17 railroad tracks. We called it the seventeenies. . . .

"The Lakes [FDR Park] was heaven. It was the only grass we had. My mom would take us. They used to have a pool there. That was heaven. And the park at Fifth and Wolf, the park was unbelievable. Used to have a guard 24 hours a day. Used to have roses in the middle. It was a beautiful park."

Leaden was born in 1915. His father, Louis, died when Leaden was four. He had worked in a garment factory and at Publickers. "My father got sick. He was 40 years old and he had eight kids, seven boys and one girl. I'm the seventh son. He got sick. My mother, Yetta, begged him to stay home, but he had no insurance, no compensation. No unions. So he went back to work at Publickers, got pneumonia, and died.

"My mother raised us. Maybe we were poor, but we always had enough to eat, and we had family. Friday nights, I remember the *lukshun* [noodles]. Mom would cut up the fish. Friday nights were unbelievable. . . .

"When the Jewish holidays came, it was like the world came to an end. Pitch black. Every store was a Jewish store, and they all closed. Holidays were really holidays in those days. On Yom Kippur and Rosh Hashana, everybody was home, everybody was so religious. It was beautiful. . . .

"I used to go and say *Yizkor* [prayer for the dead] because I lost my father, but I never felt comfortable in synagogue. I was a Jew in my heart. You know they closed some of the movie theaters on Jewish holidays. They were used for synagogues. Used to say your prayers at the Ideal. It was so Jewish around here."

He went to elementary school at Sharswood and played ball all over the neighborhood. "I played basketball for the Catholic Mount Carmel. And at one time we had a team of Jewish stars. The two Dugan brothers were Irish, and they changed their name to yours, Dubin, and played with us."

Leaden loved the Mummers, even though marching up the street was not something that Jews did back then. "The Jews never went in it, but the Jews backed it. The Jews loved it. That music, you can't beat that music. I don't why the Jews didn't get in it, but I would say it wasn't our way of life, to go out on the street and get drunk and all that. But we enjoyed it and we respected it, and we were proud of it. I used to take my daughter, Robin, and go real early in the morning on Broad Street and watch."

Abraham and Clara Goren in their grocery store at the southeast corner of Sixth and Ritner in 1915. The girl in the corner is Merle Suddock, who had just arrived from Russia and was temporarily living with the Gorens. The Catholic church across the street kept its collection money in Goren's safe and, in turn, provided a Shabbas goy to turn the store's lights on and off on the Sabbath. Goren came to Philadelphia in 1903, entering at the immigrant station on Washington Avenue. Courtesy of Drs. Stanley E. Goren and Robert A. Goren

Leaden did not grow up meekly. He used his fists, sometimes against Italians, sometimes against Irish. "The worst that would happen was a guy would punch you in the nose, or would throw a bottle. We were still the Jews. We were still the Christ killers. . . .

"I had a reputation. Every day, I used to beat a *goy* [non-Jew] up. I had a bad temper. I was a little left-handed kid, but I could hit like a horse. I used to have to fight for my gang because I carried the money for overdue books when we went to the library at Broad and Porter. You had to pass through an Italian neighborhood. They wanted to rob us. They knew the Jewish kids were coming and they figured we were rich. They didn't know we were as poor as they were."

It was a tough neighborhood, and Jews were involved in gambling and crime. "There was always gambling on the street. Shooting craps was the big thing. I never did it. I never played craps, never went to the race track, never bet on a game. I don't know why. My mother said don't gamble, and I didn't do it. Hey, I'd jump off a boxcar, I'd fight, but I didn't gamble.

"You had gangsters. Seventh and Porter, all the gangsters hung out there, and they used to bump each other off. There was a guy, Pimple-Faced Moish.

He went to school with my brother, and he was the nicest kid in my brother's room. Then he went nuts or something, and became a killer."

Leaden left Roseberry Street in 1946. He married Birdie Neiderman and moved into her family's house on Fifth Street, about six blocks from where he grew up. He worked as a garment cutter in the day and spent time at night at the corner candy store at Fifth and Wolf. Eddie "Itzy" Feinberg owned it for a while. Then Harry Sokolof, then Larry and Shirley Mazer. Summer nights were for eating polly seeds (sunflower seeds) and water ice, for talking about baseball and bragging about your children. People sat on lawn chairs in front of their homes. Electric fans and blocks of ice were the air conditioners. Weekend days were for playing ball. Leaden played basketball well into his sixties, a competitor who never forgot how to use his elbows or loft a hook shot. Life had a comfortable rhythm. No surprises.

His wife died in 1970; he left South Philadelphia the same year.

"2222 South Fifth. Birdie was born in that house, married in that house, and died in that house. Birdie, there was nobody like her. When she died, Robin used to say, 'I see Momma. I dream she's all around the house. I can't sleep.' I got a job in the Northeast and sold it. I hated to leave, but I had no alternative. I didn't think my daughter fit in there. Robin went right back the minute she got married. She moved two doors away from where we lived. She's true South Philly."

The South Philadelphia that Sam Bernstein's parents came to was one that many Jews across the Atlantic were already familiar with. Allen Meyers' grandparents arrived in South Philadelphia in 1902. They settled at Fifth and Washington, considered to be the southern outskirts at the time.

"It was right about then people started to realize that there was overcrowding north of Washington Avenue, because some of the people started migrating further south. I remember . . . my grandfather telling me that he'd write letters back to the old country. He asked for more money so he could get situated here in America, and he threatened that he would disappear below Washington Avenue unless they sent more money."

But how would his family in Kiev know what was or wasn't south of Washington Avenue?

"Some people overseas knew of Philadelphia, and thought that there was nothing south of Washington Avenue, . . . that there were forbidden lands below Washington."

Nevertheless, Jews did move south of Washington Avenue, including Meyers' grandparents, Rose and Louis Ponnock.

His grandfather was born in 1891 and came to the United States as a child. By the time he was 12, he was making a living selling fruit in the street. He lived near Second and Fitzwater, which was not a Jewish area even though it was just a few blocks away from Fourth and Bainbridge. He married in 1912 and moved to the 600 block of Mountain Street, near Morris.

"Up until the First World War, he was a house painter. During the '20s, he got involved in toys. He started out huckstering fishermen's hats and caps. Down by the seashore, people adored these caps, and he would travel from Atlantic City to Stone Harbor to Wildwood. Eventually, he gathered enough money in the '20s to open up a toy and novelty store, Ponnock's, at the corner of Fifth and Market."

Meyers would visit his grandparents two or three times a week from Strawberry Mansion.

"Zadie would take me out back and show me the roses he had planted. He would take coffee grinds and pack them along the sides to help them grow. I tried it once later—it didn't work. In South Philadelphia, it worked. We would walk along Seventh Street. We were the 1600 block South Sixth Street, and we'd walk down to about the 2500 block South Seventh Street. Seventh Street was loaded with food stores, fish stores, clothing stores, anything you wanted. A K-Mart, you might say, along the street. It was all there on South Seventh Street.

"Bubbie would treat me at the bakery shop around Seventh and Ritner. We used to get little cookies. Then she used to take me to the fish shop, Bralow's. Now it's up in the Northeast. I remember seeing the little fishes. They were big fishes in my thoughts, swimming around in these big tanks. And I remember seeing my Bubbie pointing to one and saying something in Yiddish, that's the one I wanted. The man would take a net, fish it out, wrap it up in a newspaper, and Bubbie would take it home. What do you do with a live fish? You put it in the bathtub, the kind with the feet on the floor. So it stayed in the bathtub for a day or so until she was ready to use it for gefilte fish."

Meyers' study of synagogues citywide probably taught him more than anyone wants to know about bricks and mortar, but he also learned about the lives these Jewish immigrants led.

He learned first that the synagogue expansion stopped at Porter Street. No synagogues were built south of Porter. Shari Israel at Fourth and Porter and Shari Eli at Eighth and Porter were sister synagogues, both built before 1920 and both run in the 1950s and 1960s by the same man, Rabbi Pupka, who shuttled between them. Second, very few of the larger synagogues were built to be synagogues, but were usually converted churches or houses. A good example was the Children of Moses synagogue at Fifth and Watkins, which formerly was St. Andrew's Church.

And, third, the count of 155 downtown synagogues may be an inflated number—inflated by booze.

"In the beginning of Prohibition, there was no liquor to be found unless you knew somebody. Only a few people were licensed to sell liquor, one being the *shamas* [sexton] of the synagogue because liquor was needed for religious ceremonies. People became *shamases* of synagogues, but they were really false synagogues. You had 10 buddies who weren't religious at all. They formed a synagogue. The *shamas* got his license to sell liquor. He'd sell it for his buddies. There was one right around Sixth, between Mifflin and Sigel, a small synagogue on the corner."

These sipping synagogues disappeared when Prohibition ended. Just before Prohibition, a flu epidemic killed thousands of Philadelphians, including many Jews. Word got back to Europe of the funeral wagons on the streets.

"It scared people here back into the old folk traditions. There were such things as Jewish medicine men. Did you know that? Our family, on my

mother's side, believed in the old folkways. My great-grandmother, Anna Du-binsky, was not only the cook for the synagogue at Sixth and Morris, but she was also a card thrower in the '20s and '30s. From the face and numbers and sequence of the cards, she would tell people's fortunes. She also had medical remedies for what ailed people. . . ."

It was not uncommon for babies and young children to die of disease in those days. "Some people who had passed away unexpectedly at an early age were suspected of being, quote, 'called by the dead,' which meant if you died mysteriously, it's like your dead mother was calling you to the other side. . . . People wondered if they died because of the flu, or because of the calling of the dead."

Not all the folk traditions were as macabre as that. Men and women went separately to the *shvitz* [bathhouse] to socialize and relax. It was a perspiring rite of passage when a son was finally old enough to accompany his father. Money for new furniture or a bar mitzvah was borrowed at a neighborhood-only lending institution known throughout the Jewish community as "the cor-poration." Every few blocks was another corporation.

For the first 40 or 50 years of the 1900s, many Jews stayed in South Philadelphia because of friendships and family ties and because their business was there, be it a pushcart or a store, said Meyers.

South Street was a Jewish shopping strip well into the 1960s and was known for store employees who shlepped customers inside with the promise of bargains. They are the only thing missing from this 1930 picture of the 1200 block of South. Courtesy of the Philadelphia City Archives

153

"Then you got ahead a little, maybe. You want a little bit better quarters. But more importantly, . . . when you had a little bit more money after the Second World War, you could afford not only to pay your rent from the store, now you could rent out your place upstairs and go to a new neighborhood.

"Most of the people in South Philadelphia who I've talked with, the businesses were passed on from father to son just like the power of the synagogue was passed on through father and son. But by the time of the third generation, if the synagogue lasted that long, nobody wanted to be bothered with the synagogue or the business. Things had changed drastically.

"The other part of it is that South Philadelphia has always had a poorer reputation. If you got a little bit more money, you would want to move out because that's where all the *shleppers* live, the Jewish term for the people who struggled to make a living."

There was a pull to live in the suburbs. And a pull to live in the city's better Jewish neighborhoods. Stan Sheckman's family moved to Mount Airy. Born in 1944, he grew up on the 2600 block of South Eighth Street, between Shunk and Oregon. His grandfather had a tailor shop on Lambert and Passyunk, near 19th. His father, Harry, worked at the Quartermaster Depot on Oregon Avenue. His mother, Adeline, was a school secretary.

"Your block becomes your whole world. Barsky's drugstore was on the northeast corner of Eighth and Oregon. On the opposite corner, the Democrats used it as a large meeting room. Around the corner was Dave's Candy Store on Mildred and Oregon. And our chink [handball] wall was right on the corner of Eighth and Oregon. The old age home in the middle of the block. . . . It was a brownstone front, and we used to sneak into the yard and play. . . . On my side of the street was the old corner gas station. And we had a doctor on our block, Dr. DeCherney. We had a little grocery on the other corner."

And every game a child could imagine was played on that one block. "Hit the penny. You made the penny jump. How simple can you get? We had awning ball, we had wire ball, we had pony baseball, pitch on one bounce and hit with an open hand. Street football, button hook at the Chevy. Deadbox, rub the beery caps to a high shine, take the cork out. Union Number 5 was the company that made the roller skates. Anything else was a bad imitation.

"Scooters. Half ball, there were half ball leagues. Pimple balls. Star balls. Customizing your bats out of broom handles. Roofing a half ball was a home run, chips on the ball. We played step ball. Punch blocks. That was the mason's little metal plate on the concrete. If somebody steps on it, you can punch him. . . .

"We didn't quite know what the older folks did, nor did we care. We knew our little hiding places, the cracks in the sidewalk, the punch blocks. . . . We were pretty intimate with the street itself. There was a lot, a lot of kids. I had four or five close friends just on the street alone. There were other kids that we picked on. There were other kids who picked on us, so it was that whole flow all in one block."

Then you get a little older, your world stretches, and there are more streets to explore.

Doesn't everyone have a kindergarten Halloween costume picture somewhere? This is Mrs. Horowitz's class and I'm closest to the windows, fifth from the right, dressed like a wolf, just in case you can't tell. Many of the students were Jewish, but I'll point out just two: my oldest friend, Bruce Polsky, two rows in front of me next to the pirate, and Rea Potash, in the nurse's costume, one row in front of me and all the way to the left. I kissed her playing spin the bottle. Or maybe she kissed me. Courtesy of Mary Dubin, who saves everything

Block parties on Porter Street and putting your feet in the X-ray machine at Eagle Shoes, Seventh and Ritner. Duckpin bowling on Iseminger Street, near Snyder, and basketball in the big gym at the Naval Base. Go past Frankie Avalon's house and see the gold records in the living room. The penny dances at Thomas Junior High. Go to the dances at Gelart's Ballroom in Logan, and to the most famous dance hall of all, *Bandstand.*

He was 14 and afraid that he'd be the smallest person there. They all looked so big on television. Waiting in line, he knew that he was tall enough. This was going to be great. Then he found out that it was too crowded.

"We never got to the stands, and I never got a chance to dance on *Bandstand,* but we watched from the back. We all had our favorites. I remember Frannie Giordano. When I went to Southern, everybody knew where her room was. She was a beautiful girl. . . . Italian girls were much different than the Jewish girls, more erotic or exotic, at least to me. My earliest sexual fantasies were magnificent Italian girls. Like today's expression, we called them hot. The Jewish girls were dowdy in comparison."

Those were the good memories. There are also the bad ones. Unlike Leaden Bernstein, Stan Sheckman, a school principal today, does not yearn for South Philadelphia.

When his grandfather died, his grandmother moved to East Mount Airy to live with her oldest son. "In those days, East Mount Airy was like the Valhalla of the suburbs, the wealthy section, trees and lawns and playgrounds, nothing like South Philadelphia. I suspect that my father had a lot of sibling rivalry with his brother and was intent on finding a similar house in a similar

155

neighborhood. We ended up moving into an identical house right around the corner. We got up there in 1960. I was 15 and a half.

"I was becoming disillusioned with some of the things that were going on in South Philadelphia and I was welcome to the move. There just seemed to be a stagnation, just a whole notion that the culture was frozen in time. I remember Bermuda shorts were becoming popular, but you couldn't wear them in South Philadelphia. In Mount Airy you could wear them, in Oxford Circle you could wear them. . . . Men that didn't seem to have jobs hung on the corners. It was a mediocrity that I was starting to get a sense of. And the enclave of Jewish kids diminished.

"Visiting my cousin in Mount Airy was a more enlightening experience. The kids there were doing more things. They had terrific ball fields, 12 basketball courts. I was playing baseball on cinder at 10th and Wharton.

"I remember when I was playing baseball for the South Philadelphia Optimists, we went in a van to the Somerville Playground, which was up in the Northeast. The van had no windows. We come out and here's this field, like the *Field of Dreams*. Ivy on the walls. It was fantastic. When we finished playing, we got back in the van, came back to South Philadelphia. . . . There was a world out there, green and clean and beautiful, and I was still in a ghetto-type area."

In addition to the good and the bad memories were the Jewish ones. "I went to Hebrew School at 11 and a half, which was kind of late. One of my parents was not a practicing Jew, but they were going to see that I got bar mitzvahed and I was sent to the dungeons of the Hebrew School at the Neighborhood Center, Marshall and Porter. It was the old rabbis teaching in an old-fashioned way. The kids were scorned, very little respect for kids. The bar mitzvah experience was traumatic for all of us, but when you look back on it, you learned another language, you learned to chant. In my bar mitzvah, people threw the candy down from the second floor. I was bar mitzvahed at Shari Eli, Eighth and Porter, which is now some townhomes. It was an Orthodox synagogue. The women sat upstairs. And we had a little reception at a place called Uhr's."

He asked his parents about where their parents came from, about why they left. "Before my mother died, I said, 'Mom, when I ask you all these questions, you say you don't know. Why don't you know?'

"She said, 'We never asked.' Then we talked about it. I think theirs was the generation that was so intent on becoming Americanized. They did not want to keep any of the stories. Yiddish died. My parents understood it, but never cast any of it into me. . . . In my year and a half of study, I didn't get a hell of a lot in terms of culture, and I got very little, if anything, from my parents, . . . but you knew you were a Jew."

Sheckman was born during the Second World War, a time that brought people in South Philadelphia closer together, but ultimately would split them apart.

Residents of one Jewish neighborhood published their own newspaper during the war years, "for the benefit of the Fifth and Dickinson fighting men and women."

The South Philadelphia Gazette printed only good news and bad jokes: "Raymond Weinraub, stationed at Drew Field, Fla., was promoted to corporal. . . . One of our boys is in the thick of fighting. A communique received from over there informs us that Corporal Dave Stein is one of the many Yanks battling the hell out of the Axis in Sicily. . . . Abe (Abzo) Goldstein was recently transferred to the Naval Air Station in Hollywood, Fla. Keep in touch with Gazette for further details on a new romance between Abzo and a South Philadelphia gal. . . . Did you hear about the soldier who went broke because he was confined to quarters?"

The *Gazette* kept the ties close in a Jewish neighborhood, but Sandy Wizov believes the war's aftermath destroyed the larger Jewish community in South Philadelphia. Now you could afford to leave. The suburbs beckoned.

"If you were honorably discharged, you could buy a home for no money down. The Jewish kid would have married the Jewish girl, moved in to either her house or his house. The Irish, the Italian, would have all done the same. . . . Because of the high cost of homes today, children are now starting to move in with their parents, but their parents are in the suburbs. They're not in the cities like they used to be."

That's what happened to him. He married in 1953 and moved across the bridge into New Jersey. But now, more than 40 years later, he still talks passionately about the neighborhood where he grew up. Since 1968, he has helped organize South Philadelphia reunions for as many as 500. There was one in 1991.

"Look at this, there are 325 guys out there and I know every one of them," said one participant. "Could you get 50 of your friends together? There's Fishy. And there's Mako. Mako? Meyer Gold. Hey, there's guys here I just know by their nicknames."

Let Wizov explain how special the reunions are: "There was a pool room at Fourth and Ritner, but they wouldn't let me in. In those days, if you were 12 or 13, you couldn't hang around with guys 15, 16, and 17, they just wouldn't allow it. And they couldn't hang around with guys 20 and 21. That's what makes the reunion so unique. You were once a snot-nosed little kid to a guy when he was only three years older than you. And now he's 70 and you're 67, he hugs and kisses you. It's that kind of a thing."

Wizov grew up at 423 Ritner, 2429 South Fifth, 2439 South Fifth, 2451 South Fifth, and 412 Fitzgerald Street.

"I haven't the foggiest idea why we moved so much. They never owned a home. I remember the rent was $28 when I was old enough to understand what rent was."

His father, Martin, was born in Russia, and came to Philadelphia because his own father had fled the town of Smela. "During the time of the pogrom, when the men of the village fished and hunted together leaving the women alone, they heard screams. Each man rushed back to his own home."

Wizov's grandfather killed the soldier in the house. "There was a proclamation the next day looking for Bensie Wizovsky. He ducked out, made his way to Marseilles, took the boat and landed in Philadelphia. Coincidentally, the boat was $28 to come to America. This was 1906. My father was born in 1903."

(above left)
Sitting at Fifth and Porter are Sandy Wizov's grandmother, Nessie Wizov (left) and her sister, Leah Thal. Just before this picture was taken in 1943, Leah Thal lost her husband and her third sister. She went on to marry her deceased sister's husband. Courtesy of Sandy Wizov

(above right)
That handsome 16-year-old lad with the bow tie is Sandy Wizov, who earned five dollars for the 1946 advertisement. He was "discovered" in the mail room at Stern's. By the way, there was no glass in the glasses. Courtesy of Sandy Wizov

His grandfather delivered washed laundry in Southwest Philadelphia in a horse and wagon, and soon saved enough to send for his wife and son. He later owned a mattress factory, and a furniture store on South Street. He moved to South Philadelphia at his wife's insistence when his son—Wizov's father—was born.

"Vivacious" describes Wizov as he tells the stories of his life. Animated. Joyous. Many people think their childhood was special, but he is convinced of it. The memories, the closeness of people, the reunions. For him, there was nothing like South Philadelphia.

"Eddie Fisher lived on Fifth Street across from the Taggart School. He was six months ahead of me. As a young kid, loved to sing, sing at the drop of a hat. But he was so frail that he couldn't be part of playing football or tag or baseball or anything like that. In those days, everything happened in the schoolyard. Guys played three-card Andy, where it took 10 minutes to squeeze open the cards. And he'd be the watcher, checking for the cops. . . .

"We all played the numbers for a penny, two pennies. It was an accepted thing. Even I played. I played for a dime, 60 cents a week. And I remember being sick, I was 14 or 15, and I didn't give the number writer the money that week, and I won. The number came out. Harry Bufty, I'll never forget, came into my house and put $40 or something down. I said, 'But Harry, I didn't give you any money.' He said, 'I put the 60 cents in for you.' He never did ask for the 60 cents. . . .

"There was such a camaraderie. Every house had jigsaw puzzles on bridge tables, and whole families would sit for days putting in one piece at a time at night after dinner. I'm not ancient, but even in my time a lamp lighter used to come around and turn on the lights. My father told me a story that he was stopped on the highway by a policeman because he had the first car that wasn't black. It was the 1930s. He bought a maroon car and the guy just wanted to see it. . . .

"Crazy Mae was a colored lady, the first of the bag ladies. She used to walk from Oregon Avenue to Ritner Street on Fourth or Fifth Street, up and back, up and back. Kids would tease her. She'd throw milk bottles at them and call them bastards."

Buying cottage cheese from a pile at the grocery store. Taking girls in your car to the Lakes to make out. Watching Rabbi Moskowitz give bar mitzvah lessons outdoors at Fourth and Porter. Taking the ferry to Camden. Buying knishes from Benny the Knish man.

"The Jewish corridor was Fourth, Fifth, and Sixth streets, and Seventh, too, but they were stores. It went up to McKean, then there was a gap, and then it picked up. The bulk of it was around Ritner, Wolf, Porter. . . .

"No, I'm not romanticizing the past. I feel sorry for the kids today. Kids can grow up and don't know how to make an ice cube. Just take a glass and put it into the refrigerator and push a button. I mean, we had to go steal a chunk of ice. What was wrong with growing up like that?

"You felt the neighborhood. You breathed it, you could hear people talking. If somebody hollered, you knew what the argument was. I had 20 mothers. Every one of my boyfriends' mothers was a mother to me. You want milk. You needed peaches. I couldn't go into anybody's house that they didn't feed me, or could any of my boyfriends come into my house. You don't have that today. . . . How can you grow up and not have a corner to call your own?"

8

Crime and Violence

Jean didn't know what ordinary life was like. She didn't have many childhood friends. Her parents told her not to play more than one sidewalk away, and her father did not want her in the house playing with the few friends that she had. He did not go out to work every morning like other men.

When Jean was a teenager, she was not permitted to wear makeup or go to dances. She rarely dated. Men were afraid to approach her, but those who did sometimes kissed her hand. She would marry the first man she dated at 16, a South Philadelphian she had known most of her life. It was a tragic mistake, one that she still regrets.

Her parents once whisked her out of high school to go to Florida for a month. They used other names there, and she never asked why. Jean loved her father, but was afraid for him most of her life. She knows that he loved her and understands that his life probably ruined hers. She lives with that.

Jean Bruno is the youngest child of Angelo Bruno, leader of the Cosa Nostra in Philadelphia for more than two decades until he was shot to death outside his Snyder Avenue home in 1980. Jean Bruno is also the widow of Ralph Puppo and the mother of their four children. Puppo, who was gay, died of complications due to AIDS in 1991.

"I didn't know what normal was. . . . I'm not complaining. What good would it do? I loved my father. When you love somebody, the pain is bearable. I remember one time he came into my bedroom. I have low blood sugar. I was young and I was sick and they didn't know what it was. And he looked at me and I looked at him. I always knew my father was going to die. I said to myself, 'I'm going to have to fix this look in my mind forever.'"

Violence is attached to the image of South Philadelphia like a noisy muffler on an old car. It was a way the poor tried not to be poor anymore. The violence did not begin with Jean Bruno's father. Nor did the gambling or the organized crime or the bootlegging or the prostitution. Nor did it begin with the Italians. Crime and violence has been an equal-opportunity endeavor downtown, and the names of its best-known practitioners have been Polish and Irish and Jewish and African American as well.

Actually, the first well-known bit of gambling began with the Swedes about 300 years ago.

In 1697, the minister to the Swedish community in Wicaco wanted to replace the log blockhouse that the community had been worshipping in for 20 years. But the Swedes living to the west, nearer to the Schuylkill River, wanted a new church built closer to them in Passyunk. The dispute was resolved when the names of two sites were put on pieces of paper, placed in a hat, and shaken. In Philadelphia's first ecclesiastical lottery, Wicaco won, and the Gloria Dei (Old Swedes') Church, completed in 1700 near the Delaware River, was the result.

Vice and violence are part of South Philadelphia's history. The Southwark district established a Society for the Suppression of Vice and Immorality in the late 1700s. Philadelphia was a walking city through the eighteenth century and the first half of the nineteenth, and no one wanted to live on the city's edges, so only the poor did. As dirty as the city was, the outlying districts were dirtier. As bad as some of the city's housing was, the housing in Southwark and Moyamensing was even worse. The city's police department—a system of watchmen until the 1850s—did not function well, but it did not function at all in South Philadelphia. In fact, South Street was like the Rio Grande, and pursuing city watchmen would not follow a criminal if he crossed it.

While some may blame the arrival of Irish immigrants in the 1840s or the large free black population for the tradition of crime and violence, the explanation is just not that simple. "Violence has long been an integral part of the city's native-born artisans' cultural heritage, a heritage which antedated the mass arrival of Irishmen," writes historian Michael Feldberg.

Some of the best examples of the worst violence in the city's history happened in South Philadelphia. Rampaging Moyamensing Irish weavers. Election Day donnybrooks. Native-American rioting. Racially motivated beatings and killings. And when the lineage of city street gangs is traced, the line appears to have begun in South Philadelphia.

It may have been due to poverty or the breakdown of the apprenticeship system, but gangs of violent young men and boys proliferated in South Philadelphia. The Killers, Schuylkill Rangers, Skinners, and Flayers were gangs in the mid-1800s. Some were loosely knit confederations of thieves and muggers, while others were more organized, ruling the waterfront, controlling vice, or setting fire to the houses of anyone who would not pay protection money.

The Schuylkill Rangers were a predominantly Irish gang that terrorized the Schuylkill wharves and coal yards for 26 years. An 1856 *Evening Bulletin* article suggested that the anti–Irish Catholic violence in 1844 caused the Irish living in two neighborhoods—Grays Ferry and Schuylkill, its neighbor to the north—to band together for protection. Whatever the reason, the Rangers, led by Jim Haggerty, were a force to be reckoned with. They demanded protection money from the barges bringing coal down the river, and were linked as well to murder, vice, counterfeiting, robbery, and arson. Credit for their dissolution goes to Lieutenant Flaherty, one of the few Irish police officers at the time, who went undercover to break up the Schuylkill Rangers.

On the eastern end, in Moyamensing and Southwark, the Killers held sway. Led by Charles Anderson Chester until he was killed in 1849, the Killers stole cargo on the Delaware and committed mayhem on the streets.

The Killers aligned themselves with the Moyamensing Hose Company, the volunteer fire brigade run by political leader William McMullen. They were not the only gang to join a volunteer fire company in South Philadelphia. The Bouncers were tied to Weccacoe Hose, the Shifflers to the Shiffler Hose Company. The fire fighters were neighborhood heroes to many young men, but by older residents they were feared as well as admired. The volunteer firemen could, and did, save lives, but they also forced residents to pay for fire protection and were intensely competitive with one another, often setting the fires and ambushing the arriving company.

The fights were about religion, temperance, politics, and turf. "Fighting was a time-honored tradition among firemen," writes historian Bruce Laurie. "Fights involving these companies were not brief scuffles, but riots replete with arson, shooting and murder. . . . They fought to regulate who lived near them, who socialized at their pubs and taverns, and which companies serviced the people. . . . These firemen waged battles in order to control their neighborhoods.

" . . . The Shiffler's principal opponent was the Irish Catholic and Democratic Moyamensing Hose Company. . . . The Killers' favorite tactic was to ignite a fire in Southwark, retreat to the alleys lining the Shiffler's route, ambush them, and abscond with their carriage. They launched four ambushes in the summer of 1849 before they successfully wrested away the Shiffler's carriage. Fighting intensified with each encounter, and before long neither side left for a fire without carrying muskets and duck guns."

The muskets and duck guns of the battling fire companies wounded and killed innocent bystanders as well as fire fighters. While visitors to Southwark and Moyamensing may have feared for their lives if they saw a hose company running its equipment down the street, the male visitors came to the neighborhood anyway. It was where the prostitutes were.

To find those prostitutes, the curious referred to *A Guide to the Stranger, or Pocket Companion for the Fancy Containing a List of the Gay Houses and Ladies of Pleasure in the City of Brotherly Love and Sisterly Affection*, a bawdy-house Baedeker that included numerous listings south of South Street in 1848. The guide advised readers to avoid the house run by "Sarah Ross, Passyunk Road below German [Fitzwater]. This is one of the worst conducted houses in the city. The girls, though few in number, are ugly, vulgar and drunken. . . . Shippen Street [Bainbridge], below Fourth, and Plum (Monroe), above and below Fourth, all contain houses of prostitution of the lowest grade, the resort of pickpockets and thieves. . . . The stranger is earnestly admonished not to go there."

Gaskill, Kater, Bainbridge, Monroe, and Fitzwater Streets east of Eighth were all streets of ill repute. Here is what a *New York Tribune* reporter said in 1848 of a well-known brothel on Plum, between Third and Fourth:

"Dandy Hall is the core of the rottenest and most villainous neighborhood ever populated by human beings . . . a moral Golgotha of Civilization." The writer went on to say that the three-story brick building had nightly dances and orgies on the second floor, that customers of both sexes were served three-cents-a-glass brandy and whiskey on a board lying across two barrels, that a

"Negro fiddler" provided music, and that sailors and gang members were frequent patrons. The building could not be shut down unless neighbors testified that it was a nuisance, "but the neighbors are as bad as the inmates of Dandy Hall."

Tribune reporter George G. Foster also wrote that there was a "lower and more thorough development of debasement in Philadelphia than New York. The districts, especially of Southwark and Moyamensing, swarm with these loafers, who, brave only in gangs, herd together, . . . Killers, Bouncers, Rats, Stingers, Gumballs, Smashers . . . and other . . . verminous designations, which may be seen in . . . the suburbs written in chalk or charcoal on every dead wall, fence or stable door." (Remember, before 1854 and consolidation, South Philadelphia was the suburbs.)

Italian, Jewish, and Polish immigrants in the late 1800s and early 1900s added new names and ethnic organizations to the crime-steeped traditions of the South Philadelphia neighborhoods. Before long, there would be the Cosa Nostra and the Jew Mob. Blacks introduced a new form of gambling called numbers betting. And local boys good at being bad, men like Mickey Duffy, Max "Boo Boo" Hoff, Willie Weisberg, and Angelo Bruno, became the new crime bosses.

Though no one can say which criminal organization was number one in the new century, the Italian Black Hand and Cosa Nostra were visible early. In fact, in 1928 the Black Hand attempted to extort $2,000 in protection money from Michael Bruno Annaloro, a grocery store owner. The threat was made to Annaloro's son, Angelo, who was 18 at the time. The young South Philadelphia man ignored it and testified against Black Hand member Joseph DiJulia, who was convicted. Later, the grocer's son would drop the family surname.

The first criminal luminary from downtown was Mickey Duffy, a Polish lad from Grays Ferry who was born either Michael or William Cusick—newspaper clippings disagree. Duffy, the city's beer baron during Prohibition, owned nightclubs and speakeasies in Philadelphia, ran breweries throughout New Jersey, and was involved in ancillary activities like truck hijacking, numbers, and prostitution.

He was arrested first at the age of 16 in 1908 and would be arrested on 27 other occasions and imprisoned eight times. But in the late 1920s, he was not just another ex-convict; he was a public figure who dressed well, threw lavish parties, owned a fleet of cars, and built a Moorish mansion on Haverford Avenue just west of City Avenue in Montgomery County. But he didn't stay on top long. On August 29, 1931, at the age of 39, the former street fighter and petty thief was murdered while he napped in his suite at the Ambassador Hotel in Atlantic City.

Five .38-caliber bullets to the head killed Mickey Duffy, but it was old age that took the life of the fight promoter, alcohol maker, and gambling boss Max "Boo Boo" Hoff. He died in his bed in 1953.

Hoff, who was from South Street near Eighth, joined Al Capone and Lucky Luciano at a national meeting of underworld leaders in 1928 in Atlantic City. His mortgage and investment company lent money to gangsters, and his legitimate industrial alcohol manufacturing plants turned out barrels and barrels

The man with the hat is fight manager Max "Boo Boo" Hoff. In this June 1929 photograph of his fighting stable, Ace Clark is on the left, with Tom Toner, Boo Boo, Matt Adgie, and Jack Gross. Used with permission of the Temple University Urban Archives

Max "Boo Boo" Hoff in federal court in 1934, charged with trying to pass counterfeit money. Used with permission of the Temple University Urban Archives

of illegal booze, making him the biggest bootlegger in town and one of the largest in the nation. He described himself, however, as a fight promoter and put on fights at the Philadelphia Arena for 25 years. Hoff's curious nickname was one that he acknowledged and used. His business card read, "Boo Boo Max Hoff."

Mickey and Boo Boo may have been the city's most famous drink peddlers, but the first real crime *family* was known by its last name only—Lanzetti.

South Philadelphia's six Lanzetti brothers, four of whom were named after popes, were, like Hoff and Duffy, active in the Prohibition years. In the 1930s, they became involved in prostitution, gambling, and the numbers business. The latter had been founded in the 1920s by two African Americans, Forrest White and a man known as West Indian Johnny. Their headquarters was on South Street, near 18th. White mobsters subsequently took the business over.

Leo, the eldest Lanzetti, was shot to death in South Philadelphia in 1925. Pius, the next eldest, was killed with a sawed-off shotgun on December 31, 1936, in a luncheonette at 726 South Eighth Street. The *Public Ledger* reported the next morning: "With the dying year, Pius Lanzetti, oldest brother of the Lanzetti clan of South Philadelphia hoodlums, died yesterday, victim of Gangland avengers." And Willie, dressed in gabardine with a small-caliber bullet in his brain, was found inside two sewn-together potato sacks near the stone wall of a Wynnewood estate on July 1, 1939.

Though it is not certain who killed the Lanzettis, among their enemies was the Jew Mob founded by Harry Stromberg, a New Yorker who came to Philadelphia in the 1920s. Also known as the Center City Mob and the 69th Street Mob, many of its members were from downtown. Its number-two man,

Willie Weisberg, became the boss of the sports betting and money-lending organization when Stromberg—known on the street as Nig Rosen—left town in 1950. Stromberg died in Florida in 1992.

Weisberg, originally from 35th and Wharton in Grays Ferry, was born in 1898. His education ended after the eighth grade, but his criminal accomplishments were such that he was investigated by the Kefauver and McClellan committees in the 1950s, and was described by U.S. Attorney General Robert Kennedy in 1961 as being in the "top echelon" of American racketeers.

His wife, Anna, died in 1976, and among the mourners at her funeral were Angelo Bruno and his lieutenant, Phil Testa. Weisberg died in an old age home two years later.

Which brings us to Bruno, the Docile Don, the Sicilian-born grocer's son whose rise to prominence within organized crime is well known and will be repeated only briefly here. Born in 1910, Bruno was invited to join the local Mafia family as a "soldier" in the 1930s and built a profitable numbers operation. As local Mafia leaders died or moved on, Bruno moved up. In the late 1950s, a new leader, Antonio "Mr. Migs" Polina took over and ordered Bruno killed, fearing that Bruno might lead an uprising against him.

But the assassination order was given to a soldier who was an old friend of Bruno's, and instead of killing him, he warned him. Bruno appealed to the national underworld "commission," which stripped Polina of all power and gave the control of the Philadelphia family to Bruno. Instead of executing Polina, as was expected, Bruno retired him.

What distinguished Bruno from other crime bosses was that he served not as the *capo* of a tightly knit, violence-prone crime family, but rather as the executive director of a quasi chamber of commerce, private and criminal to be sure, but less violent and less organized than people imagined. Mark H. Haller, a crime expert and professor of history, says that Bruno's advice and approval were sought when others tried new ventures, but no evidence exists that he ever sought a payment of fealty from anyone—unlike his successors.

Jean Bruno had no idea that her father might be doing something wrong, or that she should be concerned about it, until she was six or seven years old.

Head shots of Teo, Pius, Willie, and Ignatius Lanzetti. Used with permission of the Temple University Urban Archives

Pius Lanzetti was shot and killed on New Year's Eve 1936 inside Mrs. Joe Grimm's store at 726 South Eighth Street. An innocent bystander was killed as well, and a third customer was injured. Used with permission of the Temple University Urban Archives

"My cousin and I, we were in front of my house and there was a police car. I didn't think anything of it, but she said, 'Maybe they're coming for your father.' I didn't say anything. I went inside and asked my mother what daddy did for a living. She wasn't too pleased. She said he was a broker.

"I said, 'A stock broker?' She said no.

"I said, 'What kind of broker?'

" 'A money broker,' she said.

"I knew something wasn't kosher. There was a nameless fear. It wasn't a fear of the bogeyman, or the gorilla that might get out of the zoo. It was a fear you couldn't put your finger on."

She heard the story about Antonio Polina and her father when she was 12, but she never asked him about it. "He used to call me daddy and I would call him daddy. . . . When I was real little, he'd go, 'What do you want?' He's driving the car. And he had a wonderful voice. He played the violin and the piano. And he'd go, 'What do you want, daddy?' I only wanted it to last forever, but to show him that he couldn't give me what I wanted, I'd say, 'I want the moon.'

"Now, my mother would go, 'What a kid! You can't satisfy her.' But that's not what I was saying. Then they landed on the moon, and my father said to my mother, 'She wasn't so stupid. She'd be rich with the mineral rights.' "

Jean Bruno was born at St. Agnes Hospital on June 18, 1941. Her parents and her brother, Michael, older by nine years, lived across from the hospital at Broad and Mifflin. Later they would move to Snyder Avenue, near 10th. She

was named Vincentine, after her father's mother, but her mother later had her name changed to Jean.

Her mother was born Asunta Maranca in Abruzzi, but everyone called her Sue. She came to South Philadelphia as a five-year-old in about 1919. Her father, like Bruno's, was a grocer. The Marancas lived at Eighth and Annin Streets.

"My grandfather, oh, he made a statue for the church. He was very artistic. He used to make all these little wooden figures going up the mountain. You could actually see the girl going under the man's arm doing the tarantella. At 12 o'clock, the youngest child in our family would sing 'Silent Night.' And I remember those Sundays, my grandmother would dish out the macaroni. The first time I saw her without a girdle, I remember that. She was a nice woman, spoke mostly Italian. She thought she spoke English well. She'd say everything in Italian and then say something like 'ginger ale.' . . .

"Every morning, my mother used to make my hair in curls, and I used to holler because it used to tangle. And she dressed me so nice. Don't forget they didn't have permanent press. Sometimes, we had mother and daughter dresses. My mother was always one to look good. She's five feet tall. Maybe that's why she always wore high heels. My father? To me, he was enormous. I would say he was around five-nine."

She was Ange's daughter, someone very special in the neighborhood, someone who was to be treated differently.

"There was an ice cream parlor on the corner. I must have been about six years old. When I walked in, the waitresses looked at me like they hated me.

Angelo Bruno and his top aide, Phil Testa, pay their respects to Willie Weisberg at the death of his wife, Anna, in August 1976. Courtesy of the Philadelphia Police Department

Do you know why? My father took me there and said, 'Look, Jeannie, there's money on the table. Why don't you take it?' It was the tips. He'd give the waitresses a couple of dollars, and I'd walk in there and clear off all the tables. I'd go behind the booths, lift up the cushions. Now I understand why those waitresses hated me."

She loved going with her father to Delaware Avenue to look at the ships. He gave her a feeling of self-worth that no one else did. She loved him so much, but she quietly chuckled at his old-world ways. Angelo Bruno was a prude.

"My father never went to the bathroom. That's the way he was. He went to wash his hands. My nieces could never wear a bikini at the beach. One time, we stayed in a hotel [in Italy] and there was a woman who was topless on the beach. My son was a young teenager, and he was acting real naive and innocent. He goes, 'Pop, look at that woman. How come she's not wearing the top?' My father goes, 'Because she's a pig.'"

His business gave him the freedom to live a life unencumbered by most rules. But it restricted his daughter's life.

"I didn't have friends. Would you want a bunch of little kids running around the house while you were listening to the baseball scores?" People bet on the games; scores were important.

"In junior high school, I couldn't wear lipstick or go to dances like everybody else did. The only place I could go was my cousin's. And when they did have a party, my mother insisted that I wear a silk dress, with a square lace collar, with a pleated skirt. I'll never forget that. And so I sat there like a wallflower. It was a year before I went to another cousin's party and anybody asked me to dance."

When she was older, men either kept their distance or acted as if she was the daughter of a king. She would go to weddings and no one would ever ask her to dance. She was attractive. She wanted to dance. She wanted a relationship. Once, a man did walk up to her from behind, but then awkwardly walked away when he realized who she was. No one would fool around with Ange's daughter, but they would pay her homage.

"It's when I was older, at Valentino's in New Jersey, and men lined up to kiss my hand. I was kidding my girlfriend. I said, 'Penny, you have to make light of these things, because it's not reality.'

"And I said, 'Girlfriend, did we wash our hands?' We had just came out of the ladies' room. I didn't see them kissing anyone else's hand. Once, my girlfriend brought her baby, and there were a lot of people in our house. The men all lined up to kiss the baby. They didn't know exactly whose baby it was, but they figured it must be an important baby. That's the way it was."

Her brother married young and was out of the house. She couldn't approach her parents and didn't have close friends. She couldn't talk to anyone about kissing or boys or sex or the gun she found in the night table of her parent's bedroom. She checked every day to make sure it was there. It always was. She didn't know if people liked her because she was Jean, or because she was Angelo Bruno's daughter, and she didn't know how to find out. She went to Girls High and Temple University and got a job teaching in elementary school in New Jersey.

In the summer of 1962, at the age of 21, she married Ralph Puppo before 500 people at the Benjamin Franklin Hotel. She had known him since they were children. His aunt was married to her uncle. He was her first date.

The pretty blonde fourth from the left on the bottom row is Jean Bruno, celebrating her Sweet 16 birthday with two dozen friends at the Latin Casino in 1957. She remembers that Sammy Davis, Jr., was performing, but cannot recall the name of the boy next to her, a date selected by her family. She does recall that weights were sewn into the top of her dress so that if she bent over, no cleavage would show. Her mother, Sue, is on the left of the top row of adults. Courtesy of Jean Bruno

169

Angelo and Sue Bruno with their grandchildren, Marcangelo and Jeanangela, inside the Broad Street apartment of Ralph and Jean Puppo in 1965. Courtesy of Jean Bruno

Daughter Marieangela is to be christened on this day in 1974. Daughter Jeanangela on the left, proud father Ralph Puppo, Sueangela, Jean and the baby, and Marcangelo. Courtesy of Jean Bruno

"I met him at a Sweet 16 party as somebody else's date. He took a whole year before he kissed me. I should have known then, but I didn't know. . . . You know what I'm trying to say?

"Now, if I had any experience at all with men, I would never have married him. He was the only one I was really allowed to go out with. I didn't have any experience with anybody. I wanted to marry. On our wedding night, he didn't want to do anything. We were in the Presidential Suite, and there were at least three bedrooms, and he said he was so tired. Can you believe that?

"He said that he went to bed with a man when he was a kid only one time. He made it sound like child abuse, and he'd never do it again. I used to cover

170

for him, because my father didn't believe in divorce. I never told anybody because I wanted to spare my father's feelings. Then I figured it out. The only reason he married me was for my family. It's a perfect coverup, isn't it?

"See, he was a singer, and he knew my father had connections. He wanted to be in show business, but he didn't have the personality. I wanted to leave him right after my father died, but my brother said, Think of the children. That old line again. I'm angry at myself for listening."

She traded one dysfunctional relationship for another. "Being married to him. I still didn't know what normal was. I had my son, Marcangelo, right away, and things were fine because everybody was so crazy about the baby. But things were never as they should have been, because of my parents' lives and because of my husband. . . .

"I was never close to my mother. She's not the easiest person in the world to get along with. . . . It was a shame. She meant well, but she didn't know how to express herself. All those years, she resented me for marrying him. I finally said to her, 'Mom, don't hate me for something that I'm sorrier than you are for.' "

There would be three more children—Jeanangela, Sueangela, and Marieangela; there would be homes in Bala Cynwyd and Radnor; there would be a real estate career for him and allegations and an acquittal of racketeering charges. Just before he died, he was charged with money laundering.

They separated soon after she learned that he had AIDS. He hadn't told her, and they had continued, on occasion, to have sex. He had endangered her, and she was furious.

"My son always called him names, Ralphina, things like that. He was ashamed. I heard him make apologies to people. He'd say, 'Oh, don't mind my father. He never was in a fight in his life. He was raised differently.'

"But when Marc found out what his father had, he dropped out of school, did all of his cooking, drove his father around. . . . At the cemetery, Marc stands up and says, 'I'd like to say a few words. A lot of men do a lot of good in their life. Like my father getting old ladies mortgages. But it's human nature that if a man makes one mistake, that's what he's remembered for. I'm sure that my father would like to be remembered for the good he's done in his life just as much as I would like to be remembered that way.'

"I was really proud. He got in the car, and he turns around to me and says, 'Mom, God knows how many people he's stiffed.' "

Many of her father's associates are dead now, and many of their sons are dead, too, men that Jean Bruno knew as boys.

"Look at Salvi Testa. Oh, I have beautiful pictures. I remember the first day he went to kindergarten, and his father came over, just as thrilled as could be, and he said, 'I asked my son what he learned today.' And he was cute. His father did all the motions of what Salvi said. 'The Earth is a big ball, and we're in it.' Salvi used to come in and hug, and everybody would say, 'Oh, isn't that cute.'

"I've seen how the illusions can kill people. When you are cast in a role, it's almost expected of you. People judge you before you even open your mouth. You understand? He was born in a family like that. . . . He idolized his

171

father. You just knew he was going to die. It was just terrible, poor Salvi. . . ." (Salvatore Testa, 28, was found shot to death in Camden County in September 1984. A nail-packed bomb had killed his father, Philip Testa, three years before.)

"In our development, when we lived in Radnor, there was this woman whose husband died and left her very well off. . . . I was invited to this party, and she's there and she's drinking and she goes, real loud, 'I can't believe it! Lila invited that Mafia woman!' I was drinking and I said, 'Yeh, that's the most exciting thing about me.' . . .

"Sure, I wish things were different, but I wouldn't trade my father. That's my father. . . . He did the best he could. You know, he wasn't in good health. He had ulcers, and I think he had low blood sugar, like me, because he was always brushing his teeth, and I did the same thing."

Jean Bruno continues to compare men with her father, and they come up short. She knows people envied her, the daughter of the don, but they didn't understand about the violence, and she did. "I never knew any emotional security. It was like it all could be jerked out from under you."

It was jerked out from under Anthony "Butch" D'Alessandro just after his birth. His mother died and his father shipped him off to relatives.

"My mother died six months after I was born. Her name? Truthfully, I don't know. Elvira, I think. I was the youngest of 11. My father was a stone mason with 10 kids at home. He couldn't take care of me. My mother's sister raised me. Lou and Julia Alberdini. I don't know how to spell their last name. To tell you the truth, I was in and out, always on the street. I didn't go to too much school."

He was born in 1929 and today lives in Washington Township, New Jersey, a retired merchant who speaks easily about his days as a thief and as a thug. He was never connected to the Cosa Nostra. He was a small-timer, for which he makes no apologies. He doesn't blame his father or the social conditions of the day for what he did. As he likes to say, "That was the name of the game then.

"We lived on Alter Street, the little street between Eighth and Ninth just off Washington Avenue. I was more spoiled than anything else by my aunt and uncle. They came from Italy; they didn't know nothing. They thought I was doing good in school. They loved me like their own. I did anything I wanted. They always thought I was a little innocent kid."

When he was eight or nine, he was transferred to a school for students with discipline problems, the Burk School at Third and Christian. By the time he was 12, he was out of school and selling ice on an ice wagon.

"I was a bad kid, small but bad. I just didn't care about nothing. I was a little guy. I didn't take anybody's shit, and I hurt them anyway I could hurt them. I hit them with a bat, or stab the son of a gun. . . .

"See, whoever bothered my friends, I went after them. Italian, Irish, black, anything, I didn't give a damn. I used to like to fight. We had a gang, called the Mexican Gang. Teddy and me were the only Italians, two Mexicans, the rest were Irish and Polacks. We used to hang at Ninth and Christian, Sixth and Montrose. This guy, Mex, lived at Second and Pine, and I used to walk home

172

Palumbo's in 1947. Butch D'Alessandro (in the middle) shares the Outstanding Player award of the Seymour AA football team. Butch was a 135-pound lineman. Courtesy of Anthony D'Alessandro

from there at night myself, but I carried a little piece with me. I used to walk the streets all hours of the night. I didn't care."

When he was 16, his father took him back. "Then as soon as I got in, he slapped me upside the head and I went out the door. I said, 'I ain't coming back no more.' He took me back 'cause I was old enough to go to work. See, in them days, that's all they figured on. If the kid's strong enough to go to work, you go to work. After that, I was working for Pat's Steaks.

"I went back home to my aunt. See, I always called them my mother and father. In fact, when I got married the first time, they sent my father flowers, not my uncle. I said, 'If he don't get any, I don't get married.' That's the end of that ball game, 'cause he's the one that raised me. He sweated for me."

So Butch earned some money behind the counter at Pat's Steaks and earned extra money stealing.

"When the hucksters used to come down, we used to jump in back of their wagon, rob the vegetables, and have two guys running alongside and just keep on throwing it to them while we're in the back. . . .

"Remember, Gimbel's used to have a round window in the front on Eighth years and years ago. One guy threw the brick in there, the other two guys would rob the jewels and take off. That was the gimmick. Grab fast and take

Butch and his buddies had to figure out something funny to do for the 1957 Mummer's Parade. They won a $75 prize for their South Philly–Hollywood "float." That's Butch on the left. Courtesy of Anthony D'Alessandro

off, else you'd get your ass whipped. And then the newspaper stands, we used to have two groups going down both sides of the street, rob all the money off the stands. Just go right down till you get caught. One guy gets caught, the other guys come back and help him. Was the name of the game in them days."

His first wife was Rita Zangi, and he became friendly with her six brothers. "Their family used to haul food out of the food center on Dock Street. They had a truck. Like if you worked on Ninth Street and you have your packages, you used to give us a quarter a package and we'll haul it to your stand. You buy it in the morning and leave a ticket there.

"It was bad down there in them days. You had to handle yourself pretty good. If not, you got hurt because you always had a bunch of guys cutting into your territory, taking your customers. You had to knock the shit out of them to keep them out. So we'd tell you in a nice way to leave or you're going to get in trouble, and if you didn't leave, we worked you over, made sure you left. That was the name of the game in them days.

"I drove and I was like a henchman there, 'cause they used to tell you, Don't worry about the Zangis, worry about the brother-in-law, because the brother-in-law is crazy. I was the brother-in-law. I used to be a little bit goofy."

Butch and the Zangis were also strike breakers. "They called me and said, 'Hey, Butch, we got a good deal but we got to watch it, 'cause we could get hurt. Horn & Hardart is going on strike, and if we haul the stuff, we get 50 cents on everything we put on the truck.'

"We had to get it from the fruit center to Horn & Hardart. I'm not good on dates, but I think this was right after the war. Yeah, there were problems. The strikers burned one of our trucks up. One morning, I caught a black guy trying to burn my truck up. He didn't. That's the way that went."

Anthony "Butch" D'Alessandro, once a South Philadelphia tough guy, ran for a council seat in Washington Township, N.J., in the summer of 1990. He lost. Courtesy of Anthony D'Alessandro

He learned the trade of his father and worked as a stone mason. He drove through a few more picket lines, sold some bootleg liquor, and smashed some heads as a bouncer and manager in bars. In 1958, he gave it up, moved to New Jersey with his second wife, and opened a produce stand and deli. He never thought about connecting with the local Mafia.

"Know what the saying was over there? You live by the gun, you die by the gun. I didn't want that. I did all right. If I got a piece of bread, I was happy. I don't want to be no hero. We broke strikes. I made money with my brother-in-laws, and so I was content. They didn't bother us, and we didn't bother them.

"What I liked about South Philly, as bad as the people were, they never bothered any of their neighbors. They had the highest respect for anybody who lived in the neighborhood. You always had a good morning, a goodbye. If you had a fight, you had a fight, and that was it. You shook hands and forgot about it. You don't get sued. And everybody minded their own business, and we all got along good. Over here, it stinks. New Jersey, you can't trust nobody.

"Lot of people from South Philly around here 'cause it's close to the bridge and they can go and see their family. But when they get out here, they think their shit don't stink anymore. In South Philly, it was all down to earth; everybody was the same. Over here, he buys a house for 150 and you come, you want to pay 160, so you're better than him. The next guy wants to pay 170. Get the hell out of here."

He has eight children, two of them adopted. He's run for public office—unsuccessfully. He says he has been accused of trying to kill someone on four occasions, but never was convicted. He had a heart attack, so he takes it easy now, fooling around with some old cars. He doesn't bother with too many people anymore.

"You try to help people. I'm like that, but don't cross me. You cross me, then you got the devil. And if I want to tell you something, I tell you right to your face. I don't make somebody else knock on the door and tell you Butch said it." And that's the name of that game.

9

Not Irish or Black or Italian or Jew

Joseph Evancich grew up near Front and Kenilworth in the 1920s, but his parents grew up on an island near Trieste that was alternately under the rule of Austria or Croatia. Who ruled Front and Kenilworth back then is also unclear, but the neighborhood was full of Irish and Polish.

Bill Esher, a fourth-generation South Philadelphia Welshman, grew up on the 2700 block of Sheridan Street, south and west of where Evancich lived. Chinese and Filipinos lived near him in the late 1930s.

Epifanio DeJesus was born in Puerto Rico and moved to Hutchinson Street near the Italian Market as a youngster in 1954. His family were the first Puerto Ricans on the block.

And Sophal Hing was a little boy when he arrived on South 22nd Street in 1980 from a Cambodian refugee camp in Thailand.

The 1990 Census counted Hing, DeJesus, and Evancich (Esher had moved to New Jersey by that time) and about 171,000 other people living between the two rivers and south of South Street. A mix of ethnic groups and races has historically been the norm downtown. English and Germans lived in South Philadelphia in the 1700s, and English and Germans live there today, as do Laotians and Lebanese and Ukrainians. South Philadelphia never was just Irish and blacks, Italians and Jews. That same 1990 Census counted 4,758 Hispanics, 8,925 Germans, 6,948 Asians, 703 French, 53,392 Italians, 3,713 Polish, 17,281 Irish, 53,758 African Americans, and 329 West Indians. And 11,518 residents said they were born on foreign soil. Everyone originally came from foreign soil, except the indigenous Indians.

William Penn advertised throughout Europe in the late 1600s to attract settlers to his new land, but not all of the foreigners were equally welcome. In 1717 James Logan, Penn's secretary in Philadelphia and later acting governor, wrote: "We have of late great numbers of Palatinates poured in upon us, without any recommendation or notice, which gives the country some unease, for foreigners do not do so well among us as our own people." And Benjamin Franklin, famous for his pithy aphorisms, is not as famous for his 1751 complaints about the danger of the colonies' traditions being subverted by German immigrants, whom he called "Palatine boors."

Despite the concerns of Franklin and Logan, foreigners continued to pour in. Welsh, German, Irish, English, Jewish, and French newcomers all began fraternal, cultural, or self-help organizations in the city between 1759 and 1793. These groups would take many forms over the years in South Philadelphia, including baseball clubs begun by African Americans, foreign-language newspapers opened by Italians, and fire companies started by Irish Catholics.

But the percentage of foreigners coming to Philadelphia dwindled in the late 1800s, compared with the surge in other cities. In 1870, 27 percent of the city's 674,000 people were foreign-born—and the city would never have as high a percentage again. That same year, the foreign-born made up 35 percent of the population in Boston, 42 percent in Cleveland, 48 percent in Chicago, and 32 percent in Pittsburgh. No major northern city had as small a percentage as Philadelphia.

Forty years later, the European immigration influx was well under way and the city's population had jumped to more than 1.5 million, but its foreign-born component had dipped to 25 percent. New York, Pittsburgh, Chicago, Cleveland, and Detroit also had dips in 1910, but those cities still had higher percentages of foreign-born residents than Philadelphia. That may have caused Lincoln Steffens to write at the turn of the century that "Philadelphia is the most American of our greater cities."

But why? There were at least three reasons. For one thing, an inverse relationship existed between the number of foreign immigrants and the number of black residents. The city historically had more black residents than other northern cities had, and even more came following the Civil War and World War I. Their work at unskilled jobs meant that immigrants who needed unskilled work—Poles, for instance—might not prosper in Philadelphia. Poles and other immigrants also had to compete against the Irish, who already were employed, and against the Italians, who had the padrone system to help them. So many of the Polish and Slavic immigrants who landed in Philadelphia did not stay, going instead into central and western Pennsylvania, where the mining industry needed unskilled labor and where the Italians, Irish, and blacks were not a step ahead.

Second, the Irish immigration dwindled in the latter third of the 1800s. So many Irish had arrived in the early and mid-1800s that the later influx of other immigrants did not make up for the drop in Irish immigration.

The employment needs of the city's industry was another factor. By 1915, only about a dozen businesses employed more than 500 workers, not a good sign for an immigrant with a strong back but no specific skills.

But the foreign-born percentage was generally higher in South Philadelphia than in the city as a whole. For example, 25 percent of the city's residents were foreign-born in 1910, but the figure was nearly 35 percent in South Philadelphia. The part of the city that had once been so strongly Native-American had now become so foreign.

In 1852, the first Italian church and the first synagogue opened in South Philadelphia. The next year, construction began on St. Alphonsus, a German-Catholic church at Fourth and Reed Streets. St. Stanislaus, for Polish Catholics, opened on Fitzwater near Second Street in 1891, and St. Aloysius, another German-Catholic church, opened on Tasker Street in Grays Ferry three years later.

By the end of the 1800s, W. Jones, an Englishman, was selling meat and vegetables at 10th and Ellsworth while German-born Joseph Nahrgang was selling shoes at Fourth and Reed. Irishman Robert Taggart was fixing wagons and carriages on the 1200 block of Point Breeze, and Gonzalez and Silvera (Cubans perhaps?) were selling cigars on Eighth Street near Ellsworth.

And Richard Cormany, Bill Esher's German grandfather, was milking cows near where Veterans Stadium, the home of the Eagles and the Phillies, is today.

"Grandpop Cormany, my mother's father, had a dairy farm that extended almost to where the Vet Stadium is, clean down to the Navy Yard. He had about 50 head of cow. It was all farms down there. Grandpop had that up until about 1922, '23, when the politicians forced him out. The rumor was that they passed an ordinance that he couldn't have livestock in the 39th Ward, which was east of Broad, because they wanted that land. You know what for— the 1926 Sesquicentennial. He knew they wanted it for something. He sold out and moved to New Jersey, where he started another farm."

Esher was born in 1928 in his parents' bedroom at 1215 Porter Street. His family moved to Beulah and Franklin Streets when he was a little boy, and finally to the 2700 block of Sheridan, between Oregon and Johnston.

"That particular neighborhood was the greatest ethnic mix in the world. It was unbelievable. The next street over was Marshall Street, and it was 50 percent black, mostly schoolteachers, post office workers, nurses. The one thing I can still remember was when Joe Louis won his fights, they'd get out with their pots and pans and bang them and all, and parade up and down the street.

"It was a super-nice neighborhood. I would say that there's not an ethnic group you couldn't mention, including Chinese and Filipinos. We had everything. It was funny the way it broke up. Sheridan Street was quite mixed; Marshall, 2700, was half-black, but 2800 was predominantly Jewish; 2800 South Fairhill was predominantly Jewish, 2700 Fairhill was a mixture. So it was just a melting pot. You could get to know people. I belonged to a Presbyterian church at Fifth and Oregon, and they had a thing called the Pioneers. They didn't discriminate who joined, because we had the only decent indoor basketball court in the whole neighborhood. We had Jewish kids there, we had Catholic kids there, and everybody was accepted."

Esher's family was its own melting pot—his father was Welsh, his mother German and Irish. William Sr. drove a truck; Louise raised three children.

The family lived behind and above a corner store. "John Crispi's barber shop. We were paying $30 a month mortgage, and John paid us $28 a month for the barber shop. Across the street was the American store. It was a franchise; it was like the original Acme. And across the street was Schaff's, the Jewish delicatessen. On the other corner was a tailor shop. South Philly had a store on every corner. Uffe's up on the corner, dry goods store. Then Celie Fineman had a pharmacy up on the other end of Sheridan Street. Had a shoemaker store, Mr. Monica, down on Marshall Street on one corner. We had a tap room that was owned by an old-time boxer, Harry "Kid" Brown. His brother was Joe Brown, the guy who did all the sculptures down at the Vet. Joe is quite a guy.

Went to Southern High. And then there was Foreman's Candy Store. Joey Foreman became a movie star and a comedian. . . . The store was the next street down, on Marshall and Johnston.

" . . . Joey opened up an awful lot of the big shows in Vegas after he left Philadelphia. But you know what was really funny? When he was a kid, he wouldn't wait on you and he wouldn't let his mother wait on you unless you listened to his whole spiel. She was proud of him. I'll tell you where he became hot. You remember the Kefauver hearings? [He could imitate] Frank Costello, Estes Kefauver. He was on the *Ed Sullivan Show* a half a dozen times with that. Unfortunately, he passed away in the early '80s of emphysema. His dad was Abe Foreman, the local politician. He got all the tickets fixed."

After college, Esher taught school and coached basketball at Simon Gratz High School. He married in 1953 and transferred two years later to his alma mater, Southern, where he coached basketball from 1958 to 1970. Today he is alumni president.

"We send out 5,000 16-page newsletters once a year all over the world to alumni. We have a $400,000 scholarship fund, and that wasn't given by one guy. That was given by mostly with $50, $100 contributions. It's amazing. South Philly people have always been generous. I run about 20 to 30 class reunions a year. They usually ask me to come and say a few words about the school. Inevitably, the class will give a couple hundred dollars to the scholarship fund. That's nice, it's really nice.

"I have to tell you a story that a guy told at a reunion we had in California. This guy was stationed in Japan right after the war, and he was given 30 days' leave. So he goes down to Hong Kong and he walked into a store. A lot of bickering there, negotiating with the owner. He walks out. A little while later, he comes back. They start to negotiate again. Walks out. Comes back. Finally, the owner says, 'I'm giving this away to you.'

"And the South Philly guy says, 'Well, look, we had a good negotiation.' Now this is 9,000 miles away from home, and the store guy pointed at him and says, 'You know what, you must be from South Philly.' The Chinese guy said that. It's unreal."

The storekeeper in Hong Kong may have known about South Philadelphia in the 1940s, but Epifanio DeJesus' parents did not. When they arrived in the city in 1949, all they knew was that there were doctors here that could fix their son's foot.

Urbiadelia and Epifanio, Sr., arrived with a hope that someone could help their son. "They didn't know English at all, and they didn't bring me here with any referral. Someone back home said, Go to the United States, and someone else said, You should get the kid into the University of Penn. We arrived 3 o'clock in the morning at Idlewild in New York. We stayed at the airport until approximately 6 o'clock that night, when they located a relative," his mother's brother, Hector Olmo.

"We started talking to people at the airport. They knew him and that he lived in Camden. That took 12 hours, communicating in Spanish. This is what my parents told me. I was four years old, but I still remember . . . bits and pieces. The relative put us in a car, a '36 Pontiac, oil leaking. We had the oil

Albert Olmo (right), Eppi's uncle, sits with Eppi's grandparents, Maria and Pedro Olmo, in the DeJesus's first Philadelphia apartment at 10th and Spruce in 1950. The woman in the reflection is Eppi's mother. Courtesy of Eppi DeJesus

can in the car. I still remember the smell. Every so often, they would get out on Route 130. The turnpike wasn't built yet."

Twenty-four hours after they had arrived in New York, the family reached Philadelphia. "I remember the signs used to say 'Room to Let,' not room for rent. We landed at 1023 Spruce Street, second floor back."

His father was the youngest of 11 children, his mother the oldest of 13, but Eppi was their only child.

"My toes would touch the ground, but the heel would be lifted, like the way a ballet dancer would walk. But I managed. I was pretty spirited and pretty, how can I say, daring. I later became a gymnast and body builder and everything else. I remember running with kids and playing and going through the alleys.

"My friends were either Jewish or black. That area during the late '40s, early '50s was not the best area in the world. It had pimps. It had prostitutes. We didn't move to quote, unquote, Society Hill or Washington Square West. It was a slum. Usually one ethnic group was the poorest of the poor. The blacks were at that time, and we were under them because we were the newcomers.

"Those buildings are four stories high, and we lived in the back with no windows. I still remember my . . . dad and his friends, they would all hang out, quote, unquote, on the corner, 'cause that's the way you got fresh air. This is where they got the news, where they got to exchange ideas and things like that."

Through those conversations, his father found construction work and his mother found work sewing in one of the many clothing factories in Center City and North Philadelphia. Unlike their friends on the corner, they never were farm workers. Eppi was cared for by family members from Puerto Rico who had come to join them. In 1951 or 1952, a truant officer asked why this little boy playing in the street was not in school.

"They put me in school, in McCall, and the nurse asked the school doctor to see me. He said, This young man has to get an operation, that this could be corrected. My parents said fine, because that's why I was brought here. No problem. I went through first grade as a normal kid."

But he spent second grade in the hospital. Sixteen months in the hospital and then six or seven months more in a cast. The operation was a fusion of the hip bone.

"For today, it isn't really nothing major, but at that time, it was major, major. I was all cast up, whole body cast, couldn't move, just two holes, one for number one, one for number two. And my parents would carry me everywhere. We moved in 1953 to a third-floor apartment above a liquor store on Fifth Street across from the Super Fresh, between Pine and Spruce. And it was steep. Going up might not be too bad, but you can imagine coming down with a stiff body."

Soon after the operation, his family moved to the 700 block of South Hutchinson Street, close to the Ninth Street Market and to St. Paul's Church, the heart of Italian South Philly. The largest Puerto Rican community was miles away in Spring Garden.

"My father . . . heard that Philadelphia was good and clean, and he heard that South Philadelphia was much quieter than Spring Garden. . . . He's a very gentle person, and he didn't want to be where there was a lot of parties. Throughout their stay at Fifth and Spruce, they used to shop at Ninth Street. They saw this house for sale. It was yellow stucco. In 1954 they paid $6,000 for this house and the house in back on Percy Street, two houses, $3,000 each."

His family moved in on February 4, the first Puerto Ricans on the block, the first in the neighborhood.

"The date is important because that was the day that we put the sofa in, the one right there where you are sitting, and the doorbell rang and someone said to my father, 'Would you mind signing here? We're trying to get the Puerto Ricans out of the neighborhood.'

"So my father . . . looked out and said, 'Oh, so Puerto Ricans are moving out.' He was thinking, Where are they? Obviously, the man at the door didn't know what Puerto Ricans look like, because my father was darker than me. He only had a sixth-grade education, but he could read limited English. . . .

"So my father said, 'Wait a minute. I'll be right back.' He went to the kitchen, got a cleaver, came back and said, 'Where do I sign?' Since then, they love us here. We found out that the people who started the petition didn't even live on the street. They had a car garage across the street. . . . They've denied it, but all the neighbors have told us."

His father was already building homes for a contractor in Willingboro, Cherry Hill, and West Chester, but he never got to buy one of the houses he

The children of six Puerto Rican families all went to Holy Trinity Roman Catholic Church at Sixth and Spruce in 1955. Posing for their First Holy Communion picture are Eppi's mother (top row, far left), Eppi's father (top row, far right), and Eppi (top row, left). Courtesy of Eppi DeJesus

built. "He knew quality. He put on the first Permastone front in the block. Everything we did to this house, the neighbors would run out and do. We became the Joneses."

Eppi had no problems finding friends on Spruce Street and had no problems in South Philadelphia.

"I've been always very flexible, and people don't know what the hell I am anyway. I didn't have an accent. I got along. I used to do everything with the Jewish kids but be bar mitzvahed and go to Hebrew classes. With the blacks, I got along. I guess they thought I was black. Coming down here, the kids thought I was Giuseppi DeJesu, not Eppi DeJesus. They thought I was Sicilian. . . . And the fact that the neighborhood was Catholic, and we were Catholic, helped out because I grew up with their kids. I had no problem."

It was not as perfect as all that. He knew that there were lines that even someone as flexible as he could not cross.

"I didn't let myself feel prejudiced or pressured because I knew how far to go. An example is the whole dating thing. I never got to date white American girls, because there was something in us, in the whole family, that said you only go so far. And that was one of the things you didn't do at that time. It wasn't a matter of pressure from anyone, 'cause it never became an issue."

Eppi still lives in that Hutchinson Street house. He married a girl from Puerto Rico and raised two sons, another Eppi and Gabriel, both of whom are grown now and live downtown, and both of whom, their father wants you to know, dated "white American girls." He has little bad to say about the neighborhood unless you mention Darien Street.

He married in 1968 and, like most young couples, the newlyweds wanted to find their own place. They did, on the 700 block of South Darien, a block away from his parents' home.

"A block away, but 180 degrees different. The neighbors were much colder than Hutchinson Street. . . . By '68, folks knew what a Puerto Rican was or had their image of one. I was in Temple Law School, and I would come in with my law books, and you could feel the stares. You could feel the uncomfortableness. They don't know what to make of us. We were 24 years old. We certainly didn't have any parties or anything. They just felt uncomfortable that an Italian had not bought the house, that the block was broken.

"We thought of ourselves as South Philadelphians, . . . living among Italians all this time. We knew the customs, the cultural bit. And I'm saying Italian, meaning the second- or third- or fourth-generation Italian, the ones that didn't even speak Italian. We thought we'd just blend right in, but we didn't."

It was not easy back then to get newly married couples to move back with their parents, but Eppi and his wife hurried back to Hutchinson Street soon after their first son was born. An Italian bought the house on Darien Street. "We had paid $3,000 for that house. We made them pay $6,800 a year later. You want the Italians, well, we made them pay. Why not?"

No influx of Puerto Ricans followed the DeJesus family downtown. Eppi remembers just three other Hispanics at Southern. When he tells other Puerto Ricans where he lives, "there is a look in their eyes of 'You're crazy,' but then a look of 'You really must be tough.' Not just Puerto Ricans, but blacks, too.

May 25, 1968, wedding day for Eppi and Carmen on Hutchinson Street. Notice the Permastone front that Eppi's father put up. The bride is third from the left, and the future mother-in-law is next to her. The gentleman is Arturo Rodriguez, who gave Carmen away. In addition to the four bridesmaids and the flower girl, that white object in the lower left-hand corner is a '65 Pontiac Bonneville. Courtesy of Eppi DeJesus

183

This 1985 collection of sluggers and smooth fielders is the Ninth and Christian baseball team, 12- to 14-year-old league. Eppi's son, Gabriel DeJesus, is on the far right on the second row. In the upper left-hand corner is Christine Capra, the only girl on the team and, with Gabriel, one of the team's two pitchers. The uniforms were paid for by Salvatore Testa, a local mobster who was shot to death in September, 1984. Courtesy of Eppi DeJesus

And I tell them no. It's one of the safest neighborhoods I can live in. Everybody looks out for each other. Right now, they know that I have a guest. They'll know when you leave, and they can tell me what time you came in. At times, we felt that it was meddling, but at other times it's been a good thing. I've been able to have jobs that I've traveled and my wife and kids have stayed here safe. I have not had any problems. On the contrary. They make sure you have food. Can we get you anything? Every Sunday morning, there's a loaf of bread inside the screen door from the next door neighbor. It's a gift and it's been going on way beyond 20 years. If it's not that, it's other neighbors. Pasta, this, that, or whatever. . . . People share their house keys with us. We have bowls full. We share car registrations."

Eppi worked for years in the community relations office at Temple University. He spent his days in North Philadelphia and he came home to South Philadelphia, and it was a sanctuary. Today, he is a recruiter for the School District of Philadelphia, and home is still a sanctuary. The church is there, the market is there, his family, his doctor, his friends, and his memories: his son, Gabby, marching with the Oregon Brigade on New Year's; Ernest Evans, later known as Chubby Checker, singing in school; chaise longues on the sidewalk, sagging under the weight of perspiring neighbors on hot summer nights.

"Did I tell you that my best friend growing up was John Minniti? Do you know who my son Eppi's best friend was? John Minniti's son." He likes the continuity of that. His values are the same as his neighbors'. Don't bother anyone, but be a good friend. People know the difference downtown.

And the people who owned the garage, the ones who tried to chase his father out? What happened to them? "Those people have left and I'm still living here. I'm still around. We've lived in harmony."

184

Joseph Dominic Evancich lived in harmony, too, but in the beginning his brother, Mike the fighter, had to bust a few heads because the neighbors didn't like the newcomers. Evancich is a Croatian name, but the Austrians were in power when his parents left the island near Trieste, so he says he is Austrian. Not many people have anything against Austria. Joe was born in 1914 on the 100 block of Monroe, the fifth of seven children born to Nicoletta and Ed, who arrived here as teenagers.

Joseph M. Evancich is Joe's only child. He says: "I never found out the reason why they came to this country, but my grandfather came over first and my grandmother came over later. They didn't know one another. It was one of those marriages arranged by the families. She came right off the boat and then got married."

Nicoletta and Ed lived on Monroe Street, then American Street near Bainbridge, and finally Front Street near Kenilworth, the 700 block. Their son Joseph Dominic says it was a "terrific house. That house was a three-story monster, a big parlor, living room, kitchen, three bedrooms upstairs, a bath coming between, and a third floor with two bedrooms. It even had a little attic. No, no indoor plumbing. Had an outhouse in the back. We had coal heat, and we had one of them gas heaters up in the bathroom or in the kitchen, and that's the only place it was warm."

Next door lived the Lopez family. They were Italian and Polish. On the other side was a Polish family, Kenevich, but they changed their name to Conwell. Joe never changed his name, but his friends made Evancich into Evans and his mother called him Yosie, which became Yussie, so he was known as Yussie Evans.

"My father was a longshoreman. He did a lot of bridge painting and he was a rigger. I used to go down there at lunchtime, and he'd ask me to pull the ropes when he was making a net on Pier 48, Washington and Delaware Avenue. He worked off and on. He was one of them men of leisure. And I tell you, whenever he got work, he made money. When he made a lot of money, he'd go to gamble, but he was still a great guy."

His parents did not go to church often, but when they did, it was at St. Philip. "They wouldn't have been able to go to St. Stanislaus. In them days, you either had to be married to a Polish girl or be Polish. My wife went there when she was little with her brothers. They walked from Mifflin Street to Fitzwater."

Joe played ball at Stanfield Playground, Front and Lombard, and at Shot Tower, and at a filthy field at Delaware Avenue and Fitzwater that all the boys called Shitty's. His favorite candy store was Fagan's, Front and South.

He quit school after the eighth grade. "Nobody was working. That was the Depression, the '30s. I had a sister who was blind, Helen, and my sister Mary, well, she had just got married. Then it was Mike, he's the professional fighter. My brother John, my mother, father, and myself. Do you know what we were living on? Three dollars a week, and we got that from welfare, like the Salvation Army. You want to hear the story?

"We mortgaged the house on Front Street four times. I don't know how my mother did it. She was a genius. She kept that family together for all those years. She died young—65.

John Evancich, Joe D.'s older brother, playing basketball in 1933 at the Stanfield Playground, Front and Lombard. That's Front Street behind him. Courtesy of Joseph D. Evancich

"My brother Mike worked at American Bag at Water and South. Where I lived was not even a whole block from there. The machinery he was working on gave him hives, and he couldn't handle it. So my brother sent me down there to take his place, and he decided to become a boxer. The first two years, I ran three bag machines. Made paper bags. Got three dollars a week for two years. I cursed my brother I don't know how many times for those two years. It was like the salt mines."

He worked in the salt mines for 30 years. A union came in and got him better wages. In 1940, he married Jessie—Jessica Barbara Cielesz—a Polish girl he met on the Wilson Line.

"They used to have the Wilson Line going up the Delaware. Used to have music and dancing and they sold beer. Then we'd go to different clubs together. We used to go to the Silver Slipper Club on Washington Avenue between Moyamensing and Third."

His son says that his dad may have had it tough as a kid, but that his mother and her two brothers had it worse.

"Their parents, my grandparents, lived at 110 Mifflin Street. They were from, I believe, around Warsaw. He worked in the sugar house, Delaware and Reed. Worked a lot of hours. We don't know what happened to my grandmother, but somewhere in her mid-30s, I don't know if she was a manic depressive or what, but she just stopped talking. It was gradual. Eventually, they just came in the white coats and took her away. Nobody knows where. I don't know how much time after that my grandfather died.

Joseph D. Evancich, his mother, Nicoletta, and his brother, Mike, the boxer, on the right. In front of Mike is his daughter and in front of Joe is his niece. They are all in front of 710 South Front Street in 1939, the family home before the move to Fitzwater Street. Courtesy of Joseph D. Evancich

"My mother must have been about 15. Uncle Walt, the next brother, was 13, and below that was like a nine-year-old. Now, they would have been put away, foster homes, whatever they had then, but the woman who was eventually my godmother, Marie Sullivan, a neighbor on Mifflin Street who was moving up to Second and Catharine, said, 'You're not going anywhere. We have a lot of room on the third floor. You live up on the third floor.' So they lived on the third floor."

In 1941, his parents married, much to the consternation of his grandparents. "My Aunt Mary told me that they were never very happy that all their children married Polacks."

All of the children, all seven of them, married Poles? "Married Polish," says Joseph Dominic Evancich with a shrug.

At first, Joe and Jessie did not live together. "I gotta tell that story. See, I was taking care of my family, and she was taking care of her two brothers. We couldn't live together because we couldn't afford two rents. I was the only one working in my family at the time."

But somehow they found time to be together. Their son was born nine and a half months later, and they finally got a place of their own. His wife's two brothers stayed with them. Stayed 51 years.

His son says: "My dad is probably closer to his brothers-in-law than he is to his own brothers. They were my uncles, but really my brothers. Three of us slept in one room . . . bunk beds, me on top. Everybody used to ask me, Where did you ever study? 'Cause I was an honor student all the way through.

"I went to St. Stanislaus, which is where my uncles and mother went. From there, I went to LaSalle High School, which I didn't want to do because I didn't want to leave the neighborhood or the corner. To leave South Philadelphia to

Joseph M. Evancich sitting in front of his home at 145 Fitzwater in 1947. That was "the best house of all," says his father, Joseph D. "So many good times there." Courtesy of Joseph D. Evancich

go to La Salle, it was like another world. Eight years I did that. I went to LaSalle College, which is on the same campus.

"I grew up at 145 Fitzwater Street. We rented it. . . . I grew up Polish really 'cause it was predominantly Polish in the area. We had maybe a couple of Irish, and there was one Italian family. But everybody was pretty much Polish."

Except for school, he didn't leave the neighborhood much. "Once you went beyond Spruce, you were pretty much in a commercial area, and that was a boundary. And who knew where North Philly started? All we knew was that it was north of Market, but nobody really thought maybe we should go up to Fishtown or Kensington. Never no reason to.

"Well, if you went to Third or Fourth Street, you had the blacks. So you're not going up there at night. It was sort of an unspoken rule. They didn't come over east of Third, and we didn't go in there. They never came through. There was nothing to go through to. It was the river. On the other side of Third and Fourth may as well have been Europe or Asia. Was also an Italian section. My partner at work right now, Frank Abruzzi, grew up at Sixth and Wharton. I didn't know any of his friends, except maybe . . . playing ball together. No socializing. Italians . . . [didn't] date Two-Streeters. It was a pretty rough neighborhood in those days, all Polish and Irish.

"Going south, you start running into guys you knew, but it was a different territory, and you had to have good reasons for being down there. They didn't like you dating girls in their neighborhood, but they tolerated it. Washington Avenue was the boundary. You start getting downtown when you go across Washington Avenue. The funny thing is, this Polish area has always been here. Even in my mother's day, when she was young, north of the tracks, that's what they used to say, north of the tracks on Washington Avenue."

An institutional bond broker, he lives today just a few blocks north of South Philadelphia. His father lives on the 200 block of Fitzwater, across from St. Stanislaus. His son bought the house for his parents.

"My father has friends in the neighborhood, people he's known all his life. Me? I'm very proud to be from South Philly. It's one of the few neighborhoods left in the United States from what I understand. . . . When I say neighborhoods, I'm talking about people who have been there for years."

But he left, as did most of his generation. "The generation in the '60s and '70s, we didn't get married and buy a house three doors away in the same neighborhood. We were going to college. We were doing different things. . . . There's another world, and it's hard to live in that world if you were living around your uncles and aunts. You stay in the parish or stand on the corner, and people started to say they were being left behind. So all those people left, and now they sit around and talk about where they're from. . . . It's funny how people now are coming back to the city, back to South Philly.

"Most of the people who grew up in neighborhoods like South Philly usually have a lot of street smarts, and it helps them in life. Sure, there's some people who never saw beyond the corner, who never thought there was anything else they needed in life. A guy quits to get a job right out of high school, he doesn't go to college. You're studying every night with no money in your pocket, and this guy got a new car, he's buying whiskey from the bar when all you can afford is a Rolling Rock. That's the only drawback I can see. They don't realize that there's an outside world. They think this is the only world."

His father listens. There are no drawbacks for him. "You'll never me get me out. I just love the place, that's all."

It will not be as hard to get Sophal Hing to leave. Studying quantum physics at Fifth and Cross Streets is not what he has in mind.

He has lived in South Philadelphia since 1980, except for a year in West Philadelphia. Never at one address more than two years. West of Broad Street, east of Broad, he doesn't remember all the houses. His mother was married twice. He was born in 1975, oldest child of three. His sister, five years younger, is Chan Than. His brother, nine years younger, was born in Philadelphia. "My mom, when she first came here, was driving a lot. The only name she could think of was King of Prussia." His brother's name is Prussia.

That's amusing. Getting to this country was not. "It was the post-Vietnamese war, and the Vietnamese were still in Cambodia. The reason we left our home and tried to escape was because my mom thought my dad had died. He was a Khmer Rouge. He had left to go off to fight. She never heard from him again, so there was nothing there for us.

"I was a little boy, and my sister was not born yet. We escaped and went to a refugee camp in Thailand. Then, all of a sudden, my aunt, my mother's sister, got married, and she came here with her husband. Here to Philadelphia, and she sponsored us in 1980. I think we were in the camp less than a year. I was about five. We came in the fall."

The first house was on 22nd Street, he's not sure where. The family moved a lot, but he spent most of his school years at Kirkbride, at Seventh and Dickinson, and at Central High School, in the Olney section of the city.

189

When he was little, he stayed close to his mother and the house. "I was inside most of the time. Didn't really go out, didn't talk much. The only Cambodian friends I knew was at school. I was shy. The first time I went to kindergarten, I was afraid, but I did not want to cry because I was the oldest one in the class. I did not understand the teacher that much. All I did was eat snacks, play, sleep, and write ABC, so it wasn't hard. After a while I got used to it. The others kids were mostly Italians and Spanish, and black. The Asians came later on."

His first friend in kindergarten was Nicholas Meitzler. They didn't talk much, but they didn't fight, either. "We were together since kindergarten, but it wasn't until fifth, sixth grade they included me in what they did. We were good friends.

"When I was small, all I did was go to school and come home, and my friends in school were not that racist. . . . Now, and a couple of years ago, when I walk down the streets, people are calling me names. . . . Eighth Street and Ninth, sometimes Fifth, people going, 'Gook, go back to where you came from.'"

Maybe they were calling him names when he was smaller too, he concedes, but he didn't notice.

"Seventh and eighth grade, I changed. Class friends started inviting me to things. I went to South Street. Never saw South Street until a few years ago. I never went past my house, past my neighborhood. This neighborhood I lived in the most, around Dickinson Street, Fifth, Sixth. I've always lived in houses right close to here. The people here, I know them. I don't really know them, but I see their faces, they see my face."

His mother still speaks to him in Cambodian, but he knows as many English words as he does Cambodian. Other than language, not much in his life is Cambodian anymore. He dreams in English.

"My mom still does all the Cambodian stuff. She goes to the Cambodian New Year, she goes to the temple, has parties and dresses up. I'm the only Christian in my family. I don't really participate in any of their rituals. My sister and my brother are Buddhist like my mother, but they really don't believe.

"The food is still Cambodian, but I can tell the difference between my mom's cooking and my aunt's. I go to my aunt's and my grandmother's place, and they still make the Cambodian foods that I used to eat. My mom's added her own little style, and it's not Cambodian food as I remember it. Instead of frying the chicken and adding little spices, she puts barbecue sauce on it."

His father is still alive and is the strongest link Sophal has to Cambodia. "When my father writes me, I think back. He's remarried and I have half-brothers and sisters over there. It takes so long for letters to go back and forth."

His mother, Sokhom Hing, is on public assistance. In the warm weather, she joins the fruit pickers on New Jersey farms. Once those pickers were Puerto Rican, but today many are Southeast Asian immigrants from South Philadelphia.

High school has taken him out of South Philadelphia, and it is a trip he doesn't mind. He has made new friends. "The bad part is we only meet in school. The good part is they tell me stuff about their neighborhoods. One of

*Sophal Hing outside the
Academy of Music, following
his graduation from Central
High School in June 1995. If
you look closely, you can see
the reflection of the photographer—his brother, Prussia.
Courtesy of Sophal Hing*

my friends lives in a house somewhere, it's like a suburban lifestyle thing. Not
too much crime there. This other friend lives in North Philadelphia, and he tells
me there's a lot of drugs and shootin'.

"When I asked my friends about South Philadelphia, everybody keeps saying this bad stuff. They say that it's the worst place to be; you can get killed
walking up the neighborhood down there. I said I didn't think it was that bad.
One of my friends who lives in North Philadelphia was scared to come here
alone."

Sophal is a member of the Youth Task Force, a local group of adults and
teenagers that works to reduce violence. "We split up in different groups. We
raise money for the homeless, we have response teams that respond to news articles. We've participated in anti-drug marches, opened a day camp for children, and we throw parties to keep kids off the street at night."

But he will probably not be in that organization much longer. Sophal began college at St. Joseph's in September 1995, commuting from South Philadelphia. He wants to say goodbye to the neighborhood as soon as he can.

"I want to study quantum physics. . . . I want to do research, and I don't
think South Philadelphia is the right place for me to do that. I want to move
somewhere more quiet, somewhere like the suburbs."

191

10

One Family: Bennie Dubin's Story

My father's mouth used to round itself into an exagerated little O and his eyebrows would erupt in glee when I Hit the Penny. Sometimes he would split a Tastykake Junior in half and put ice cream in the middle and share it with me. He had good card sense and won a lot of money playing knock rummy. "I knock 'em dead," he'd say. He used to slip me a few bucks after he had won.

When I was little, he used to call me a genius in front of people. Maybe I should have gotten used to his boastful pride, but I never did. When I got older and went to work for newspapers, he would introduce me as "my son, the writer," and embarrass me.

I've been thinking—daydreaming, really—a lot about my dad. I'm not much of a believer in God or heaven and that's become troubling for the first time. See, if there isn't any heaven, then I'll never see my dad again or hear him exaggerate about me. I try not to have that daydream much, because it makes me cry.

My father, Benjamin Dubin, 74, died in February of a sudden heart attack. There were no momentous last words that I didn't say that I should have. He knew I loved him. He was not a man who said "I love you" very often to me, but I was always warmed by his love and kindness. He praised me all my life.

After he died, my daughter Minna, who is seven and a half, accused me of being a liar. I had told her that Grandpa's stroke would keep him in the hospital for a while. And he might not be able to pick her up like he used to, but don't worry, Grandpa would be OK.

"Daddy, you lied. Grandpa's dead."

I explained the best I could, but I don't think she was satisfied.

A couple of months later, I was telling her about a colleague who had a heart transplant that had saved his life. After questions about the operation— "You mean they took his heart out? Gross. How did he live?"—she asked, "Why didn't Grandpa get a heart transplant?"

I explained the best I could, but I don't think she was satisfied.

I was 30 minutes away from visiting him that Sunday morning when the doctor called to tell me he had bad news. I didn't know what bad news he could be talking about. It was just a stroke. There would be rehabilitation, maybe a year of it, but he'd be OK. His mind was fine, his spirits were fine, and he could move both legs and one arm. He'd deal one-handed if necessary. He'd be fine.

It was a massive heart attack, the doctor said on the phone. He had eaten his breakfast. When the attendant came back for the tray, my dad didn't look good. A nurse was summoned and she called the code, I learned later. Just like on television. They tried to bring him back, but it was too late.

Myocardial infarction is what the death certificate said. My dad would have mispronounced it. Some words he just mispronounced, but he mangled the language more than he had to. It was his way of getting me, his way of pushing the buttons that would make me crazy. Sometimes, he would start laughing before I could correct him. I miss his laugh.

When I was little, he'd ask not just how I did in my tests, but if the teacher announced the marks in class. As an adult, he often asked what the "big bosses" said about my stories. He worried that I didn't earn enough, but was always reluctant to ask how much money I made. A couple of months before he died, he asked if I earned "at least $30,000." When I told him I earned more than that, he was so pleased.

My father was a giver—toys to his granddaughter, jokebooks to his grandson, a couple of dollars to a friend who needed it. My dad never drove, but he always seemed to be in Chinatown on Sundays, down the shore on weekends and in the mountains for a week or so in the summer. People took my dad places. He didn't hear very well and didn't see very well, but everybody liked Bennie Dubin and wanted him with them. He was good times, a nice guy with a big heart.

I guess a fella can't ask for a better legacy. It's funny. I've spent a lot of my life feeling awkward and uncomfortable with my dad's boastful and, sometimes, blind praise of me. (It wasn't just me; he bragged about my mother, who's probably the only one of us who deserved it, my big brother, sisters-in-law, nieces, nephews.) But here I am, boasting about my father. I'm my father's son, aren't I? My dad would have gotten a big kick out of that.

That was written in July 1989, five months after my father died. He was born in June 1914, the oldest of Minnie Cohen and Aaron (everyone called him Sam) Dubin's three sons. Sam was the second of nine children born to Beryl Dubinsky and Etta Beck, of Chanuble, about 12 kilometers from Kiev and a long way from South Philadelphia.

Isaac was their first-born child. Over the next 20 years came Sam, Ida, Rose, and Yussel, whose name was never Americanized because he died over there in a childhood swimming accident. Then Harry, Max, Mamie, and Abe. Sam was five-foot-six, the tallest Dubinsky. This family of shrimps fled the pogroms in 1905 with six children and one grandchild, Morris, Isaac's son. Mamie and Abe would be born in New Jersey.

How they came to New Jersey is a question. No papers exist to explain, and no one alive ever thought to ask, so we have only family lore to tell the story.

The Dubinskys did not go through Ellis Island, living first on a Wisconsin farm. Beryl had worked as a forester in Russia (*Dube* is Russian for oak; it is likely that my lineage is one of wee woodsmen), so he might have been comfortable working outdoors. But the family was not happy in Wisconsin and stayed less than a year. Why they picked New Jersey is unclear, but someone must have had a relative there, perhaps Etta, my great-grandmother. The

It is 1930, and here are four generations of Dubins. The man with the white beard is Beryl Dubin. Seated across from him is his oldest child, Isaac. Looming above them is Morris, Isaac's son. And in Beryl's hands is his grandaughter, Phyllis, Morris' daughter. Courtesy of Joe Dubin

family was in Camden, the 600 block of Ferry Street, not too long after 1905. The *-SKY* was gone by now, and the short people now had a shorter name. Beryl was a *shamas* in a local synagogue, a tiny man, perhaps four-foot-nine, with blue eyes and a full beard, who made a little money selling this and that from a pushcart in Philadelphia. His favorite word in English was "bum." He liked to swim around Steel Pier in Atlantic City, floating on his back to rest, elfin body barely underwater, beard buoyant and white like a life preserver.

Etta was sick a lot, and by the late 1920s she was not well enough to cook for her children and grandchildren when they would come to visit on the ferry from Philadelphia for Sukkot and Passover. Mamie, the youngest daughter, made the *matzoh brie* for the family. My father and the other grandchildren mixed club soda with the sweet red wine. Mamie and Abe took care of their mother until her death in about 1931. Beryl died nine years later.

None of Beryl and Etta's children graduated from high school. They lived in the Jewish enclaves of Strawberry Mansion, West Philadelphia, and South Philadelphia, and in Camden. Isaac, or Itzie, the oldest, was a cabinet finisher and the most religious. Abe, the youngest and most Americanized, was the head of Camden's Sanitation Commission, a feisty pol known as "Abie the Jew."

Ida, the oldest daughter, married Hymie Cohen, a furrier. Hymie and Ida were part of a double relationship in the family involving my grandparents. A brother and a sister, Hymie and Minnie Cohen, married a sister and a brother, Ida and Sam Dubin.

Ida and Hymie had brothers and sisters, but no children. When she died in the 1960s, each of her nieces and nephews, including my father, was bequeathed $2,500.

Sister Rose, five-foot-three, was taller than most of the Dubin men. Like Ida, she married a furrier. His name was Dandy and he had a toupee. Their four children have died.

Harry had a shoe store in Camden around the corner from his parents' home. He couldn't make a living, so he and his wife, Pearl, moved and opened a restaurant-bakery near Sixth and Poplar in Philadelphia. It was not terribly successful, either.

Max earned the most money of Beryl and Etta's children, and lost the most as well. He sewed dresses, designed gowns, and managed factories in the needle trade. He had the first car in the family and lived in Ohio, New York, and Philadelphia. He bought the only boat in the family and was the Dubin's first bankruptcy. He bounced back. Lillian's, the dress shop that he named after his daughter, was on South Seventh Street for years. He and Abie were the bulldogs in the family.

Mamie the nurturer took care of her mother and, later, her sister Ida. Late in life, she married Leonard Ramov, a hotel clerk. They had one son, Eddie, a sickly youngster who was picked on by other boys, often non-Jews. He became a high school math teacher and the leader of the Jewish Defense League in Philadelphia. He died in 1984 at the age of 47.

Sam, my grandfather, and Mamie were the poorest of the children. He worked on Pine Street for a cousin named Beck, cleaning and polishing antiques. He bought things at auctions and tried to peddle them from a horse and wagon. Sam was a gentle man with a soft voice and a strong back, a failed entrepreneur with no bulldog in him. He didn't make much money, but worked long hours trying. When he wasn't working, he was in the synagogue at Sixth and Wolf. He was the first Dubin in South Philadelphia.

He and Minnie had three boys: Benjamin, born in 1914; Louis, born in 1916 and known in the family by his Jewish name, Label; and Isadore, or Eddie, in 1918. No one in the family called him Isadore or Eddie. He was Bibbs.

Sam had problems paying rent, and the family moved a lot. Bibbs was born at 334 Washington Avenue, just a few doors down from a Polish club. When he was small, they moved south to 416 Wilder Street, between Dickinson and Reed. The rent was usually cheaper the further south you went. No indoor bathroom, not much light. Too poor to own bikes, the boys had to rent them, and Ben never learned how to ride (nor did either of his sons). The times that they had a few extra pennies, they'd go to the Penn Movies on Wilder, just a couple of blocks east of their house. Ben was good in school, Label was the ballplayer, Bibbs was very sick with bronchial asthma. The doctors thought he wouldn't survive childhood. He did.

In 1928, the family moved again, this time south to 444 Durfor, just south of Wolf, one of South Philadelphia's many toothpick-thin, one-way, park-on-one-side-only streets. Learn to drive and park there, you can drive and park anywhere. Later they would move to 451, closer to Fifth Street. Durfor Street was good for the Dubins. They didn't get rich, but all the boys met the women they would marry: Bibbs met Clara, Label met Lillian, and Ben met Mary Alterman, my mother.

The Altermans weren't rich either, but their pockets were full compared with the Dubins'.

The Dubins were gone from Russia when Morris Alterman and Sara Sokoletsky married. Their first son, Sam, was born in the Ukraine in 1908. Morris came to the United States several years later and lived with his wife's sister in South Philadelphia. His wife and son arrived in 1913. He sewed linings into fur coats, a finisher in the business, a furrier to everyone else. He was active in the fur workers' union. There would be three more children, Louis, Mary, and Hyman, and a move to 608 Mifflin, a street of Jews and Italians, immigrants all.

In the mid-1920s, they rented their home and moved to Fifth and Wolf Streets, leasing the candy store on the northeast corner from the Abramowitz family. But the Abramowitzes kept raising the rent, so after a year or two the Altermans bought the property next door on Fifth Street and opened their own candy store. Their former store was vacant.

Hymie Alterman: "I think my mother thought the Abramowitzes were going to open up some sort of a little 5 and 10, but they opened up a candy store. It was two stores, wall to wall. I was, like, six years old, and they had these

One Family:
Benny Dubin's Story

The Altermans on the 600
block of Mifflin Street in 1943.
That's Lou on the left, sister
Mary next to him, oldest
brother Sam with the tie, and
the baby of the family, Hymie,
just 22 at the time. The little
boy watching is Donnie, Lou's
son, who would grow up to be
a policeman. Courtesy of
Hymie Alterman

water ice boxes outside. The kids coming to Taggart School from Jackson Street would have to pass our store first. So my mother would stand out there, 'Here's the water ice, here's the water ice, give a penny, a penny.' And the other lady, they couldn't get to her 'cause they had to get past my mother first. My mother would almost grab them by the neck and drag them in. . . ."

His sister and two older brothers helped out, but it was his mother who was in control. "My father couldn't work in the store too good. In those days, a person came with a large pitcher and they'd say, 'Give me for five cents, cherry soda.' So you filled up a large pitcher. Now the fountains were full, just push a thing and flavor would shoot right out. He would come home and would get very upset when he'd give them their nickel's worth in a large pitcher and they'd say, 'Make it a little sweeter.' He'd get very angry. 'You know how much this flavor costs? What the hell do you want for a nickel? I'm giving you a pitcher, giving you eight glasses of good soda.' They'd say, 'But make it sweeter.' He'd go nuts. So my mother was mostly in the store."

Living in a candy store at Fifth and Wolf was not a bad way to grow up. You knew everyone, everyone knew you, and the candy and ice cream was right there. Across the street was the park, a square block of green called Mifflin Square, even though Mifflin Street was four blocks away.

Mary (Alterman) Dubin: "It used to have flowers in the center, and there was water coming out like a spray, a fountain. It was very pretty. People used to picnic in the park. We always felt safe. Everybody felt safe, put blankets out and ate there. And when it got very hot, a lot of people would sleep out there.

"In the store, there was always lots of people, young men that were friendly with my brothers, and they were kidding, teasing. I was the only girl, so my mother, she was always kissing and hugging me. She called me 'Mumala'

197

The bride and groom. Mary Dubin went to a new hairdresser just before the wedding and was disappointed with the results, but her husband thought she looked beautiful. The marriage lasted 52 years. Photo in possession of the author

Mr. and Mrs. M. Alterman
Mr. and Mrs. S. Dubin
request the honor of your presence at the marriage
of their children

Mary

to

Mr. Benjamin Dubin

Saturday evening, March sixth
nineteen hundred and thirty-seven
eight-thirty o'clock sharp

at Savoy Plaza
835-37 N. Broad Street
Philadelphia, Pa.

Bride's Residence
608 Mifflin Street

The 1939 wedding invitation of Benjamin Dubin and Mary Alterman. Courtesy of Mary Dubin.

[little mother]. And I remember thinking it funny when one of the fellas who wasn't Jewish called me *Mumala.*"

Sara worked 14 to 16 hours a day and would sometimes ask one of her children to work while she rested on the leather sofa in the dining room behind the store. Near the sofa was a big radio and a dark-wood buffet, with a big gold and cherry sugar bowl, a tea set, and two large plates on top. The second floor had a living room in the front and three bedrooms, one for the boys, one for Mary, and one for their parents.

The store was full of stuff—fountain counter painted to look like marble, penny candies in jars laid out on the shelves, popsicles in the freezer, jars of coconut chunks that Mary liked, ice cream cones, two cents for a small one, nickle for a large, Tastykakes, frozen bananas dipped in chocolate that Sara made herself, and cigarette packs piled high like Lincoln Logs. Sara couldn't read or write English, but she knew the prices of each pack by its color. And two brown booth phones, ORegon 10–100 and ORegon 10–101. Most people did not have telephones at home in the mid-1920s.

Hymie: "When they would call, I'd pick up the phone, 'Hello?' 'Yeah, listen, can you do me a favor and get Raymond Rivel on the phone?' Well, I knew who Raymond Rivel was, 446 Wolf. I'd say, 'Okay, hold the wire.' I went right away, but they may hold five, ten minutes. . . . I'd wait until he gets done talking, sit right near that phone. He'd come out, 'Here, kid,' hand me a nickel. My sister Mary loved to grab the nickels, too. They used to give her dimes once in a while. I'd get mad."

Ben Dubin spent a lot of time at that candy store, talking to Mary and buying malteds for 15 cents.

Mary: "There was a lot of competition with malteds. Other places made them with a lot of ice in it, so they looked bigger. There was a store, Feldman's, on Snyder Avenue. My mother didn't use ice, just ice cream and milk and malt, and it was good. He'd come in to buy a malted. Mom made him real nice malteds. We used to talk, and we went out together a couple times. My mother asked me whether I liked him. I said, 'He's nice.' So she said, 'Well, you don't think he's coming in here to see me, do you?'"

They married in March 1937. She was 19, he was almost 23, and, at 6 feet, the tallest of Beryl and Etta's grandchildren.

Mary: "My parents liked him. At one time, maybe at a time things were a little better, Mom said to me, 'Maybe we ought to try to help him go to college.' I thought it would look like he's marrying me for money or something, and I didn't know how much money my mother could spare. She had to really sweat over money. So I said, 'No, we'll manage.' Afterward, I regretted it."

The Ben Dubin I knew was a warm, generous man who loved to talk, who laughed and wasn't ashamed to cry, a born salesman who wanted to be a pharmacist but was born too poor to try, a man unable to make the simplest household repair but always able to find people who could, who had no car but loved to be driven, who wanted his sandwiches uncut because they felt bigger that way, a man with small dreams who avoided problems and turned his head when he saw one, someone who *really* enjoyed airplane food. He would grow older and become cautious and worry. He would brag about others, never him-

It is about 1944, and soldier Lou "Label" Dubin visits Mifflin Street and his nephew, Stanley, who is ready with his "gun." Courtesy of Mary Dubin

self. He took no big chances, placed no more big bets. But it wasn't always that way.

The Altermans ultimately lost the candy store wars and moved back to 608 Mifflin in the early 1930s. The newlyweds would live there briefly and then move to an apartment seven doors away. Ben's first job as a married man was selling paper goods.

People had a hard time saying no to his paper cups and plates. After two weeks, it was time to receive a promised salary and a fat commission, but his boss didn't want to pay it all. They argued, and my father, a man I never saw angry enough to hit anyone or do anything to endanger his job, slugged him. The police came, but no one was arrested. It's a story he never told me, but one I would love to have heard.

He went to work on the trains, a candy butcher on the seven-minute run from North Philadelphia Station to 30th Street, seven minutes to sell newspapers and candies and chewing gum from a tray around his neck, seven minutes of hustling on swaying trains on the same route over and over again. During the war, he sold more of everything, including sandwiches to soldiers, and started making money. He'd walk around with a hundred dollars in change in his pockets, his dollar bills crumpled together every which way. Never kept money in a wallet. He had his own table at Leibowitz's Steak House and liked to treat friends. Drive him the four blocks from his house and the dinner was on him. He bet the horses, bet them big, and lost more often than he won.

Hymie: "But the good thing about it was his wife. If he gave her $200, she put $210 in the bank. Where she got the extra $10, I'll never know. Whatever he gave her, she put in more. I don't know how, but she squeezed it."

Ben's brothers Label and Bibbs weren't gamblers, but his brothers-in-law were. Hymie—everyone called him Beezel—and Louie liked to play craps. Beezel even worked for the numbers boys for a while.

When the family moved back to Mifflin Street, Beezel was a teenager who wanted to grow up and be a baseball player like Hank Greenberg. Beezel could hit, but he had a heart murmur. So in 1937 he was a 16-year-old spending his time not on the field, but at Mr. Yuberman's candy store at Sixth and Mifflin. Eddie Serota was always there, sitting in the back at a round marble table.

Hymie: "People would come in and play numbers with him. He sat near a telephone on a wall, an old Keystone telephone. He never wrote anything on paper. Everything was written on this marble table in pencil and he had a wet rag on the table at all times. If somebody hollered, 'Hey, the cops are coming,' he took this wet rag and gave it one wipe and everything disappeared. He'd memorize it in his head. . . . I used to go in and out of the small streets picking up the numbers for him. I'd write it down on a little piece of paper. He used to give me five dollars a week, that mother humper. I used to walk in and out of Hoffman Street from Fifth to Seventh, Dudley from Fifth to Seventh. . . .

"His girlfriend was a stripper. Her name was Amber Dean. This was in 1939. He had a brand new '39 Chrysler. And while he'd be hanging with the racket guys and doing his numbers, he would say, 'Beeze, take Amber to work.' And she would only want me to drive her. She used to say, 'Thomas, let's go to work. Thomas, you gotta wear a chauffeur's hat for me.' So I'd wear a black chauffeur's hat. Thomas sounded more chauffeur-y than Beeze. She worked on the Boulevard; it was called Maggie's on the Boulevard. I'd stand up against the bar and wait for her to get done. I didn't like beer, so I'd drink ginger ale. And this bastard Eddie maybe gave me seven dollars a week for taking numbers and driving her all hours of the night. Then one day I went to him and said, 'Ed, you gotta give me more money, it's getting hot out there, the vice squads, the cops. I'm getting scared.' He said, What, are you crazy? He gave me hell. So I stopped working for him."

Beezel, who would later be a longshoreman, drive a cab, and work at the Philadelphia International Airport, had one more job with the racket guys. Merle, the oldest of his three children, was seven at the time and had just had her tonsils taken out. Ben and Mary's oldest son, Stanley, had been a bar mitzvah the year before; I was six. It was 1953.

"I was working for a syndicate of number backers, and I used to ride the streets and pick up the numbers from the people who had written all their numbers, you know, the take for the day. . . . I got the job through a guy who was working for this guy. He says, Beeze, they need a pick-up man. I was known to be a pick-up man. I had experience when I worked for Eddie Serota in 1939. They were giving me a couple hundred a week to start, two hours a day is all I worked. . . . I would have to go pick up at seven or eight places. I went to a place at Front and Porter to pick up numbers. I went to Fourth and Wolf. I went to a place at Sixth and Oregon and at Sixth and Fitzwater. I met this colored lady at Eighth and Bainbridge. I'd had $50,000 worth of numbers, pieces of paper, hidden in my car."

The numbers were hidden in the car's heater. The heater was under the car, and no one but Beezel knew that if you turned it a certain way, a compartment would open and you could put your arm in there. "But yet 10,000 people would sit there and kick it with their feet and all they saw was a heater that drew heat.

"One day, I'm coming down Bainbridge and let's say I had to be there 2:30; the lady's waiting for me on the corner, and she had this little package in her hand. As I approached her, like I'm ten houses away, I look in my mirror to make sure that nobody is around. This car was behind me. . . . Plainclothes cops. I knew they were cops. I knew it. As I'm getting to her, I'm going 'Back off, back off,' but she comes right out and stops me. It was either stop or run her over. I'm telling her to get away, get away, but she couldn't understand. She stopped me cold turkey in the middle of the street and says, Here, and they saw it.

"When she gave it to me, I ducked down to open the thing, got rid of it fast. I had to go down Sixth Street, there was a guy waiting for me on Christian, and here I was at Eighth and Bainbridge. I got as far as Sixth Street, and they pulled me over. 'Where's the package the lady gave you?'

"I said, 'What lady?' They were pretty sure there was numbers slips. They threw my seats out on the street. They said, 'Look, we saw this son of a bitch bend down, we saw it. We saw him take it. Where's the package?'

"I said, "Look, officer, my cigarettes fell out of my pocket while I was driving so I only bent down to pick them up.'

"'The thing that she gave you, don't tell us, we saw.'

"I said, 'I never got nothing off of her. She was trying to hustle me or something.' They had my seats, like I say, outside on the street. They couldn't find nothing. They turned me loose right there."

Beezel and his wife, Elizabeth, known as Leah to the family, were already living on the 500 block of Tree, between Jackson and Wolf. Ben and Mary had stayed in the apartment on Mifflin Street until 1947, when she was pregnant with me. Then they moved to a home on the 400 block of Wolf, half a block from where the candy store had been. Leah's father had done the renovation. Their little boy, Stanley, was eight years old, and he didn't want to leave his friends on Mifflin Street.

Stanley Dubin: "The 400 block of Wolf was a bigger street, and the houses were newer than on Mifflin. The houses had showers. We didn't have showers on Mifflin Street."

He made new friends—Barry Fishbein, whose parents had the grocery at Fourth and Wolf, and Sheldon and Stanley Goldstein, who lived across the street. He played ball at the park, at the Taggart and Sharswood schools, and at Furness, the junior high. He played ping pong and learned to box at the Police Athletic League at Fourth and Snyder, just a few doors from where Uncle Louie lived. Louie and Sam were his mother's eldest brothers, and they each had one son, Sam's Arthur and Louie's Don. The three cousins learned how to swim together at the YMHA on Pine Street. On weekends, Lou and Sam would take the boys down to the Lakes to play football and baseball. Ben sometimes played basketball with his son, shooting a two-hand set shot and laughing at his lost skills, but he worked more often than he played. All the men played

ball, all the boys played ball. Ben took his son to Connie Mack Stadium for Phillies' twi-nighters, taking the subway to Broad and Lehigh and walking up to 21st with the crowds, Ben holding the sandwiches that Mary had made. The walk and the crowds were as much fun as the game.

Sometimes Ben, Mary, and Stanley would see a show uptown at the Earle Theater and eat out. They'd go in town, or in the neighborhood at Gansky's or Uhr's. All of Stanley's grandparents and four of his five uncles lived within five blocks of his home. Only Ben's brother Label had moved out, and he would come back to visit. Uncle Sam lived at 610 Mifflin, next door to his parents, and all the family was on Mifflin Street each Sunday. Someone was always in the house on Wolf Street—Hymie making Ben laugh, Sam kidding his little sister, Mary, *Bubba* Minnie eating in the kitchen and telling everyone not to worry because God will help. Lots of family.

Stanley: "Everybody was about the same. All the fathers worked. All the mothers stayed home. . . . Well, some people had more, like Mr. and Mrs. Goldstein, and there was a magistrate, John O'Malley, and maybe a few others. I mean, the Goldsteins had the first TV. They had the first car. They had a pinball machine downstairs. . . . And that was a status in that time, having a pinball machine. We had a cellar; they had a basement. They had the nicest house on the block, but there was no jealousy. The Goldsteins, they were so nice. They invited everybody to watch the TV and play the pinball machine."

Stanley is married now, lives in Overbrook Park, has a grown son, and has been out of South Philadelphia since 1966. He says South Philadelphia in the 1950s was the best. It was polly seeds and half ball, hanging with your friends

In March 1947, Mary Dubin is eight months pregnanat with her second son. That's her against the wall, second from the left. Her husband, Ben, is on one side, and her niece, Layne, Sam's daughter, is on the other. Leah Alterman is to the right, next to her husband, Hymie. On the front row, there's Don Alterman on the left. Then come his parents, Lou and Mary Alterman, Mary's mother-in-law, Sara Alterman, and her second husband, David Checker. Courtesy of Hymie Alterman

Stanley Dubin, 13 years old, became a bar mitzvah in 1952. His parents, Mary and Ben, and his little brother, Murray, stand with him in this family photo. Photo in possession of the author

on the corner. Itzie had the store for a while, then it was Harry's, then Shirley's, but it didn't matter. Your father was there sometimes, your uncles, even your little brother, and everyone knew everyone. It was sitting on the porch with your dad, transistor radio at his ear, listening to the Phillies. It was going across the street to the Romanos on Christmas Eve. Frank's Soda was delivered to the house, and the best knishes were at the block parties on Ritner Street.

"It was an easy time. There is nothing now that's as good as before. Look at these streets here. Look how crowded with the cars. Look at the crime. There isn't the closeness in family, closeness in neighborhood. I've lived in this neighborhood 25 years, I know eight people. In 1950, there was a hundred houses, I knew a hundred people. Why is that? You have to have a car nowadays. [Stanley, like his father, doesn't drive.] You go to the corner now, there's no movie theater. If I want to go to the movies, I have to take a bus or go in town. You want to go shopping, you got to walk six blocks. In those days, everything was so convenient. It was perfect. Everything was there, you had the stores, you had the shopping. I wish I can bring those times and push them here, 'cause this is bad and it's going to get worse. That's my opinion. South Philadelphia was great in the '50s."

He's back in South Philadelphia about once a month now. "I visit my mom. She still lives in the same house on Fourth and Wolf. Our house is still nice, the block's nice. When I'm there, I feel very comfortable, it's like I never left. The street, most of the people have passed away. There's still a few neighbors that are still there from when I was a kid, and it's nice to see them, but they're all getting old. There's still the candy store. It's a different name now, but that brings back memories. The park is still there. There's a lot of young kids. There's a lot of drugs. There's a lot of crime in the general area. It's not as safe to walk, but that's all over, not just South Philadelphia. A lot of houses are boarded up in the area, and I'd walk past and say, 'Boy, my friend lived there, and look at that house now.'

"Things have just changed. I guess it's just like the decaying of the world. Wolf Street, it's just part of the world. You can't go out at night. Where there used to be synagogues or homes, it's parking lots. Nothing is like it used to be. It's constant changes. It's not for the better. . . . I know a lot of people who lived in South Philadelphia, they never go back because they only want to remember how it was, not how it is. When they had kids, they used to bring them down there and say, This is where I went to school. This is the barber shop I went to. This is where I did this. Now if they go, it gives them a heart pang feeling. South Philadelphia never will be the same."

Stanley's Uncle Bibbs left South Philadelphia as a young married man because his wife wanted to live in the Northeast. He moved there, hated it, and came back alone. He lives today in poor health on Tasker Street, enjoying the familiarity of the community he grew up in. He'll never leave, and he is the only descendant of Beryl and Etta to remain.

All of Stan's other uncles—Sam, Louie, Label, and Hymie—have died. Hymie's wife, Leah, remains downtown, as does Dawn, her daughter, and Dawn's family. But none of the other Altermans or Dubins live downtown anymore, except for Mary, Stanley's mother.

She has good friends (Leah among them), old neighbors who have been on Wolf Street for years, and new neighbors as well. She has the senior center at Marshall and Porter, the synagogue at Marshall and Ritner. She shops on Seventh Street in the daytime only. She lives simply, still squeezing money from somewhere, never wanting to ask for help. She still cuts out her son's newspaper stories and brags about her grandchildren to friends, but not nearly as often or with as much exaggeration as her husband once did. It's not her style.

She knows that South Philadelphia doesn't look like anything special, rowhouse streets intersecting each other, gray on gray, but it's always been a special place for her and her family. Everyone was nice. Everyone got along. Everyone worked hard. Loved ones have died, the children have left, but that's just the way life is. Her family helped build the neighborhood, the neighborhood helped build her family. No regrets. She's there for the duration.

Appendix:
History by the Numbers

1640s   Handful of Swedish settlers, unhappy with Governor Johan Printz, leave Delaware and Delaware County for Wicaco, now part of Queen Village.

1643   Lieutenant Swen Schute, veteran of the Thirty Years War, arrives.

1653   Queen Cristina of Sweden grants South Philadelphia to Schute.

1654   Governor Johan Rising of New Sweden refuses to approve Schute's grant.

1655   Dutch end the rule of the Swedes, but leave Wicaco residents alone.

1664   English take over from the Dutch and rule benignly.

1665   Schute dies, never having lived in South Philadelphia.

1669   Peter Gunnarsson Rambo owns 300 acres in Passyunk.

1677   Swedes use a small blockhouse in Wicaco for the area's first church, attracting residents from Bucks and Chester counties.

1678   Passyunk landholder Lasse Cock dies.

1682   William Penn establishes Philadelphia with South Street as its southern boundary.

1687   Map lists Moyamensing and Passyunk as areas south of city.

1696   Travelers crossing the Schuylkill use Grays Ferry Road.

1700   Gloria Dei (Old Swedes') Church is erected, replacing the blockhouse.

1720   Many men in Wicaco and Southwark make their living by the sea.

1744   Fortification built at Front and Federal by the British.

1750   Southwark has about 150 residences.

1759   Patrons hear the first theater orchestra (two violins) play the music of "Theodosis" in a building on South Street west of Front.

1762   Southwark becomes first municipality outside the city.

1763   English astronomers Charles Mason and Jeremiah Dixon use an astronomical observatory to create the Mason-Dixon line in their South Street office.

1766   Southwark Theater built on South Street, just west of Fourth.

1767   *The Prince of Parthia,* first play written by an American and performed by professional players, is staged at Southwark Theater.

1769   Southwark has about 600 houses.

1776   Southwark has more than 750 houses and about 1,200 people. Broad Street ends at South, and the eastern end of Washington Avenue is Love Lane.

1777   Hessian stationed near League Island writes home that he is living in the Neck.

1789   Hundreds cheer George Washington as he crosses Grays Ferry Bridge from Mount Vernon to be sworn in as president.

1790	Mummers already strutting.
1793	Secretary of State Thomas Jefferson lives in a three-room house between Reed and Dickinson on the east banks of the Schuylkill.
1796	Federal Street open from Grays Ferry to Southwark.
1800	900 people live in Passyunk; about 1,600 in Moyamensing.
1801	Navy Yard opens.
1808	Shot Tower built at Front and Carpenter for sportsmen.
1812	Moyamensing incorporated as township.
1821	Southwark Theater destroyed by fire.
1828	Dickinson Street (spelled "Dickson") appears on area maps.
1829	Average working man earns $58 a year.
1830s	Moyamensing Prison and the Navy's first training academy open downtown.
1832	Passyunk described as "covered with gardens and meadows."
1834	Whites and blacks riot in Moyamensing.
1835	Seeking a 10-hour day, Irish coal heavers walk off jobs on the Schuylkill docks.
1836	Southwark District divided into five political wards.
1838	Department store mogul John Wanamaker is born.
1839	Point Breeze Inn is one of several hotels on the Schuylkill.
1840	Streets as far south as McKean appear on area maps.
1850	39,000 people live in Southwark; 27,000 in Moyamensing; and 1,600 in Passyunk.
1854	City consolidates suburban districts, eliminating Passyunk, Southwark, and Moyamensing. South Philadelphia now makes up about 10 percent of the city's 130 square miles.
1857	St. Paul's parochial school has 500 children.
1858	City's first horse-drawn streetcar runs on Fifth and Sixth Streets beginning at Morris.
1861	Most of the Navy Yard's 285 workers come from South Philadelphia.
1862	Sixteen die in cartridge factory fire at 10th and Reed.
1863	Blacks fleeing Confederate army's advance to Gettysburg find shelter at House of Industry.
1864	Captured in Grays Ferry is George Bane, the only Confederate soldier ever caught in the city.
1865	More than 2,800 workers employed at the Navy Yard as the Civil War ends.
1866	Pythians, a black baseball team featuring Octavius Catto at shortstop, begins playing baseball on Wharton Street field.
1867	Packer Street appears on maps.
1868	Pythians denied entry to state white-team-only baseball league.
1870	Cantrell Street first appears in street directories.
1871	Five blacks die within three blocks of Seventh and South in Election Day riots.
1876	Navy Yard moves to land near League Island at the end of Broad Street.
1880s	P. T. Barnum amusement park—featuring Jumbo the elephant—opens at Broad and Morris.
1882	Snellenburg's Department Store opens at Fifth and South.
1891	Louis Sherman opens an ice cream store at Fourth and McKean.

1892   C. C. Baldi leads Columbus Day parade through South Philadelphia.

1894   St. Aloysius, a church for German Catholics, opens at 26th and Tasker.

1895   James P. McGranery, U.S. attorney general in 1952, is born.

1898   Jew Mob boss Willie Weisberg is born in Grays Ferry.

1899   Graphic Sketch Club, first free art school in nation, opens downtown.

1900   South Philadelphia has 282,000 residents.

1910   Boat trip from Sicily costs about $30; first class graduates from Southern High School.

1911   Passyunk Avenue Bridge opens; gangster Teo Lanzetti and artist Biagio Pinto are born.

1912   First public library in South Philadelphia opens at Fifth and Ellsworth.

1913   Girard Estates starts renting houses.

1914   Bennie Dubin is born.

1919   16-ounce loaf of bread costs eight cents; cotton socks are 20 cents.

1920   South Philadelphia's population peaks at 375,000; Frank Rizzo is born.

1921   Mario Lanza is born.

1922   Kirschbaum's clothing factory on Carpenter Street is bombed in labor dispute.

1923   Dusolina Giannini makes her concert debut at the Met in New York.

1926   Sesquicentennial celebration at south end of Broad Street fails to attract anticipated crowds.

1933   St. Paul's gets its first priest of Italian descent.

1934   Southeast Catholic opens at Seventh and Christian; William Vare dies.

1935   Melrose Diner opens.

1940   Italian Market has 159 stores and 131 sidewalk stalls.

1942   Tasker Homes opens with a victory garden and a football team, the Tasker Tigers.

1943   Weekly dances begin at Southeast Catholic; Frank Rizzo becomes a policeman.

1947   South Philadelphia's Bernard Samuel elected mayor.

1948   Neighborhood Center for Jewish children opens at Marshall and Porter Streets.

1953   Bootlegger and fight promoter Max "Boo Boo" Hoff dies in bed.

1954   Wilson Park housing project opens over objections of Irish and Italian neighbors; Point Breeze Community Council distributes a welcoming booklet.

1956   Bishop Neumann High School opens.

1959   Mario Lanza dies; Angelo Bruno takes over the South Philadelphia crime family.

1962   James McGranery dies in Florida.

1970   Ship building stops at Navy Yard; overhauls and refitting still carried on.

1978   Former Jew Mob boss Willie Weisberg dies at 79 in a home for the aged.

1980   Downtown population about 188,000; Angelo Bruno is killed.

1983   Frank Palumbo dies.

1990   South Philadelphia has about 171,000 residents.

1994   Palumbo's, the city's oldest nightclub, is destroyed by fire.

1995   Naval Base closes.

Sources

PREFACE

For more information about the immigrant history of Philadelphia's neighborhoods, see Dennis Clark, *The Irish in Philadelphia: Ten Generations of Urban Experience* (Philadelphia: Temple University Press, 1973), and Caroline Golab, *Immigrant Destinations* (Philadelphia: Temple University Press, 1977).

INTRODUCTION

Interviews with the late Dennis Clark (January 23, 1992) and Harry Silcox (December 30, 1993) taught me a great deal about working-class life in South Philadelphia.

The landscape of early South Philadelphia is described in *Southwark, Moyamensing, Passyunk and Dock Ward* (Philadelphia: Quaker Publishing Co., 1892). Harry C. Silcox, *Philadelphia Politics from the Bottom Up: The Life of Irishman William McMullen, 1824–1901* (Philadelphia: Balch Institute Press, 1989), sketches that landscape in the nineteenth century and also offers a broader picture of working-class life as well as a detailed closeup of the career of South Philadelphia's first political boss. The division of that landscape into political wards is examined by John Daly and Allen Weinberg, "Genealogy of Philadelphia County Subdivisions" (Department of Records, City of Philadelphia, 1966). Two helpful maps are Benjamine Easburn's Map of Philadelphia, 1776, and Charles Ellet's Map of Philadelphia, 1839. Both can be found in the main branch of the Free Library of Philadelphia.

Books offering a good view of working-class life in the city in the eighteenth and nineteenth centuries include Billy Gordon Smith, *Struggles of the Lower Sort: The Lives of Philadelphia's Laboring People, 1750–1800* (Berkeley and Los Angeles: University of California Press, 1981); W. E. B. Du Bois, *The Philadelphia Negro* (1899; New York: Schocken Books, 1967); and *The Peoples of Philadelphia: A History of Ethnic Groups and Lower Class Life, 1790–1940*, edited by Allen F. Davis and Mark H. Haller (Philadelphia: Temple University Press, 1973).

Specifically focusing on the history of South Philadelphia are C. A. Morello, *Beyond History: The Times and People of St. Paul's Roman Catholic Church, 1843–1993* (Philadelphia: Jefferies and Manz, 1992); the W.P.A. Pennsylvania Historical Survey, 1938–1941 (available on microfilm at the Balch Institute for Ethnic Studies); Philadelphia Historical Commission, "Report on Southwark" (1961); M. Antonia Lynch, *The Old District of Southwark* (Philadelphia: City History Society, 1909), vol. 1.; and John Maneval, "An Ethnic History of South Philadelphia" (Balch Institute for Ethnic Studies, 1991).

The history of the city—and glimpses of South Philadelphia—are seen in Joseph Jackson, *Encyclopedia of Philadelphia* (Philadelphia: National Historical Association,

1931), vols. 3, 4); Charles E. Welch, *Oh! Dem Golden Slippers* (New York: Thomas Nelson, 1970); and, of course, *History of Philadelphia* (Philadelphia: L. H. Everts, 1884) by Thomas J. Scharf and Thompson Westcott.

The books by Du Bois, Clark, Morello, and Silcox also offer insight into vice, crime, and violence. For more information, see Michael Feldberg, "Urbanization as a Cause of Violence: Philadelphia as a Test Case," and "Crime Patterns in Philadelphia, 1840–1870," both in *The Peoples of Philadelphia; A Guide to the Stranger, or Pocket Companion for the Fancy, Containing a List of the Gay Houses and Ladies of Pleasure in the City of Brotherly Love and Sisterly Affection* (no author or publisher, 1849), and George G. Foster, "Philadelphia in Slices," *New York Tribune,* October 30, 1848, November 17, 1848.

For the theatrical tradition, see *The Old District of Southwark.* For Mummers' tradition, see *Oh! Dem Golden Slippers;* Du Bois, *Philadelphia Negro,* also refers to the Mummers (p. 37).

For the growth of Catholic churches, see "Historical Sketches of the Catholic Churches and Institutions of Philadelphia" (Daniel H. Mahoney, 1895). Frank H. Taylor, *Philadelphia in the Civil War, 1861–1865,* covers the birth of the naval academy as well as the role of South Philadelphia in the war. "Pennsylvania Arts and Sciences: A Guide to Philadelphia" (Philadelphia Society for Promotion of Arts and Sciences, 1935) and an article by Joseph A. Slobodzian in the *Philadelphia Inquirer,* April 19, 1991, recount the history of the Navy Yard.

Murray Dubin, "Buddhist Temple Isn't Fitting In," *Philadelphia Inquirer,* October 14, 1987, and Ralph Cipriano, "Year Dawns on a New Roof—Vietnamese in Phila. Celebrate a Temple of Their Own," *Philadelphia Inquirer,* February 1, 1995, are stories about the growth of the Asian population. Jeff Gelles and Walter F. Roche, Jr., "Fire Engulfs Palumbo's Restaurant—Famed Club Was Closed at the Time," *Philadelphia Inquirer,* June 21, 1994, chronicles Palumbo's history.

CHAPTER 1 IRISH

This chapter draws on interviews with the historian Dennis Clark (January 23, 1992) and with the following South Philadelphians: the Reverend John J. Cox (December 12, 1991); Jean DiElsi (March 12, 1992); Jimmy Fox (October 19, 1991); Bill Patridge (April 9, 1992); John Pooler (September 20, 1991); and Joseph Slavin (September 2, 1990).

Billy Gordon Smith, *Struggles of the Lower Sort: The Lives of Philadelphia's Laboring People, 1750–1800* (Berkeley and Los Angeles: Univesity of California Press, 1981); Dennis Clark, *The Irish in Philadelphia: Ten Generations of Urban Experience* (Philadelphia: Temple University Press, 1973); and Harry C. Silcox, *Philadelphia Politics from the Bottom Up: The Life of Irishman William McMullen, 1824–1901* (Philadelphia: Balch Institute Press, 1989) are important sources for Irish neighborhoods and politics. John K. Alexander, "Poverty, Fear and Continuity: An Analysis of the Poor in Late Eighteenth-Century Philadelphia," in *The Peoples of Philadelphia: A History of Ethnic Groups and Lower Class Life, 1790–1940,* ed. Allen F. Davis and Mark H. Haller (Philadelphia: Temple University Press, 1973), and Michael Feldberg, "Urbanization as a Cause of Violence: Philadelphia as a Test Case," ibid. (esp. pp. 61–63), deal specifically with crime, poverty, and labor violence. C. A. Morello, *Beyond History: The Times and People of St. Paul's Roman Catholic Church, 1843–1993* (Philadelphia: Jefferies and Manz, 1992), discusses waterfront labor (p. 27).

See Clark for the Irish temperance movement (pp. 103–4), occupations in the Civil War era (pp. 41, 73, 76–77), and the proliferation of Catholic churches (p. 95). "Historical Sketches of the Catholic Churches and Institutions of Philadelphia" (Daniel H. Mahoney, 1895), pp. 103–4, 111, 122, 163, also traces church construction. Richard A. Varbero, "Philadelphia's South Italians in the 1920s," in Haller and Davis, *Peoples of Philadelphia*, records the Raggio–Brown wedding (p. 265).

CHAPTER 2 THE ARTS

For this chapter I interviewed Carmen Dee (October 25, 1991); Anthony DiRienzi (January 2, 1992); Henry Meadows (February 21, 1992); Donald Montanaro (April 27, 1992); Cozy Morley (March 30, 1992); LaVaughn Robinson (February 11, 1992); Bobby Rydell (June 3, 1991, in Penn Valley); and Elliott Tessler (March 10, 1992).

See Joseph Jackson, *Encyclopedia of Philadelphia* (Harrisburg, Pa.: National Historical Association, 1931), 3:919 (singing at Old Swedes), 4:1138 (*Within the Law* at the Dunbar Theater); M. Antonia Lynch, *The Old District of Southwark* (Philadelphia: City History Society, 1909), 1:108—9 *(Prince of Parthia* and *School for Scandal)*. John F. Watson, *Watson's Annals of Philadelphia* (Philadelphia: E. L. Carey and A. Hart, 1830), records Washington's theater attendance (p. 410).

Other sources for the arts are: "Pennsylvania Arts and Sciences: A Guide to Philadelphia" (Pennsylvania Society for Promotion of Arts and Sciences, 1935); the annual report of St. Martha's House for 1904–5; the W.P.A. Pennsylvania Historical Survey, 1938–1941; *Who's Who in American Art, 1938–1939* (Washington, D.C.: American Federation of Arts, 1937).

CHAPTER 3 BLACKS

This chapter is based on interviews with Renee Branham and Jean Branham (July 2, 1991); Nick Cooper (November 5, 1991); Falaka Fattah (January 29, 1992); Lillian Fauntleroy (July 2, 1991); Bill Lawson (November 6, 1991, in Wilmington); Jerry Moore (March 18, 1991); and Catherine Williams (November 5, 1991). Dennis Clark and Harry Silcox also provided historical background on relations between African and Irish Americans.

The Passyunk district census of 1683 is in the American Swedish Historical Museum. Other sources: Richard R. Wright, Jr., "The Negro in Pennsylvania" (M.A. thesis, University of Pennsylvania, 1912); Edward Raymond Turner, *The Negro in Pennsylvania: Slavery–Servitude–Freedom* (Washington, D.C.: American Historical Association, 1911); W. E. B. Du Bois, *The Philadelphia Negro* (1899; New York, Schocken Books, 1967); Sam Bass Warner, *The Private City* (Philadelphia: University of Pennsylvania Press, 1987); Allen F. Davis and Mark H. Haller, eds., *The Peoples of Philadelphia: A History of Ethnic Groups and Lower Class Life, 1790–1940* (Philadelphia: Temple University Press, 1973), esp. the Introduction by Allen F. Davis and the chapter by Russell F. Weigley, "A Peaceful City: Public Order in Philadelphia from Consolidation Through the Civil War"; Harry C. Silcox, *Philadelphia Politics from the Bottom Up: The Life of Irishman William McMullen, 1824–1901)* (Philadelphia: Balch Institute Press, 1989); Dorothy Gondos Beers, "The Centennial City," in *Philadelphia: A 300 Year History*, edited by Russell F. Weigley (New York: Norton, 1982); John Maneval, "An Ethnic History of South Philadelphia, 1870–1980" (Philadelphia: Balch Institute for Ethnic Studies, 1991).

For the riot of 1834, see Du Bois, *Philadelphia Negro*, pp. 27–29; Warner, *Private City*, pp. 128–29. Frederick Douglass is quoted in Davis, Introduction, p. 11. For conditions in the 1840s, see Edward Needles, "Ten Years of Progress; or: A Comparison of the State and Conditions of the Colored People in the City and County of Philadelphia from 1837–1847" (Merrihew and Thompson, 1849); Lucille Klinghoffer, "The

United Communities, Southeast Philadelphia: The House of Industry, Historical Background, 1847–1900" (Philadelphia Society for the Employment and Instruction of the Poor, 1972). Frank H. Taylor, *Philadelphia in the Civil War, 1861–1865* (Philadelphia: City of Philadelphia, 1913), p. 13, notes the arrival of former slaves during the Civil War. For the streetcar campaign, see Silcox, *Politics from the Bottom Up,* pp. 62–63; for the murder of Octavius Catto, see pp. 80–81. Du Bois, *Philadelphia Negro,* describes Catto's funeral (pp. 41–42) and quotes Robert Adger's obituary (pp. 121–22).

The figures on population growth in the early twentieth century are from Maneval, "Ethnic History."

CHAPTER 4   POLITICS

The following people discussed South Philadelphia politics with me: Henry J. Cianfrani (July 9, August 1, 1991); Alfred Ford (March 19, 1992); Thomas J. Kelly (February 25, 1992); Martin Weinberg (October 9, 1992).

On McMullen, see Harry C. Silcox, *Philadelphia Politics from the Bottom Up: The Life of Irishman William McMullen, 1824–1901* (Philadelphia: Balch Institute Press, 1989). Russell F. Weigley, "A Peaceful City: Public Order in Philadelphia from Consolidation Through the Civil War," in *The Peoples of Philadelphia: A History of Ethnic Groups and Lower Class Life, 1790–1940,* ed. Allen F. Davis and Mark H. Haller (Philadelphia: Temple University Press, 1973), talks about McMullen on pp. 161–62.

The *Evening Bulletin,* October 16, 1922, and the *Evening Public Ledger,* October 17, 1922, reported on the Committee of 70 challenge to Edwin Vare. Stefano Luconi, "Bringing Out the Italian Vote in Philadelphia," *Pennsylvania Magazine of History and Biography* 117 (1993): 251–85, is about the Vares and other Republican power brokers. Joseph Howlett's comment appeared in the *Philadelphia Inquirer,* June 2, 1994.

CHAPTER 5   ITALIANS

Richard Juliani, sociology professor at Villanova University, has written well and often about Italian urban settlement. I interviewed him on February 16, 1994. Other interviews: Sally, David, and Sal Auriemma (December 9, 1991, in Norristown); Nicholas Cipriani (November 7, 1991); the Reverend Michael Gambone (October 3, 1991); Gabriella LaBella (July 10, 1992); Dorothy Marcucci (October 16, 1991); Arlene Notoro Morgan (July 11, 1991, in Nanticoke, Pa.); Marie Mobilio Stapinski (July 11, 1991, in Nanticoke, Pa.).

Father Alfred M. Natali is the author of a brochure: "Saint Mary Magdalen de Pazzi Parish—The First Italian Church in the U.S.A." (St. Mary Magdalen de Pazzi Church, 1992). Other sources: the W.P.A. Pennsylvania Historical Survey, 1938–1941; Richard A. Varbero, "Philadelphia's South Italians in the 1920s," in *The Peoples of Philadelphia: A History of Ethnic Groups and Lower Class Life, 1790–1940,* ed. Allen F. Davis and Mark H. Haller (Philadelphia: Temple University Press, 1973).

For men's jobs see Caroline Golab, *Immigrant Destinations* (Philadelphia: Temple University Press, 1977), p. 60; for women's, see Barbara Mary Klaczynska, "Working Women in Philadelphia—1910–1930" (Ph.D. diss., Temple University, 1975); for teenage employment, see Golab, p. 58, and Varbero, pp. 259–62.

For housing see John F. Sutherland, "Housing the Poor in the City of Homes: Philadelphia at the Turn of the Century," in Davis and Haller, *Peoples of Philadelphia.*

CHAPTER 6   SPORTS

For this chapter I interviewed Samuel Bernstein (April 22, 1991); David Dabrow (December 4, 1991); Pearl Perkins Nightingale (October 27, 1992); Adolph Ritacco (January 30, 1992); Alexander "Petey" Rosenberg (November 12, 1991); Jerry Rullo (September 9, 1991); Bob Vetrone (October 1, 1991).

Other sources were Ron Avery, *Philadelphia Jewish Life, 1940–1985,* ed. Murray Friedman (Ardmore, Pa.: Philadelphia Jewish History Project, Seth Press, 1986), esp. pp. 301 (Feinberg), 292 (Rosenberg); Joseph Jackson, *Encyclopedia of Philadelphia* (Harrisburg, Pa.: National Historical Association, 1931), 4:1092 (ice skating), 2:322 (boxing).

The description of South Philadelphia in the 1600s and 1700s comes from *Southwark, Moyamensing, Passyunk and Dock Ward* (Philadelphia: Quaker Publishing Co., 1892), pp. 10, 11; the *Public Ledger* is quoted in Nicholas B. Wainwright, *Philadelphia in the Romantic Age of Lithography* (Philadelphia: Historical Society of Pennsylvania, 1958), p. 294.

William Carl Bolivar wrote about black baseball in "Pencil Pusher Points," *Philadelphia Tribune,* Aug. 24, 1912, May 3, 1913.

CHAPTER 7 JEWS

This chapter is based on interviews with Allen Meyers, historian of city synagogues (December 23, 1991, in Cherry Hill, N.J.); Samuel Bernstein (April 22, 1991); Stanley Sheckman (August 6, 1991); and Sanford Wizov (November 20, 1991, in Westville, N.J.).

Important published sources are: Edwin Wolf 2d and Maxwell Whiteman, *The History of the Jews of Philadelphia—From Colonial Times to the Age of Jackson* (Philadelphia: Jewish Publication Society of America, 1956); Henry Samuel Morais, *Jews of Philadelphia* (publisher unknown, 1893); Maxwell Whiteman, "Philadelphia's Jewish Neighborhoods," in *The Peoples of Philadelphia: A History of Ethnic Groups and Lower Class Life, 1790–1940,* ed. Allen F. Davis and Mark H. Haller (Philadelphia: Temple University Press, 1973); John Maneval, "An Ethnic History of South Philadelphia, 1870–1980" (Philadelphia: Balch Institute for Ethnic Studies, 1991); and the W.P.A. Pennsylvania Historical Survey, 1938–1941. Information on early synagogues can also be found in articles in the *Philadelphia Inquirer,* November 28, 1926, January 8, 1948; and the *Evening Bulletin,* September 13, 1928; and a press release from Congregation Rodeph Shalom, April 15, 1965, in the Balch Institute. The wartime issues of the *South Philadelphia Gazette* quoted here (August 15, 1943, February 6, 1944) are in the Jewish Archives Center of the Balch Institute.

See Wolf and Whiteman, *History,* for "Concillor Israel" (p. 11).

CHAPTER 8 CRIME AND VIOLENCE

Jean Bruno spoke to me on several occasions in Philadelphia and Radnor: August 12, 1991; August 28, 1991; November 5, 1991; July 8, 1992; May 30, 1993. I also interviewed Mark H. Haller, historian and expert on organized crime (February 3, 1993); and Anthony "Butch" D'Alessandro (November 26, 1991, in Washington Township, N.J.).

For the Wicaco lottery, see *Southwark, Moyamensing, Passyunk and Dock Ward* (Philadelphia: Quaker Publishing Co., 1892), p. 95. For early crime, vice, and violence, see John K. Alexander, "Poverty, Fear and Continuity: An Analysis of the Poor in Late Eighteenth-Century Philadelphia," and Michael Feldberg, "Urbanization as a Cause of Violence: Philadelphia as a Test Case," both in *The Peoples of Philadelphia: A History of Ethnic Groups and Lower Class Life, 1790–1940,* ed. Allen F. Davis and Mark H. Haller (Philadelphia: Temple University Press, 1973). Two nineteenth-century observers are *A Guide to the Stranger, or Pocket Companion for the Fancy, Containing a*

List of the Gay Houses and Ladies of Pleasure in the City of Brotherly Love and Sisterly Affection (no author or publisher, 1849), and George G. Foster, "Philadelphia in Slices," *New York Tribune,* October 30, 1848, November 17, 1848.

Irish gangs are described in Dennis Clark, *The Irish in Philadelphia: Ten Generations of Urban Experience* (Philadelphia: Temple University Press, 1973), esp. p. 115 (Rangers); Harry C. Silcox, *Philadelphia Politics from the Bottom Up: The Life of Irishman William McMullen, 1824–1901)* (Philadelphia: Balch Institute Press, 1989), esp. p. 45 (fire brigades); and Bruce Lurie, "Fire Companies and Gangs in Southwark: The 1840s," in Davis and Haller, *Peoples of Philadelphia,* pp. 77–81.

For the Black Hand incident, see *Philadelphia Inquirer,* March 23, 1980; for Duffy and Hoff, see *Philadelphia Inquirer,* October 14, 1958, and *Sunday Bulletin,* May 12, 1968. Also on Hoff: Mark H. Haller, "Bootleggers and American Gambling 1920–1950" (Commission on the Review of National Policy Toward Gambling, Gambling in America, 1976); Jim Riggio, "The Over the Hill Mob," *Philadelphia Magazine,* November 1972. Lanzettis: *Philadelphia Inquirer,* January 1, 1937, July 2, 1939; Riggio, "Over the Hill." Weisberg: Riggio, "Over the Hill"; *Evening Bulletin,* December 26, 1978; *Philadelphia Daily News,* December 26, 1978; *Philadelphia Inquirer,* March 13, 1956, December 26, 1978. Bruno: *Philadelphia Inquirer,* March 23, 1980.

CHAPTER 9 NOT IRISH OR BLACK OR ITALIAN OR JEW

For this chapter I interviewed Epifanio DeJesus (September 7, 1991); William Esher (November 14, 1991, in Haddon Township, N.J.); Joseph D. and Joseph M. Evancich (June 25, 1992); Sophal Hing (July 12, 1994).

Published sources: John Maneval, "An Ethnic History of South Philadelphia, 1870–1980" (Philadelphia: Balch Institute for Ethnic Studies, 1991); Caroline Golab, *Immigrant Destinations* (Philadelphia: Temple University Press, 1977), pp. 203–5 (immigration), 207–12 (employment); "Historical Sketches of the Catholic Churches and Institutions of Philadelphia" (Daniel H. Mahoney, 1895); *Southwark, Moyamensing, Passyunk and Dock Ward* (Philadelphia: Quaker Publishing Co., 1892).

CHAPTER 10 ONE FAMILY: BENNIE DUBIN'S STORY

The column about my father originally appeared in the *Philadelphia Inquirer Magazine,* July 23, 1989.

Interviewed for this chapter were: Hyman Alterman (May 11, 1991); Mary Dubin (July 22, 1991); Joseph Dubin (Max's son, August 19, 1991); Edward "Bibbs" Dubin (September 15, 1991); Stanley Dubin (September 21, 1992). Hyman Alterman died in October 1994.

Bibliography

BOOKS

Alotta, Robert I. *Mermaids, Monasteries, Cherokees and Custer: The Stories Behind Philadelphia Street Names.* Chicago: Bonus Books, 1990.

Anastasia, George. *Blood and Honor: Inside the Scarfo Mob—The Mafia's Most Violent Family.* New York: William Morrow, 1991.

Campbell, William Burke. *Old Towns and Districts of Philadelphia.* Philadelphia: City History Society of Philadelphia, 1942.

Clark, Dennis. *The Irish in Philadelphia: Ten Generations of Urban Experience.* Philadelphia: Temple University Press, 1973.

Craig, Peter Stebbins. *The 1693 Census of the Swedes on the Delaware.* Winter Park, Fla.: SAG Publications, 1993.

Davis, Allen F., and Haller, Mark H., eds. *The Peoples of Philadelphia: A History of Ethnic Groups and Lower Class Life, 1790–1940.* Philadelphia: Temple University Press, 1973.

Du Bois, W. E. B. *The Philadelphia Negro.* 1899. New York: Schocken Books, 1967.

Ershkowitz, Miriam, and Zikmund, Joseph, eds. *Black Politics in Philadelphia.* New York: Basic Books, 1973.

Feldberg, Michael. *The Philadelphia Riots of 1844: A Study of Ethnic Conflict.* Westport, Conn.: Greenwood Press, 1975.

Friedman, Murray, ed. *Philadelphia Jewish Life, 1940–1985.* Ardmore, Pa.: Philadelpha Jewish History Project, Seth Press, 1986.

Golab, Caroline. *Immigrant Destinations.* Philadelphia: Temple University Press, 1977.

Greene, Victor R. *American Immigration Leaders: 1800–1910.* Baltimore: Johns Hopkins University Press, 1987.

Jackson, Joseph. *Encyclopedia of Philadelphia.* Harrisburg, Pa.: National Historical Association, 1931.

Juliani, Richard N. "The Italian Community of Philadelphia." In *Little Italies in North America,* ed. Robert F. Harney and J. Vincenza Scarpaci. Toronto: Multicultural Society of Ontario, 1981.

Lewis, John Frederick. *The History of an Old Philadelphia Land Title.* Philadelphia: Patterson and White, 1934.

Lynch, M. Antonia. *The Old District of Southwark.* Philadelphia: City History Society, 1909.

Miller, Fredric M.; Vogel, Morris J.; and Davis, Allen F. *Philadelphia Stories: A Photographic History, 1920–1960.* Philadelphia: Temple University Press, 1988.

———. *Still Philadelphia: A Photographic History, 1890–1940.* Philadelphia: Temple University Press, 1983.

Morais, Henry Samuel. *Jews of Philadelphia*. No publisher, 1893.

Morello, C. A. *Beyond History: The Times and People of St. Paul's Roman Catholic Church, 1843–1993*. Philadelphia: Jefferies and Manz, 1992.

Morley, Christopher. *Travels in Philadelphia*. David McKay, 1920.

Nash, Gary B. *Forging Freedom: The Formation of Philadelphia's Black Community, 1720–1840*. Cambridge: Harvard University Press, 1988.

Paolantonio, S. A. *Rizzo: The Last Big Man in Big City America*. Philadelphia: Camino Books, 1993.

Paxon, Henry D. *Where Pennsylvania History Began*. George H. Buchanan, 1926.

Reider, Jonathan. *Canarsie: The Jews and Italians Against Liberalism*. Cambridge: Harvard University Press, 1985.

Scharf, J. Thomas, and Westcott, Thompson. *History of Philadelphia*. L.H. Everts, 1884.

Scranton, Philip, and Licht, Walter. *Work Sights: Industrial Philadelphia, 1890–1950*. Philadelphia: Temple University Press, 1986.

Silcox, Harry C. *Philadelphia Politics from the Bottom Up: The Life of Irishman William McMullen, 1824–1901*. Philadelphia: Balch Institute Press, 1989.

Smith, Billy Gordon. *Struggles of the Lower Sort: The Lives of Philadelphia's Laboring People, 1750–1800*. Berkeley and Los Angeles: University of California Press, 1981.

Southwark, Moyamensing, Passyunk and Dock Ward. Philadelphia: Quaker Publishing Co., 1892.

Taylor, Frank H. *Philadelphia in the Civil War, 1861–1865*. Philadelphia: City of Philadelphia, 1913.

Turner, Edward Raymond. *The Negro in Pennsylvania: Slavery–Servitude–Freedom, 1639–1861*. Washington, D.C.: American Historical Association, 1911.

Wainwright, Nicholas B. *Philadelphia in the Romantic Age of Lithography*. Philadelphia: Historical Society of Pennsylvania, 1958.

Warner, Sam Bass. *The Private City: Philadelphia in Three Periods of Growth*. Rev. ed. Philadelphia: University of Pennsylvania Press, 1987.

Watson, John F. *Watson's Annals of Philadelphia*. Philadelphia: E. L. Carey and A. Hart, 1830.

Weigley, Russell F., ed. *The Centennial City: Philadelphia—A 300 Year History*. New York: Norton, 1982.

Welch, Charles E. *Oh! Dem Golden Slippers*. New York: Thomas Nelson, 1970.

Weslager, C. A. *New Sweden on the Delaware: 1638–1655*. Wilmington, Del.: Middle Atlantic Press, 1988.

Who's Who in American Art, 1938–1939. Washington, D.C.: American Federation of Arts, 1937.

Wolf, Edwin 2nd, and Whiteman, Maxwell. *The History of the Jews of Philadelphia—From Colonial Times to the Age of Jackson*. Philadelphia: Jewish Publication Society of America, 1956.

BOOKLETS, PAMPHLETS, REPORTS

Bacon, Benjamin C. "Statistics of the Colored Peoples of Philadelphia." Board of Education of the Pennsylvania Society for the Abolition of Slavery, 1856.

"Census of the People of Color of the City and Districts of Philadelphia." Society of Friends, 1848.

Clark, Dennis. "The Irish in Pennsylvania: A People Share a Commonwealth." Pennsylvania Historical Studies no. 22. Pennsylvania Historical Association, 1991.

Commemorating the 110th Anniversary Celebration. South Street Business Association, 1980.

Daly, John, and Weinberg, Allen. *Genealogy of Philadelphia County Subdivisions.* Department of Records, City of Philadelphia, 1966.

A Guide to the Stranger, or Pocket Companion for the Fancy, Containing a List of the Gay Houses and Ladies of Pleasure in the City of Brotherly Love and Sisterly Affection. 1848.

"Historical Sketches of the Catholic Churches and Institutions of Philadelphia." Daniel H. Mahoney, 1895.

"Housing Today and Tomorrow: A Reappraisal of Goals." Philadelphia: Philadelphia Housing Association, 1950.

"The Improvement of a Street." Octavia Hill Association, 1906.

Klinghoffer, Lucille. "The United Communities, Southeast Philadelphia: The House of Industry, Historical Background, 1847–1900." Philadelphia Society for the Employment and Instruction of the Poor, 1972.

"Life and Adventures of Charles Anderson Chester, the Notorious Leader of the Killers." Historical Society of Pennsylvania, 1850.

Maneval, John. "An Ethnic History of South Philadelphia, 1870–1980." Balch Institute for Ethnic Studies, 1991.

Michael, Jennifer, ed. "Philadelphia FolkLife Resources: A Guide to Local Folk Traditions." Philadelphia Folklore Project, 1991.

Natali, Reverend Alfred M. "Saint Mary Magdalen de Pazzi Parish—The First Italian Church in the U.S.A." Saint Mary Magdalen de Pazzi Church, 1992.

Needles, Edward. "Ten Years of Progress, or: a Comparison of the State and Conditions of the Colored People in the City and County of Philadelphia from 1837–1847." Merrihew and Thompson, 1849.

"Pennsylvania Arts and Sciences: A Guide to Philadelphia." Pennsylvania Society for Promotion of Arts and Sciences, 1935.

"Plans for the Day Care of Children—Tasker Homes Area." Philadelphia Committee on Day Care for Children, 1942.

St. Martha's House. Annual reports, 1902–15.

Souder, Caspar. "The Mysteries and Miseries of Philadelphia: A Sketch of the Conditions of the Most Degraded Classes of the City." Historical Society of Pennsylvania, 1853.

South Philadelphia High School Alumni Association. Newsletters. 1973–90.

"Report on Southwark." Philadelphia Historical Commission, 1961.

"A Study of the Housing and Social Conditions in Selected Districts of Philadelphia." Henry Phipps Institute, University of Pennsylvania, 1915.

"A Study of Redlining in Four Philadelphia Neighborhoods." Housing Association of the Delaware Valley, 1976.

"Survey of Negro Babies." Philadelphia Health and Tuberculosis Committee, 1925.

"Survey of War-Time Housing, Oregon Avenue Area." Philadelphia Housing Association, 1935.

"Whitman Conservation Area Survey." Department of Licenses and Inspection, Department of Housing, 1963.

"Wilson Park." Point Breeze Community Council, 1954.

Workman Place House. Annual reports, 1908–46.

W.P.A. Pennsylvania Historical Survey, 1938–1941. Pennsylvania Historical and Museum Commission, State Archives, on microfilm, Balch Institute for Ethnic Studies.

DISSERTATIONS

Greifer, Julian L. "Neighborhood Center: A Study of the Adjustments of a Cultural Group in America." Ph.D. dissertation, New York University, 1948.

Klaczynska, Barbara Mary. "Working Women in Philadelphia: 1910–1930." Ph.D. dissertation, Temple University, 1975.

Peltz, Rachmiel. "Speaking Yiddish in South Philadelphia: Changes in Language and Identity." Ph.D. dissertation, Columbia University, 1988.

Wright, Richard R., Jr. "The Negro in Pennsylvania." Ph.D. dissertation, University of Pennsylvania, 1912.

JOURNAL ARTICLES

Bolivar, William Carl. "Pencil Pusher Points. *Philadelphia Tribune,* August 24, 1912; May 3, 1913.

Carlisle, Marcia. "Disorderly City, Disorderly Women—Prostitution in Ante-Bellum Philadelphia." *Pennsylvania Magazine of History and Biography* 110 (1986): 549–68.

Ericksen, Eugene P., and Yancey, William L. "Work and Residence in Industrial Philadelphia." *Journal of Urban History* 5, no. 2 (1979): 141–81.

Foster, George G. "Philadelphia in Slices." *New York Tribune,* October 30, 1848; November 17, 1848.

Kenn, Gregory B. "The Courts of Pennsylvania in the 17th Century." *Pennsylvania Magazine of History and Biography* 5 (1881).

Luconi, Stefano. "Bringing out the Italian Vote in Philadelphia." *Pennsylvania Magazine of History and Biography* 117 (1993): 251–85.

Nicholson, Jim. "Taken Under the Gun." *Philadelphia Magazine,* August 1974.

Riggio, Jim. "The Over the Hill Mob." *Philadelphia Magazine,* November 1972.

Silcox, Harry C. "Nineteenth Century Philadelphia Black Militant: Octavius V. Catto (1839–1871)." *Pennsylvania Magazine of History and Biography* 44 (1977): 53–76.

South Philadelphia Gazette, August 15, 1943; February 6, 1944. Jewish Archives Center, Balch Institute.

Index

Page references in roman type indicate text. Page references in italic type indicate illustrations.

221